OCA Java SE 8 Programmer Study Guide (Exam 1Z0-808)

Budi Kurniawan

OCA Java SE 8 Programmer Study Guide (Exam 1Z0-808)

First Edition: July 2015

ISBN: 9781771970228

Book and Cover Designer: Brainy Software Team

Technical Reviewer: Paul Deck
Indexer: Chris Mayle

About the Author

Known for his clear writing style, Budi Kurniawan is a senior developer at Brainy Software and the author of *How Tomcat Works*, *Servlet and JSP: A Tutorial*, *Struts 2 Design and Programming*, and others. He has written software that is licensed by major corporations worldwide.

Table of Contents

Introduction

Welcome to *OCA Java SE 8 Programmer Study Guide (Exam 1Z0-808)*.

This book is designed for people who want to pass the Oracle Certified Associate, Java SE 8 Programmer exam. I assume you already know Java and have used it to write programs. If you are completely new to Java, then I recommend that you start with a Java tutorial book such as my own *Java: A Beginner's Tutorial, Fourth Edition* (ISBN 9780992133047).

If you have programmed in Java before but are not up to date with the current Java language and technologies, you can still use this book as it comes with a Java refresher. In fact, the Java refresher includes all the materials you need to master to pass the exam. Each of the eight chapters in the Java refresher comes with ten questions to test your knowledge on the subjects discussed in the chapter. These questions are similar to what you would expect in a real exam. In addition, at the end of the book you will find a full mock exam to test how prepared you are to take the exam. It is a good idea to try the mock exam before you take the real test. Even if you have several years experience with Java, you might still fail or might not pass with flying colors. Why? Because there may be questions that might surprise you, that you as a developer may never have thought about. Bear in mind that if you fail the exam, you will have to pay again to retake it. It currently costs a couple hundred dollars, so make sure you only take the exam when you are really ready.

Registering for the Exam

This and other Oracle exams are operated by Pearson VUE. Before you can take the exam, you need to register and pay. To register, visit http://pearsonvue.com/oracle and create an account. Once you have an account, you can log in and choose a test center and an exam date/time that suits you. Finally, before you can complete your registration, you have to pay. You can pay with a credit card or with an exam voucher from Oracle. Alternatively, you can visit a test center if there is one near you and schedule an exam and pay there.

If you successfully register online, you will receive an email confirming your exam time and location.

Taking the Exam

The exam consists of 77 multiple choice questions with a passing score of 65%. This means, you have to get at least 51 questions right. You will be given 150 minutes to complete the exam. As there is no penalty for wrong answers, make sure you answer all the questions. Note that a question may have multiple correct answers and you must choose all the correct answers.

Your exam may contain unscored questions in addition to the scored questions. In other words, the total number of questions that are presented to you may be greater than the number shown on the exam page. You will not be told which questions are unscored but you will get extra time if your exam contains unscored questions.

The number of questions and passing score are accurate at the time of writing. They might change in the future.

If you pass the exam, you can check your score by signing in to http://certview.oracle.com. A printed certificate can be ordered from Oracle.

Should you fail, you have to wait 14 days before you can retake the exam. Oracle may have different sets of questions, so the questions on a subsequent test may be entirely different.

Exam Topics

The following are the exam topics. To the right of each topic you can find the book section(s) that discusses the topic.

Java Basics

- Define the scope of variables (3.1 Variable Scope)
- Define the structure of a Java class (3.2 Java Classes)
- Create executable Java applications with a main method**; run a Java program from the command line; including console output** (3.2 Java Classes)
- Import other Java packages to make them accessible in your code (3.6 Java Packages, 3.7 Encapsulation and Access Control)
- **Compare and contrast the features and components of Java such as: platform independence, object orientation, encapsulation, etc. (3.3 Creating An Object, 3.6 Java Packages, 3.7 Encapsulation and Access Control)**

Working With Java Data Types

- Declare and initialize variables **(including casting of primitive data types)** (1.4 Variables, 1.5 Constants, 1.6 Literals)
- Differentiate between object reference variables and primitive variables (1.4 Variables, 3.8 The this Keyword)
- **Know how to** read or write to object fields (3.3 Creating An Object)
- Explain an object's lifecycle (creation, "dereference **by reassignment**" and

garbage collection) (3.4 The null Keyword, 3.5 Memory Allocation for Objects)
- **Develop code that uses wrapper classes such as Boolean, Double, and Integer (4.4 Primitive Wrappers)**

Using Operators and Decision Constructs

- Use Java operators; **including parentheses to override operator precedence** (1.8 Operators)
- Test equality between Strings and other objects using == and equals() (4.2 java.lang.String)
- Create if and if/else **and ternary** constructs (2.2 The if Statement)
- Use a switch statement (2.8 The switch Statement)

Creating and Using Arrays

- Declare, instantiate, initialize and use a one-dimensional array (5.1 Array Overview, 5.2 Iterating over an Array, 5.3 The java.util.Arrays Class)
- Declare, instantiate, initialize and use multi-dimensional array (5.1 Array Overview, 5.2 Iterating over an Array, 5.3 The java.util.Arrays Class, 5.7 Multidimensional Arrays)

Using Loop Constructs

- Create and use while loops (2.3 The while Statement)
- Create and use for loops including the enhanced for loop (2.5 The for Statement, 5.2 Iterating over an Array, 5.8 ArrayList)
- Create and use do/while loops (2.4 The do-while Statement)
- Compare loop constructs (2.3 The while Statement, 2.5 The for Statement)
- Use break and continue (2.6 The break Statement, 2.7 The continue Statement)

Working with Methods and Encapsulation

- Create methods with arguments and return values**; including overloaded methods** (3.2 Java Classes, 3.15 Method Overloading)
- Apply the static keyword to methods and fields (3.11 Static members)
- **Create and overload constructors; including impact on default constructors** (3.2 Java Classes)
- Apply access modifiers (3.7 Encapsulation and Access Control)
- Apply encapsulation principles to a class (3.7 Encapsulation and Access Control)
- Determine the effect upon object references and primitive values when they are passed into methods that change the values (3.17 By Value or By Reference?)

Working with Inheritance

- **Describe inheritance and its benefits** (6.1 Inheritance Overview)
- Develop code that demonstrates the use of polymorphism; **including overriding and object type versus reference type** (7.4 Polymorphism, 7.5 Polymorphism in Action)
- Determine when casting is necessary (6.6 Type Casting)
- Use super and this to access objects and constructors (6.4 Calling the Constructors of the Superclass, 6.5 Calling the Hidden Members of the Superclass)

- Use abstract classes and interfaces (7.1 The Concept of Interface, 7.2 The Interface, Technically Speaking, 7.3 Abstract Classes)

Handling Exceptions

- Differentiate among checked exceptions, **unchecked exceptions**, and Errors (8.1 Catching Exceptions)
- Create a try-catch block and determine how exceptions alter normal program flow (8.3 Catching Multiple Exceptions)
- **Describe the advantages of Exception handling** (8.1 Catching Exceptions)
- **Create and** invoke a method that throws an exception (8.6 Throwing an Exception from a Method)
- **Recognize common exception classes (such as NullPointerException, ArithmeticExcpetion, ArrayIndexOutOfBoundsException, ClassCastException)** (8.5 The java.lang.Exception Class)

Working with Selected classes from the Java API

- Manipulate data using the StringBuilder class and its methods (4.3 java.lang.StringBuilder and java.lang.StringBuffer)
- Creating and manipulating Strings (4.2 java.lang.String)
- Create and manipulate calendar data using classes from java.time.LocalDateTime, java.time.LocalDate, java.time.LocalTime, java.time.format.DateTimeFormatter, java.time.Period (9.1 Date and Time API Overview, 9.3 LocalDate, 9.4 Period, 9.5 LocalDateTime, 9.9 Formatting A Date-Time)
- Declare and use an ArrayList of a given type (5.8 ArrayList)
- Write a simple Lambda expression that consumes a Lambda Predicate expression (10.2 Why Lambda Expressions?, 10.5 Predefined Functional Interfaces)

About This Book

This book contains a Java refresher and a full mock exam. The Java refresher consists of eight chapters of introductory Java. Each chapter has a self test section with ten multiple choice questions.

The following presents the overview of each chapter.

Chapter 1, "Language Fundamentals" teaches you the Java language syntax. You will be introduced to topics such as character sets, primitives, variables, operators, etc.

Chapter 2, "Statements" explains Java statements **for**, **while**, **do-while**, **if**, **if-else**, **switch**, **break**, and **continue**.

Chapter 3, "Objects and Classes," is the first OOP lesson in this book. It starts by explaining what a Java object is an how it is stored in memory. It then continues with a discussion of classes, class members, and two OOP concepts (abstraction and encapsulation).

Chapter 4, "Core Classes" covers important classes in the Java core libraries: **java.lang.Object**, **java.lang.String**, **java.lang.StringBuffer** and **java.lang.StringBuilder**, as well as wrapper classes. This is an important chapter because the classes explained in this chapter are some of the most commonly used classes in Java.

Chapter 5, “Arrays” discusses arrays, a special language feature of Java that is widely used. This chapter also covers a utility class for manipulating arrays.

Chapter 6, “Inheritance” discusses an OOP feature that enables code extendibility. This chapter teaches you how to extend a class, affect the visibility of a subclass, override a method and so forth.

Chapter 7, “Interfaces, Abstract Classes and Polymorphism” explains the concept of interface and abstract classes and discusses polymorphism. The latter is one of the main pillars of OOP.

Undoubtedly, error handling is an important feature of any programming language. As a mature language, Java has a very robust error handling mechanism that can help prevent bugs from creeping in. Chapter 8, “Error Handling” is a detailed discussion of this mechanism.

Chapter 9, “Dates and Times” and Chapter 10, “Lambda Expressions” discuss new features in Java 8. Chapter 9 introduces the new Date and Time API and Chapter 10 the new language construct. Both are subjects that you need to study to pass the exam.

Appendix A, “Mock Exam 1” contains the first full mock exam and Appendix B, “Mock Exam 1 Answers” provides the answers to and explanations for the questions.

Appendix C, “Mock Exam 2” contains the second full mock exam and Appendix D, “Mock Exam 2 Answers” provides the answers to and explanations for the questions.

Downloading Program Examples

The program examples accompanying this book can be downloaded from the publisher’s website:

```
http://books.brainysoftware.com
```

Extract the zip file to a working directory and you are good to go.

Chapter 1
Language Fundamentals

Java is an object-oriented programming (OOP) language, therefore an understanding of OOP is of utmost importance. Chapter 3, "Objects and Classes" is the first lesson of OOP in this book. However, before you explore OOP features and techniques, you should first study Java language fundamentals.

1.1 ASCII and Unicode

Traditionally, computers in English speaking countries only used the ASCII (American Standard Code for Information Interchange) character set to represent alphanumeric characters. Each character in the ASCII is represented by 7 bits. There are therefore 128 characters in this character set. These include the lower case and upper case Latin letters, numbers, and punctuation marks.

The ASCII character set was later extended to include another 128 characters, such as the German characters ä, ö, ü and the British currency symbol £. This character set is called extended ASCII and each character is represented by 8 bits.

ASCII and the extended ASCII are only two of the many character sets available. Another popular one is the character set standardized by the ISO (International Standards Organization), ISO-8859-1, which is also known as Latin-1. Each character in ISO-8859-1 is represented by eight bits as well. This character set contains all the characters required for writing text in many of the western European languages, such as German, Danish, Dutch, French, Italian, Spanish, Portuguese and, of course, English. An eight-bit-per-character character set is convenient because a byte is also 8 bits long. As such, storing and transmitting text written in an 8-bit character set is most efficient.

However, not every language uses Latin letters. Chinese and Japanese are examples of languages that use different character sets. For example, each character in the Chinese language represents a word, not a letter. There are thousands of these characters and eight bits are not enough to represent all the characters in the character set. The Japanese use a different character set for their language too. In total, there are hundreds of different character sets for all the world languages. To unify all these characters sets, a computing standard called Unicode was created.

Unicode is a character set developed by a non-profit organization called the Unicode Consortium (www.unicode.org). This body attempts to include all characters in all languages in the world into one single character set. A unique number in Unicode represents exactly one character. Currently at version 7, Unicode is used in Java, XML, ECMAScript, LDAP, etc.

Initially, a Unicode character was represented by 16 bits, which were enough to represent more than 65,000 different characters. 65,000 characters are sufficient for encoding most of the characters in major languages in the world. However, the Unicode consortium planned to allow for encoding for as many as a million more characters. With this amount, you then need more than 16 bits to represent each character. In fact, a 32 bit system is considered a convenient way of storing Unicode characters.

Now, you see a problem already. While Unicode provides enough space for all the characters used in all languages, storing and transmitting Unicode text is not as efficient as storing and transmitting ASCII or Latin-1 characters. In the Internet world, this is a huge problem. Imagine having to transfer 4 times as much data as ASCII text!

Fortunately, character encoding can make it more efficient to store and transmit Unicode text. You can think of character encoding as analogous to data compression. And, there are many types of character encodings available today. The Unicode Consortium endorses three of them:

- UTF-8. This is popular for HTML and for protocols whereby Unicode characters are transformed into a variable length encoding of bytes. It has the advantages that the Unicode characters corresponding to the familiar ASCII set have the same byte values as ASCII, and that Unicode characters transformed into UTF-8 can be used with much existing software. Most browsers support the UTF-8 character encoding.
- UTF-16. In this character encoding, all the more commonly used characters fit into a single 16-bit code unit, and other less often used characters are accessible via pairs of 16-bit code units.
- UTF-32. This character encoding uses 32 bits for every single character. This is clearly not a choice for Internet applications. At least, not at present.

ASCII characters still play a dominant role in software programming. Java too uses ASCII for almost all input elements, except comments, identifiers, and the contents of characters and strings. For the latter, Java supports Unicode characters. This means, you can write comments, identifiers, and strings in languages other than English.

1.2 Separators

Java uses certain characters as separators. These special characters are presented in Table 1.1.

Symbol	Name	Description
( )	Parentheses	Used in: 1. method signatures to contain lists of arguments. 2. expressions to raise operator precedence. 3. narrowing conversions. 4. loops to contain expressions to be evaluated
{ }	Braces	Used in: 1. declaration of types. 2. blocks of statements 3. array initialization.
[ ]	Brackets	Used in: 1. array declaration. 2. array value dereferencing
< >	Angle brackets	Used to pass parameter to parameterized types.
;	Semicolon	Used to terminate statements and in the **for** statement to separate the initialization code, the expression, and the update code.
:	Colon	Used in the **for** statement that iterates over an array or a collection.
,	Comma	Used to separate arguments in method declarations.
.	Period	Used to separate package names from subpackages and type names, and to separate a field or method from a reference variable.

Table 1.1: Java separators

It is important that you are familiar with the symbols and names, but don't worry if you don't understand the terms in the Description column for now.

1.3 Primitives

When writing an object-oriented (OO) application, you create an object model that resembles the real world. For example, a payroll application would have **Employee** objects, **Tax** objects, **Company** objects, etc. In Java, however, objects are not the only data type. There is another data type called *primitive*. There are eight primitive types in Java, each with a specific format and size. Table 1.2 lists Java primitives.

Primitive	Description	Range
byte	Byte-length integer (8 bits)	-128 (-2^7) to 127 (2^7-1)
short	Short integer (16 bits)	-32,768 (-2^{15}) to 32,767 ($-2^{15}-1$)
int	Integer (32 bits)	-2,147,483,648 (-2^{31}) to 2,147,483,647 ($-2^{31}-1$)
long	Long integer (64 bits)	-9,223,372,036,854,775,808 (-2^{63}) to 9,223,372,036,854,775,807 ($2^{63}-1$)
float	Single-precision floating point (32-bits)	Smallest positive nonzero: $14e^{-45}$ Largest positive nonzero: 3.4028234^{e38}
double	Double-precision floating point (64-bits)	Smallest positive nonzero: $4.9e\text{-}^{324}$ Largest positive nonzero: $1.7976931348623157e^{308}$
char	A Unicode character	[See Unicode 6 specification]
boolean	A boolean value	true or false

Table 1.2: Java primitives

The first six primitives (**byte**, **short**, **int**, **long**, **float**, **double**) represent numbers. Each has a different size. For example, a **byte** can contain any whole number between -128 and 127. To understand how the smallest and largest numbers for an integer were obtained, look at its size in bits. A byte is 8 bits long so there are 2^8 or 256 possible values. The first 128 values are reserved for -128 to -1, then 0 takes one place, leaving 127 positive values. Therefore, the range for a byte is -128 to 127.

If you need a placeholder to store number 1000000, you need an **int**. A **long** is even larger, and you might ask, if a **long** can contain a larger set of numbers than a **byte** and an **int**, why not just use a **long**? It is because a **long** takes 64 bits and therefore consume more memory space than a **byte** or an **int**. Thus, to save space, you want to use a primitive with the smallest possible data size.

The primitives **byte**, **short**, **int**, and **long** can only hold integers or whole numbers, for numbers with decimal points you need either a **float** or a **double**. A float is a 32-bit value that conforms to the Institute of Electrical and Electronics Engineer (IEEE) Standard 754. A double is a 64-bit value that conforms to the same standard.

A **char** can contain a single Unicode character, such as 'a', '9' or '&'. The use of Unicode allows **chars** to also contain characters that do not exist in the English alphabet. A **boolean** can contain one of two possible states (**false** or **true**).

Note

The reason why not everything in Java is an object is speed. Objects are more expensive to create and operate on than primitives. In programming an operation is said to be expensive if it is resource intensive or consumes a lot of CPU cycles to complete.

Now that you know that there are two types of data in Java (primitives and objects), let's continue by studying how to use primitives. Let's start with variables.

1.4 Variables

Variables are data placeholders. Java is a strongly typed language, therefore every variable must have a declared type. There are two data types in Java:

- reference types. A variable of reference type provides a reference to an object.
- primitive types. A variable of primitive type holds a primitive.

How Java Stores Integer Values

You must have heard that computers work with binary numbers, which are numbers that consists of only zeros and ones. This section provides an overview that may come in useful when you learn mathematical operators.

A byte takes eight bits, meaning there are eight bits allocated to store a byte. The leftmost bit is the sign bit. 0 indicates a positive number, and 1 denotes a negative number. 0000 0000 is the binary representation of 0, 0000 0001 of 1, 0000 0010 of 2, 0000 0011 of 3, and 0111 1111 of 127, which is the largest positive number that a byte can contain.

Now, how do you get the binary representation of a negative number? It's easy. Get the binary representation of its positive equivalent first, and reverse all the bits and add 1. For example, to get the binary representation of -3 you start with 3, which is 0000 0011. Reversing the bits results in

```
1111 1100
```

Adding 1 gives you

```
1111 1101
```

which is -3 in binary.

For **int**s, the rule is the same, i.e. the leftmost bit is the sign bit. The only difference is that an **int** takes 32 bits. To calculate the binary form of -1 in an **int**, we start from 1, which is

```
0000 0000 0000 0000 0000 0000 0000 0001
```

Reversing all the bits results in:

```
1111 1111 1111 1111 1111 1111 1111 1110
```

Adding 1 gives us the number we want (-1).

```
1111 1111 1111 1111 1111 1111 1111 1111
```

In addition to the data type, a Java variable also has a name or an identifier. There are a few ground rules in choosing identifiers.

1. An identifier is an unlimited-length sequence of Java letters and Java digits. An identifier must begin with a Java letter.
2. An identifier must not be a Java keyword (given in Table 1.3), a **boolean** literal, or the **null** literal.
3. It must be unique within its scope. Scopes are discussed in Chapter 3, "Objects and Classes."

Java Letters and Java Digits

Java letters include uppercase and lowercase ASCII Latin letters A to Z (\u0041-\u005a—note that \u denotes a Unicode character) and a to z (\u0061-\u007a), and, for historical reasons, the ASCII underscore (_ or \u005f) and the dollar sign ($, or \u0024). The $ character should be used only in mechanically generated source code or, rarely, to access preexisting names on legacy systems.
Java digits include the ASCII digits 0-9 (\u0030-\u0039).

abstract	continue	for	new	switch
assert	default	if	package	synchronized
boolean	do	goto	private	this
break	double	implements	protected	throw
byte	else	import	public	throws
case	enum	instanceof	return	transient
catch	extends	int	short	try
char	final	interface	static	void
class	finally	long	strictfp	volatile
const	float	native	super	while

Table 1.3: Java keywords

Here are some legal identifiers:

```
salary
x2
_x3
row_count
```

Here are some invalid variables:

```
2x
java+variable
```

2x is invalid because it starts with a number. **java+variable** is invalid because it contains a plus sign.

Also note that names are case-sensitive. **x2** and **X2** are two different identifiers.

You declare a variable by writing the type first, followed by the name plus a semicolon. Here are some examples of variable declarations.

```
byte x;
int rowCount;
char c;
```

In the examples above you declare three variables:

- The variable **x** of type **byte**
- The variable **rowCount** of type **int**
- The variable **c** of type **char**

x, **rowCount** and **c** are variable names or identifiers.

It is also possible to declare multiple variables having the same type on the same line, separating two variables with a comma. For instance:

```
int a, b;
```

which is the same as

```
int a;
int b;
```

However, writing multiple declarations on the same line is not recommended as it reduces readability.

Finally, it is possible to assign a value to a variable at the same time the variable is declared:

```
byte x = 12;
int rowCount = 1000;
char c = 'x';
```

Naming Convention for Variables

Variable names should be short yet meaningful. They should be in mixed case with a lowercase first letter. Subsequent words start with capital letters. Variable names should not start with underscore _ or dollar sign $ characters. For example, here are some examples of variable names that are in compliance with Sun's code conventions: **userName**, **count**, **firstTimeLogin**.

1.5 Constants

In Java constants are variables whose values, once assigned, cannot be changed. You declare a constant by using the keyword **final**. By convention, constant names are all in upper case with words separated by underscores.

Here are examples of constants or final variables.

```
final int ROW_COUNT = 50;
final boolean ALLOW_USER_ACCESS = true;
```

1.6 Literals

From time to time you need to assign values to variables in your program, such as number 2 to an **int** or the character 'c' to a **char**. For this, you need to write the value representation in a format that the Java compiler understands. This source code representation of a value is called *literal*. There are three types of literals: literals of primitive types, string literals, and the **null** literal. Only literals of primitive types are discussed in this chapter. The **null** literal is discussed in Chapter 3, "Objects and Classes" and string literals in Chapter 4, "Core Classes."

Literals of primitive types have four subtypes: integer literals, floating-point literals, character literals and boolean literals. Each of these subtypes is explained below.

Integer Literals

Integer literals may be written in decimal (base 10, something we are used to), hexadecimal (base 16) or octal (base 8). For example, one hundred can be expressed as **100**. The following are integer literals in decimal:

```
2
123456
```

As another example, the following code assigns 10 to variable **x** of type **int**.

```
int x = 10;
```

Hexadecimal integers are written by using the prefixes **0x** or **0X**. For example, the hexadecimal number 9E is written as 0X9E or 0x9E. Octal integers are written by prefixing the numbers with 0. For instance, the following is an octal number 567:

```
0567
```

Integer literals are used to assign values to variables of types **byte**, **short**, **int**, and **long**. Note, however, you must not assign a value that exceeds the capacity of a variable. For instance, the highest number for a **byte** is 127. Therefore, the following code generates a compile error because 200 is too big for a **byte**.

```
byte b = 200;
```

To assign a value to a **long**, suffix the number with the letter **L** or **l**. L is preferable because it is easily distinguishable from digit 1. A **long** can contain values between -9223372036854775808L and 9223372036854775807L (2^{63}).

Beginners of Java often ask why we need to use the suffix l or L, because even without it, such as in the following, the program still compiles.

```
long a = 123;
```

This is only partly true. An integer literal without a suffix L or l is regarded as an **int**. Therefore, the following will generate a compile error because 9876543210 is larger than the capacity for an **int**:

```
long a = 9876543210;
```

To rectify the problem, add an L or l at the end of the number like this:

```
long a = 9876543210L;
```

Longs, ints, shorts, and bytes can also be expressed in binaries by prefixing the numbers with **0B** or **0b**. For instance:

```
byte twelve = 0B1100; // = 12
```

If an integer literal is too long, readability suffers. For this reason, starting from Java 7 you can use underscores to separate digits in integer literals. For example, these two have the same meaning but the second one is obviously easier to read.

```
int million = 1000000;

int million = 1_000_000;
```

It does not matter where you put the underscores. You can use one every three digits, like the example above, or any number of digits. Here are some more examples:

```
short next = 12_345;

int twelve = 0B_1100;

long multiplier = 12_34_56_78_90_00L;
```

Floating-Point Literals

Numbers such as 0.4, 1.23, $0.5e^{10}$ are floating point numbers. A floating point number has the following parts:

- a whole number part
- a decimal point
- a fractional part
- an optional exponent

Take 1.23 as an example. For this floating point, the whole number part is 1, the fractional part is 23, and there is no optional exponent. In $0.5e^{10}$, 0 is the whole number part, 5 the fractional part, and 10 is the exponent.

In Java, there are two types of floating points:

- **float**. 32 bits in size. The largest positive float is 3.40282347e+38 and the smallest positive finite nonzero float is 1.40239846e-45.
- **double**. 64 bits in size. The largest positive double is 1.79769313486231570e+308 and the smallest positive finite nonzero double is 4.94065645841246544e-324.

In both **float**s and **double**s, a whole number part of 0 is optional. In other words, 0.5 can be written as .5. Also, the exponent can be represented by either e or E.

To express float literals, you use one of the following formats.

```
Digits . [Digits] [ExponentPart] f_or_F
. Digits [ExponentPart] f_or_F
Digits ExponentPart f_or_F
Digits [ExponentPart] f_or_F
```

Note that the part in brackets is optional.

The *f_or_F* part makes a floating point literal a **float**. The absence of this part makes a float literal a **double**. To explicitly express a double literal, you can suffix it with D or d.

To write double literals, use one of these formats.

```
Digits . [Digits] [ExponentPart] [d_or_D]
. Digits [ExponentPart] [d_or_D]
Digits ExponentPart [d_or_D]
Digits [ExponentPart] [d_or_D]
```

In both floats and doubles, *ExponentPart* is defined as follows.

```
ExponentIndicator SignedInteger
```

where *ExponentIndicator* is either **e** or **E** and *SignedInteger* is .

Sign_{opt} *Digits*

and *Sign* is either + or - and a plus sign is optional.

Examples of **float** literals include the following:

```
2e1f
8.f
.5f
0f
3.14f
9.0001e+12f
```

Here are examples of **double** literals:

```
2e1
8.
.5
0.0D
3.14
9e-9d
7e123D
```

Boolean Literals

The **boolean** type has two values, represented by literals **true** and **false**. For example, the following code declares a **boolean** variable **includeSign** and assigns it the value of **true**.

```
boolean includeSign = true;
```

Character Literals

A character literal is a Unicode character or an escape sequence enclosed in single quotes. An escape sequence is the representation of a Unicode character that cannot be entered using the keyboard or that has a special function in Java. For example, the carriage return and linefeed characters are used to terminate a line and do not have visual representation. To express a linefeed character, you need to escape it, i.e. write its character representation. Also, single quote characters need to be escaped because single quotes are used to enclosed characters.

Here are some examples of character literals:

```
'a'
'Z'
'0'
'ü'
```

Here are character literals that are escape sequences:

```
'\b'   the backspace character
'\t'   the tab character
'\\'   the backslash
'\''   single quote
'\"'   double quote
'\n'   linefeed
```

```
'\r'   carriage return
```

In addition, Java allows you to escape a Unicode character so that you can express a Unicode character using a sequence of ASCII characters. For example, the Unicode code for the character £ is 00A3. You can write the following character literal to express this character:

```
'£'
```

However, if you do not have the tool to produce that character using your keyboard, you can escape it this way:

```
'\u00A3'
```

1.7 Primitive Conversions

When dealing with different data types, you often need to perform conversions. For example, assigning the value of a variable to another variable involves a conversion. If both variables have the same type, the assignment will always succeed. Conversion from a type to the same type is called identity conversion. For example, the following operation is guaranteed to be successful:

```
int a = 90;
int b = a;
```

However, conversion to a different type is not guaranteed to be successful or even possible. There are two other kinds of primitive conversions, the widening conversion and the narrowing conversion.

The Widening Conversion

The widening primitive conversion occurs from a type to another type whose size is the same or larger than that of the first type, such as from **int** (32 bits) to **long** (64 bits). The widening conversion is permitted in the following cases:

- **byte** to **short**, **int**, **long**, **float**, or **double**
- **short** to **int**, **long**, **float**, or **double**
- **char** to **int**, **long**, **float**, or **double**
- **int** to **long**, **float**, or **double**
- **long** to **float** or **double**
- **float** to **double**

A widening conversion from an integer type to another integer type will not risk information loss. At the same token, a conversion from **float** to **double** preserves all the information. However, a conversion from an **int** or a **long** to a **float** may result in loss of precision.

The widening primitive conversion occurs implicitly. You do not need to do anything in your code. For example:

```
int a = 10;
long b = a; // widening conversion
```

The Narrowing Conversion

The narrowing conversion occurs from a type to a different type that has a smaller size, such as from a **long** (64 bits) to an **int** (32 bits). In general, the narrowing primitive conversion can occur in these cases:

- **short** to **byte** or **char**
- **char** to **byte** or **short**
- **int** to **byte**, **short**, or **char**
- **long** to **byte**, **short**, or **char**
- **float** to **byte**, **short**, **char**, **int**, or **long**
- **double** to **byte**, **short**, **char**, **int**, **long**, or **float**

Unlike the widening primitive conversion, the narrowing primitive conversion must be explicit. You need to specify the target type in parentheses. For example, here is a narrowing conversion from **long** to **int**.

```
long a = 10;
int b = (int) a; // narrowing conversion
```

The **(int)** on the second line tells the compiler that a narrowing conversion should occur.

The narrowing conversion may incur information loss, if the converted value is larger than the capacity of the target type. The preceding example did not cause information loss because 10 is small enough for an **int**. However, in the following conversion, there is some information loss because 9876543210L is too big for an **int**.

```
long a = 9876543210L;
int b = (int) a; // the value of b is now 1286608618
```

A narrowing conversion that results in information loss introduces a defect in your program.

1.8 Operators

A computer program is a collection of operations that together achieve a certain function. There are many types of operations, including addition, subtraction, multiplication, division, and bit shifting. In this section you will learn various Java operations.

An operator performs an operation on one, two or three operands. Operands are the targets of an operation and the operator is a symbol representing the action. For example, here is an additive operation:

```
x + 4
```

In this case, **x** and 4 are the operands and + is the operator.

An operator may or may not return a result.

Note

Any legal combination of operators and operands are called an expression. For example, **x + 4** is an expression. A boolean expression results in either **true** or

false. An integer expression produces an integer. And, the result of a floating-point expression is a floating point number.

Operators that require only one operand are called unary operators. There are a few unary operators in Java. Binary operators, the most common type of Java operator, take two operands. There is also one ternary operator, the **? :** operator, that requires three operands.

Table 1.4 list Java operators.

```
=    >    <    !    ~    ? :  instanceof
==   <=   >=   !=   &&   ||   ++   --
+    -    *    /    &    |    ^    %    <<    >>    >>>
+=   -=   *=   /=   &=   |=   ^=   %=   <<=   >>=   >>>=
```

Table 1.4: Java operators

In Java, there are six categories of operators.

- Unary operators
- Arithmetic operators
- Relational and conditional operators
- Shift and logical operators
- Assignment operators
- Other operators

Each of these operators is discussed in the following sections.

Unary Operators

Unary operators operate on one operand. There are six unary operators, all discussed in this section.

Unary Minus Operator –

The unary minus operator returns the negative of its operand. The operand must be a numeric primitive or a variable of a numeric primitive type. For example, in the following code, the value of **y** is -4.5;

```
float x = 4.5f;
float y = -x;
```

Unary Plus Operator +

This operator returns the value of its operand. The operand must be a numeric primitive or a variable of a numeric primitive type. For example, in the following code, the value of **y** is 4.5.

```
float x = 4.5f;
float y = +x;
```

This operator does not have much significance since its absence makes no difference.

Increment Operator ++

This operator increments the value of its operand by one. The operand must be a variable of a numeric primitive type. The operator can appear before or after the operand. If the operator appears before the operand, it is called the prefix increment operator. If it is written after the operand, it becomes the postfix increment operator.

As an example, here is a prefix increment operator in action:

```
int x = 4;
++x;
```

After **++x**, the value of **x** is 5. The preceding code is the same as

```
int x = 4;
x++;
```

After **x++**, the value of **x** is 5.

However, if the result of an increment operator is assigned to another variable in the same expression, there is a difference between the prefix operator and its postfix twin. Consider this example.

```
int x = 4;
int y = ++x;
// y = 5, x = 5
```

The prefix increment operator is applied *before* the assignment. **x** is incremented to 5, and then its value is copied to **y**.

However, check the use of the postfix increment operator here.

```
int x = 4;
int y = x++;
// y = 4, x = 5
```

With the postfix increment operator, the value of the operand (**x**) is incremented *after* the value of the operand is assigned to another variable (**y**).

Note that the increment operator is most often applied to **int**s. However, it also works with other types of numeric primitives, such as **float** and **long**.

Decrement Operator --

This operator decrements the value of its operand by one. The operand must be a variable of a numeric primitive type. Like the increment operator, there are also the prefix decrement operator and the postfix decrement operator. For instance, the following code decrements **x** and assigns the value to **y**.

```
int x = 4;
int y = --x;
// x = 3; y = 3
```

In the following example, the postfix decrement operator is used:

```
int x = 4;
int y = x--;
// x = 3; y = 4
```

Logical Complement Operator !

This operator can only be applied to a **boolean** primitive or an instance of **java.lang.Boolean**. The value of this operator is **true** if the operand is **false**, and **false** if the operand is **true**. For example:

```
boolean x = false;
boolean y = !x;
// at this point, y is true and x is false
```

Bitwise Complement Operator ~

The operand of this operator must be an integer primitive or a variable of an integer primitive type. The result is the bitwise complement of the operand. For example:

```
int j = 2;
int k = ~j; // k = -3; j = 2
```

To understand how this operator works, you need to convert the operand to a binary number and reverse all the bits. The binary form of 2 in an integer is:

```
0000 0000 0000 0000 0000 0000 0000 0010
```

Its bitwise complement is

```
1111 1111 1111 1111 1111 1111 1111 1101
```

which is the representation of -3 in an integer.

Arithmetic Operators

There are four types of arithmetic operations: addition, subtraction, multiplication, division, and modulus. Each arithmetic operator is discussed here.

Addition Operator +

The addition operator adds two operands. The types of the operands must be convertible to a numeric primitive. For example:

```
byte x = 3;
int y = x + 5; // y = 8
```

Make sure the variable that accepts the addition result has a big enough capacity. For example, in the following code the value of **k** is -294967296 and not 4 billion.

```
int j = 2000000000; // 2 billion
int k = j + j; // not enough capacity. A bug!!!
```

On the other hand, the following works as expected:

```
long j = 2000000000; // 2 billion
long k = j + j; // the value of k is 4 billion
```

Subtraction Operator –

This operator performs subtraction between two operands. The types of the operands must be convertible to a numeric primitive type. As an example:

```
int x = 2;
int y = x - 1;      // y = 1
```

Multiplication Operator *

This operator perform multiplication between two operands. The type of the operands must be convertible to a numeric primitive type. As an example:

```
int x = 4;
int y = x * 4;      // y = 16
```

Division Operator /

This operator perform division between two operands. The left hand operand is the dividend and the right hand operand the divisor. Both the dividend and the divisor must be of a type convertible to a numeric primitive type. As an example:

```
int x = 4;
int y = x / 2;      // y = 2
```

Note that at runtime a division operation raises an error if the divisor is zero.

The result of a division using the / operator is always an integer. If the divisor does not divide the dividends equally, the remainder will be ignored. For example

```
int x = 4;
int y = x / 3;      // y = 1
```

The **java.lang.Math** class, explained in Chapter 4, "Core Classes," can perform more sophisticated division operations.

Modulus Operator %

The modulus operator perform division between two operands and returns the remainder. The left hand operand is the dividend and the right hand operand the divisor. Both the dividend and the divisor must be of a type that is convertible to a numeric primitive type. For example the result of the following operation is 2.

```
8 % 3
```

Equality Operators

There are two equality operators, == (equal to) and **!=** (not equal to), both operating on two operands that can be integers, floating points, characters, or **boolean**. The outcome of equality operators is a **boolean**.

For example, the value of **c** is **true** after the comparison.

```
int a = 5;
int b = 5;
boolean c = a == b;
```

As another example,

```
boolean x = true;
boolean y = true;
boolean z = x != y;
```

The value of **z** is **false** after comparison because **x** is equal to **y**.

Relational Operators

There are five relational operators: <, >, <=, and >= and **instanceof**. The first four operators are explained in this section. **instanceof** is discussed in Chapter 6, "Inheritance."

The <, >, <=, and >= operators operate on two operands whose types must be convertible to a numeric primitive type. Relational operations return a **boolean**.

The < operator evaluates if the value of the left-hand operand is less than the value of the right-hand operand. For example, the following operation returns **false**:

```
9 < 6
```

The > operator evaluates if the value of the left-hand operand is greater than the value of the right-hand operand. For example, this operation returns **true**:

```
9 > 6
```

The <= operator tests if the value of the left-hand operand is less than or equal to the value of the right-hand operand. For example, the following operation evaluates to **false**:

```
9 <= 6
```

The >= operator tests if the value of the left-hand operand is greater than or equal to the value of the right-hand operand. For example, this operation returns **true**:

```
9 >= 9
```

Conditional Operators

There are three conditional operators: the AND operator **&&**, the OR operator ||, and the **? :** operator. Each of these is detailed below.

The && operator

This operator takes two expressions as operands and both expressions must return a value that must be convertible to **boolean**. It returns **true** if both operands evaluate to **true**. Otherwise, it returns **false**. If the left-hand operand evaluates to **false**, the right-hand operand will not be evaluated. For example, the following returns **false**.

```
(5 < 3) && (6 < 9)
```

The || Operator

This operator takes two expressions as operands and both expressions must return a value that must be convertible to **boolean**. || returns **true** if one of the operands evaluates to **true**. If the left-hand operand evaluates to **true**, the right-hand operand will not be evaluated. For instance, the following returns **true**.

```
(5 < 3) || (6 < 9)
```

The ? : Operator

This operator operates on three operands. The syntax is

```
expression1 ? expression2 : expression3
```

Here, *expression1* must return a value convertible to **boolean**. If *expression1* evaluates to **true**, *expression2* is returned. Otherwise, *expression3* is returned.

For example, the following expression returns 4.

```
(8 < 4) ? 2 : 4
```

Shift Operators

A shift operator takes two operands whose type must be convertible to an integer primitive. The left-hand operand is the value to be shifted, the right-hand operand indicates the shift distance. There are three types of shift operators:

- the left shift operator <<
- the right shift operator >>
- the unsigned right shift operator >>>

The Left Shift Operator <<

The left shift operator bit-shifts a number to the left, padding the right bits with 0. The value of **n << s** is **n** left-shifted **s** bit positions. This is the same as multiplication by two to the power of s.

For example, left-shifting an **int** whose value is 1 with a shift distance of 3 (1 << 3) results in 8. Again, to figure this out, you convert the operand to a binary number.

```
0000 0000 0000 0000 0000 0000 0000 0001
```

Shifting to the left 3 shift units results in:

```
0000 0000 0000 0000 0000 0000 0000 1000
```

which is equivalent to 8 (the same as $1 * 2^3$).

Another rule is this. If the left-hand operand is an **int**, only the first five bits of the shift distance will be used. In other words, the shift distance must be within the range 0 and 31. If you pass an number greater than 31, only the first five bits will be used. This is to say, if **x** is an **int**, **x << 32** is the same as **x << 0**; **x << 33** is the same as **x << 1**.

If the left-hand operand is a **long**, only the first six bits of the shift distance will be used. In other words, the shift distance actually used is within the range 0 and 63.

The Right Shift Operator >>

The right shift operator >> bit-shifts the left-hand operand to the right. The value of **n >> s** is **n** right-shifted **s** bit positions. The resulting value is **$n/2^s$**.

As an example, **16 >> 1** is equal to 8. To prove this, write the binary representation of 16.

```
0000 0000 0000 0000 0000 0000 0001 0000
```

Then, shifting it to the right by 1 bit results in.

```
0000 0000 0000 0000 0000 0000 0000 1000
```

which is equal to 8.

The Unsigned Right Shift Operator >>>

The value of **n >>> s** depends on whether **n** is positive or negative. For a positive **n**, the value is the same as **n >> s**.

If **n** is negative, the value depends on the type of **n**. If **n** is an **int**, the value is **(n>>s)+(2<<~s)**. If **n** is a **long**, the value is **(n>>s)+(2L<<~s)**.

Assignment Operators

There are twelve assignment operators:

```
=  +=  -=  *=  /=  %=  <<=  >>=  >>>=  &=  ^=  |=
```

Assignment operators take two operands whose type must be of an integral primitive. The left-hand operand must be a variable. For instance:

```
int x = 5;
```

Except for the assignment operator =, the rest work the same way and you should see each of them as consisting of two operators. For example, += is actually + and =. The assignment operator <<= has two operators, << and =.

The two-part assignment operators work by applying the first operator to both operands and then assign the result to the left-hand operand. For example **x += 5** is the same as **x = x + 5**.

x -= 5 is the same as **x = x - 5**.

x <<= 5 is equivalent to **x = x << 5**.

x &= 5 produces the same result as **x = x &= 5**.

Integer Bitwise Operators & | ^

The bitwise operators **&** | ^ perform a bit to bit operation on two operands whose types must be convertible to **int**. **&** indicates an AND operation, | an OR operation, and ^ an exclusive OR operation. For example,

```
0xFFFF & 0x0000 = 0x0000
0xF0F0 & 0xFFFF = 0xF0F0
0xFFFF | 0x000F = 0xFFFF
0xFFF0 ^ 0x00FF = 0xFF0F
```

Logical Operators & | ^

The logical operators **&** | ^ perform a logical operation on two operands that are convertible to **boolean**. **&** indicates an AND operation, | an OR operation, and ^ an exclusive OR operation. For example,

```
true & true  = true
true & false = false
true | false = true
false | false = false
true ^ true = false
false ^ false = false
false ^ true = true
```

Operator Precedence

In most programs, multiple operators often appear in an expression, such as.

```
int a = 1;
int b = 2;
int c = 3;
int d = a + b * c;
```

What is the value of **d** after the code is executed? If you say 9, you're wrong. It's actually 7.

Multiplication operator * takes precedence over addition operator +. As a result, multiplication will be performed before addition. However, if you want the addition to be executed first, you can use parentheses.

```
int d = (a + b) * c;
```

The latter will assign 9 to **d**.

Table 1.5 lists all the operators in the order of precedence. Operators in the same column have equal precedence.

<table>
<tr><th>Operator</th><th></th></tr>
<tr><td>postfix operators</td><td>[ ] . (params) expr++ expr--</td></tr>
<tr><td>unary operators</td><td>++expr --expr +expr -expr ~ !</td></tr>
<tr><td>creation or cast</td><td>new (type)expr</td></tr>
<tr><td>multiplicative</td><td>* / %</td></tr>
<tr><td>additive</td><td>+ -</td></tr>
<tr><td>shift</td><td><< >> >>></td></tr>
<tr><td>relational</td><td>< > <= >= instanceof</td></tr>
<tr><td>equality</td><td>== !=</td></tr>
<tr><td>bitwise AND</td><td>&</td></tr>
<tr><td>bitwise exclusive OR</td><td>^</td></tr>
<tr><td>bitwise inclusive OR</td><td>|</td></tr>
<tr><td>logical AND</td><td>&&</td></tr>
<tr><td>logical OR</td><td>||</td></tr>
<tr><td>conditional</td><td>? :</td></tr>
<tr><td>assignment</td><td>= += -= *= /= %= &= ^= |= <<= >>= >>>=</td></tr>
</table>

Table 1.5: Operator precedence

Note that parentheses have the highest precedence. Parentheses can also make expressions clearer. For example, consider the following code:

```
int x = 5;
int y = 5;
boolean z = x * 5 == y + 20;
```

The value of **z** after comparison is **true**. However, the expression is far from clear.

You can rewrite the last line using parentheses.

```
boolean z = (x * 5) == (y + 20);
```

which does not change the result because * and + have higher precedence than ==, but this makes the expression much clearer.

Promotion

Some unary operators (such as +, -, and ~) and binary operators (such as +, -, *, /) cause automatic promotion, i.e. elevation to a wider type such as from **byte** to **int**. Consider the following code:

```
byte x = 5;
byte y = -x; // error
```

The second line surprisingly causes an error even though a byte can accommodate -5. The reason for this is the unary operator - causes the result of **-x** to be promoted to **int**. To rectify the problem, either change **y** to **int** or perform an explicit narrowing conversion like this.

```
byte x = 5;
byte y = (byte) -x;
```

For unary operators, if the type of the operand is **byte**, **short**, or **char**, the outcome is promoted to **int**.

For binary operators, the promotion rules are as follows.

- If any of the operands is of type **byte** or **short**, then both operands will be converted to **int** and the outcome will be an **int**.
- If any of the operands is of type **double**, then the other operand is converted to **double** and the outcome will be a **double**.
- If any of the operands is of type **float**, then the other operand is converted to **float** and the outcome will be a **float**.
- If any of the operands is of type **long**, then the other operand is converted to **long** and the outcome will be a **long**.

For example, the following code causes a compile error:

```
short x = 200;
short y = 400;
short z = x + y;
```

You can fix this by changing **z** to **int** or perform an explicit narrowing conversion of **x + y**, such as

```
short z = (short) (x + y);
```

Note that the parentheses around **x + y** is required, otherwise only **x** would be converted to **int** and the result of addition of a **short** and an **int** will be an **int**.

1.9 Comments

It is good practice to write comments throughout your code, sufficiently explaining what functionality a class provides, what a method does, what a field contains, and so forth.

There are two types of comments in Java, both with syntax similar to comments in C and C++.

- Traditional comments. Enclose a traditional comment in /* and */.
- End-of-line comments. Use double slashes (//) which causes the rest of the line after // to be ignored by the compiler.

For example, here is a comment that describes a method

```
/*
  toUpperCase capitalizes the characters of in a String object
*/
public void toUpperCase(String s) {
```

Here is an end-of-line comment:

```
public int rowCount; //the number of rows from the database
```

Traditional comments do not nest, which means

```
/*
  /* comment 1 */
  comment 2 */
```

is invalid because the first */ after the first /* will terminate the comment. As such, the comment above will have the extra **comment 2** */, which will generate a compiler error.

On the other hand, end-of-line comments can contain anything, including the sequences of characters /* and */, such as this:

```
// /* this comment is okay */
```

Self Test

Question 1

Which of the following are Java primitives? (Choose all that apply)

A. int
B. Long
C. short
D. boolean
E. String

Question 2

Which of the following are Java legal identifiers? (Choose all that apply)

A. tempCounter
B. long
C. $
D. _rows
E. game_users

Question 3

Which of the following are valid variable declarations? (Choose all that apply)

A. int int;
B. long Long;
C. boolean $true;
D. short #x2;
E. int a, b, c;

Question 4

Which of the following are valid value assignments? (Choose all that apply)

A. float f = 123;
B. float g = 123.45;
C. double h = 123.45;
D. long i = 123;
E. int j = 12345_12345_12345;
F. long k = 12345_12345_12345;

Question 5

Which of the following are valid value assignments? (Choose all that apply)

A. float f = 123;
B. float g = 123.45F;
C. double h = 123.45D;
D. long i = 123L;
E. int j = 12345_12345_12345;
F. long k = 12345_12345_12345L;

Question 6

Given

```
int temp = 1 + 2 * 3;
```

What is the value of temp?

A. 9
B. 7
C. 2
D. None of the above

Question 7

Given

```
int temp = (1 + 2) * 3;
```

What is the value of temp?

A. 9
B. 7
C. 2
D. None of the above

Question 8

Which of these statements create a variable whose value cannot be changed?

A. public static final int TEMP = 5;
B. public static int TEMP = 5;
C. private static final int TEMP = 5;
D. final int TEMP = 5;

Question 9

Given the following code

```
1.  long a = 1000_000_000L;
2.  int b = a - 999_999_999L;
3.  int c = (int) a - 999_999_999L;
```

```
4.   int d = (int) (a - 999_999_999L);
```

What will happen if you try to compile the code?

A. The code will compile with no reported errors;
B. Compile error at line 2;
C. Compile error at line 3;
D. Compile error at line 4;

Question 10

Which of the following are valid comments?

A. // This is a comment
B. /* This is a comment */
C. /* This is a /* good */ comment */
D. // /* This is a /* good */ comment */

Answers to Self Test

Question 1

Which of the following are Java primitives? (Choose all that apply)

A. int
B. Long
C. short
D. boolean
E. String

Answer: A, C, D.

int, **short** and **boolean** are some of Java primitives, and so is **long**, but not **Long**. **String** is a Java class and is not a primitive.

Question 2

Which of the following are Java legal identifiers? (Choose all that apply)

A. tempCounter
B. long
C. $
D. _rows
E. game_users

Answer: A, C, D, E.

B is not a valid identifier because **long** is a Java primitive. Note that **$** can be used in a Java identifier but its use is normally reserved for machine-generated code.

Question 3

Which of the following are valid variable declarations? (Choose all that apply)

A. int int;
B. long Long;
C. boolean $true;
D. short #x2;
E. int a, b, c;

Answer: B, C, E.

A is invalid because **int** is a primitive and cannot be used as an identifier. B is valid because **Long** can be used as a variable name, even though it happens to be the name of a popular Java class. C is legal because $ can be used in an identifier. D is invalid because it contains the character #. E is also valid and declares three **int**s.

Question 4

Which of the following are valid value assignments? (Choose all that apply)

A. float f = 123;
B. float g = 123.45;
C. double h = 123.45;
D. long i = 123;
E. int j = 12345_12345_12345;
F. long k = 12345_12345_12345;

Answer: A, C, D.

B is invalid because 123.45 is a **double** and cannot be assigned to a float. E is invalid because the value is too big for an **int**. F is invalid because literal 12345_12345_12345 is considered an **int** and its value is too big for an **int**.

Question 5

Which of the following are valid value assignments? (Choose all that apply)

A. float f = 123;
B. float g = 123.45F;
C. double h = 123.45D;
D. long i = 123L;
E. int j = 12345_12345_12345;
F. long k = 12345_12345_12345L;

Answer: A, B, C, D, F.

E is invalid because the value is too big for an int. All the other options are correct.

Question 6

Given

```
int temp = 1 + 2 * 3;
```

What is the value of temp?

A. 9
B. 7
C. 2
D. 6

Answer: B.

2 * 3 is evaluated first because * has precedence over +. The result (6) is then added to 1.

Question 7

Given

```
int temp = (1 + 2) * 3;
```

What is the value of temp?

A. 9
B. 7
C. 2
D. 6

Answer: A.

The bracket has precedence over *, so 1 + 2 is evaluated first. The result (3) is then multiplied by 3.

Question 8

Which of these statements create a variable whose value cannot be changed?

A. public static final int TEMP = 5;
B. public static int TEMP = 5;
C. private static final int TEMP = 5;
D. final int TEMP = 5;

Answer: A, C, D.

The **final** keyword makes a variable a constant.

Question 9

Given the following code

```
long a = 1000_000_000L;
int b = a - 999_999_999L;
int c = (int) a - 999_999_999L;
int d = (int) (a - 999_999_999L);
```

What will happen if you try to compile the code?

A. The code will compile with no reported errors;

B. Compile error at line 2;
C. Compile error at line 3;
D. Compile error at line 4;

Answer: B, C.

The expression at line 2 returns a **long** and assigning a **long** to an **int** results in a compile error. At line 3 variable **a** is converted to an **int**, which is legal. However, subtracting a **long** from an **int** results in a **long**, so the expression at line 3 returns a **long**. Attempting to assign a **long** value to an **int** causes a compile error. Line 4 performs the subtraction first and then the result is converted to an **int** and assigned to an **int** variable. Therefore, line 4 does not cause a compile error.

Question 10

Which of the following are valid comments?

A. // This is a comment
B. /* This is a comment */
C. /* This is a /* good */ comment */
D. // /* This is a /* good */ comment */

Answer: A, B, D.

C is invalid because the comment is nested. D is valid because the statement comments out everything to the right of //.

Chapter 2
Statements

A computer program is a compilation of instructions called statements. There are many types of statements in Java and some—such as **if**, **while**, **for**, and **switch**—are conditional statements that determine the program flow. This chapter discusses Java statements, starting with an overview and then providing details of each of them. The **return** statement, which is the statement to exit a method, is discussed in Chapter 3, "Objects and Classes."

2.1 Overview

In programming, a statement is an instruction to do something. Statements control the sequence of program execution. Assigning a value to a variable is an example of a statement.

```
x = z + 5;
```

Even a variable declaration is a statement.

```
long secondsElapsed;
```

By contrast, an *expression* is a combination of operators and operands that gets evaluated. For example, **z + 5** is an expression.

In Java a statement is terminated with a semicolon and multiple statements can be written in a single line.

```
x = y + 1; z = y + 2;
```

However, writing multiple statements in a single line is not recommended as it obscures code readability.

Note

In Java, an empty statement is legal and does nothing:

```
;
```

Some expressions can be made statements by terminating them with a semicolon. For example, **x++** is an expression. However, this is a statement:

```
x++;
```

Statements can be grouped in a block. By definition, a block is a sequence of the following programming elements within braces:

- statements
- local class declarations
- local variable declaration statements

A statement and a statement block can be labeled. Label names follow the same rule as Java identifiers and are terminated with a colon. For example, the following statement is labeled **sectionA**.

```
sectionA: x = y + 1;
```

And, here is an example of labeling a block:

```
start: {
    // statements
}
```

The purpose of labeling a statement or a block is so that it can be referenced by the **break** and **continue** statements.

2.2 The if Statement

The **if** statement is a conditional branch statement. The syntax of the **if** statement is either one of these two:

```
if (booleanExpression) {
    statement(s)
}

if (booleanExpression) {
    statement(s)
} else {
    statement(s)
}
```

If *booleanExpression* evaluates to **true**, the statements in the block following the **if** statement are executed. If it evaluates to **false**, the statements in the **if** block are not executed. If *booleanExpression* evaluates to **false** and there is an **else** block, the statements in the **else** block are executed.

For example, in the following **if** statement, the **if** block will be executed if **x** is greater than 4.

```
if (x > 4) {
    // statements
}
```

In the following example, the **if** block will be executed if **a** is greater than 3. Otherwise, the **else** block will be executed.

```
if (a > 3) {
    // statements
} else {
    // statements
```

```
}
```

Note that the good coding style suggests that statements in a block be indented.

If you are evaluating a boolean in your if statement, it's not necessary to use the == operator like this:

```
boolean fileExist = ...
if (fileExist == true) {
```

Instead, you can simply write

```
if (fileExists) {
```

By the same token, instead of writing

```
if (fileExists == false) {
```

write

```
if (!fileExists) {
```

If the expression to be evaluated is too long to be written in a single line, it is recommended that you use two units of indentation for subsequent lines. For example.

```
if (numberOfLoginAttempts < numberOfMaximumLoginAttempts
        || numberOfMinimumLoginAttempts > y) {
    y++;
}
```

If there is only one statement in an **if** or **else** block, the braces are optional.

```
if (a > 3)
    a++;
else
    a = 3;
```

However, this may pose what is called the dangling else problem. Consider the following example:

```
if (a > 0 || b < 5)
    if (a > 2)
        System.out.println("a > 2");
    else
        System.out.println("a < 2");
```

The **else** statement is dangling because it is not clear which **if** statement the **else** statement is associated with. An **else** statement is always associated with the immediately preceding **if**. Using braces makes your code clearer.

```
if (a > 0 || b < 5) {
    if (a > 2) {
        System.out.println("a > 2");
    } else {
        System.out.println("a < 2");
    }
}
```

If there are multiple selections, you can also use **if** with a series of **else** statements.

```
if (booleanExpression1) {
    // statements
} else if (booleanExpression2) {
    // statements
}
...
else {
    // statements
}
```

For example

```
if (a == 1) {
    System.out.println("one");
} else if (a == 2) {
    System.out.println("two");
} else if (a == 3) {
    System.out.println("three");
} else {
    System.out.println("invalid");
}
```

In this case, the **else** statements that are immediately followed by an **if** do not use braces. See also the discussion of the **switch** statement in the section "The switch Statement" later in this chapter.

2.3 The while Statement

In many occasions, you may want to perform an action several times in a row. In other words, you have a block of code that you want executed repeatedly. Intuitively, this can be done by repeating the lines of code. For instance, a beep can be achieved using this line of code:

```
java.awt.Toolkit.getDefaultToolkit().beep();
```

And, to wait for half a second you use these lines of code.

```
try {
    Thread.currentThread().sleep(500);
} catch (Exception e) {
}
```

Therefore, to produce three beeps with a 500 milliseconds interval between two beeps, you can simply repeat the same code:

```
java.awt.Toolkit.getDefaultToolkit().beep();
try {
    Thread.currentThread().sleep(500);
} catch (Exception e) {
}
```

```
java.awt.Toolkit.getDefaultToolkit().beep();
try {
    Thread.currentThread().sleep(500);
} catch (Exception e) {
}
java.awt.Toolkit.getDefaultToolkit().beep();
```

However, there are circumstances where repeating code does not work. Here are some of those:

- The number of repetition is higher than 5, which means the number of lines of code increases five fold. If there is a line that you need to fix in the block, copies of the same line must also be modified.
- If the number of repetitions is not known in advance.

A much cleverer way is to put the repeated code in a loop. This way, you only write the code once but you can instruct Java to execute the code any number of times. One way to create a loop is by using the **while** statement, which is the topic of discussion of this section. Another way is to use the **for** statement, which is explained in the next section.

The **while** statement has the following syntax.

```
while (booleanExpression) {
    statement(s)
}
```

Here, *statement(s)* will be executed as long as *booleanExpression* evaluates to **true**. If there is only a single statement inside the braces, you may omit the braces. For clarity, however, you should always use braces even when there is only one statement.

As an example of the **while** statement, the following code prints integer numbers that are less than three.

```
int i = 0;
while (i < 3) {
    System.out.println(i);
    i++;
}
```

Note that the execution of the code in the loop is dependent on the value of **i**, which is incremented with each iteration until it reaches 3.

To produce three beeps with an interval of 500 milliseconds, use this code:

```
int j = 0;
while (j < 3) {
    java.awt.Toolkit.getDefaultToolkit().beep();
    try {
        Thread.currentThread().sleep(500);
    } catch (Exception e) {
    }
    j++;
}
```

Sometimes, you use an expression that always evaluates to **true** (such as the **boolean** literal **true**) but relies on the **break** statement to escape from the loop.

```
int k = 0;
while (true) {
    System.out.println(k);
    k++;
    if (k > 2) {
        break;
    }
}
```

You will learn about the **break** statement in the section, “The break Statement” later in this chapter.

2.4 The do-while Statement

The **do-while** statement is like the **while** statement, except that the associated block always gets executed at least once. Its syntax is as follows:

```
do {
    statement(s)
} while (booleanExpression);
```

With **do-while**, you put the statement(s) to be executed after the **do** keyword. Just like the **while** statement, you can omit the braces if there is only one statement within them. However, always use braces for the sake of clarity.

For example, here is an example of the **do-while** statement:

```
int i = 0;
do {
    System.out.println(i);
    i++;
} while (i < 3);
```

This prints the following to the console:

```
0
1
2
```

The following **do-while** demonstrates that at least the code in the **do** block will be executed once even though the initial value of **j** used to test the expression **j < 3** evaluates to **false**.

```
int j = 4;
do {
    System.out.println(j);
    j++;
} while (j < 3);
```

This prints the following on the console.

```
4
```

2.5 The for Statement

The **for** statement is like the **while** statement, i.e. you use it to enclose code that needs to be executed multiple times. However, **for** is more complex than **while**.

The **for** statement starts with an initialization, followed by an expression evaluation for each iteration and the execution of a statement block if the expression evaluates to **true**. An update statement will also be executed after the execution of the statement block for each iteration.

The **for** statement has following syntax:

```
for ( init ; booleanExpression ; update ) {
    statement(s)
}
```

Here, *init* is an initialization that will be performed before the first iteration, *booleanExpression* is a boolean expression which will cause the execution of *statement(s)* if it evaluates to **true**, and *update* is a statement that will be executed *after* the execution of the statement block. *init*, *expression*, and *update* are optional.

The **for** statement will stop only if one of the following conditions is met:

- *booleanEpression* evaluates to **false**
- A **break** or **continue** statement is executed
- A runtime error occurs.

It is common to declare a variable and assign a value to it in the initialization part. The variable declared will be visible to the *expression* and *update* parts as well as to the statement block.

For example, the following **for** statement loops three times and each time prints the value of **i**.

```
for (int i = 0; i < 3; i++) {
    System.out.println(i);
}
```

The **for** statement starts by declaring an **int** named **i** and assigning 0 to it:

```
int i = 0;
```

It then evaluates the expression **i < 3**, which evaluates to **true** since **i** equals 0. As a result, the statement block is executed, and the value of **i** is printed. It then performs the update statement **i++**, which increments **i** to 1. That concludes the first loop.

The **for** statement then evaluates the value of **i < 3** again. The result is again **true** because **i** equals 1. This causes the statement block to be executed and **1** is printed on the console. Afterwards, the update statement **i++** is executed, incrementing **i** to 2. That concludes the third loop.

Next, the expression **i < 3** is evaluated and the result is **true** because **i** equals 2. This causes the statement block to be run and 2 is printed on the console. Afterwards, the update statement **i++** is executed, causing **i** to be equal to 3. This concludes the second loop.

Next, the expression **i < 3** is evaluated again, and the result is **false**. This stops the **for** loop.

This is what you see on the console:

```
0
1
2
```

Note that the variable **i** is not visible anywhere else since it is declared within the **for** loop.

Note also that if the statement block within **for** only consists of one statement, you can remove the braces, so in this case the above **for** statement can be rewritten as:

```
for (int i = 0; i < 3; i++)
    System.out.println(i);
```

However, using braces even if there is only one statement makes your code clearer.

Here is another example of the **for** statement.

```
for (int i = 0; i < 3; i++) {
    if (i % 2 == 0) {
        System.out.println(i);
    }
}
```

This one loops three times. For each iteration the value of **i** is tested. If **i** is even, its value is printed. The result of the **for** loop is as follows:

```
0
2
```

The following **for** loop is similar to the previous case, but uses **i += 2** as the update statement. As a result, it only loops twice, when **i** equals 0 and when it is 2.

```
for (int i = 0; i < 3; i += 2) {
    System.out.println(i);
}
```

The result is

```
0
2
```

A statement that decrements a variable is often used too. Consider the following **for** loop:

```
for (int i = 3; i > 0; i--) {
    System.out.println(i);
}
```

which prints:

```
3
2
1
```

The initialization part of the **for** statement is optional. In the following **for** loop, the variable **j** is declared outside the loop, so potentially **j** can be used from other points in the code outside the **for** statement block.

```
int j = 0;
for ( ; j < 3; j++) {
    System.out.println(j);
}
// j is visible here
```

As mentioned previously, the update statement is optional. The following **for** statement moves the update statement to the end of the statement block. The result is the same.

```
int k = 0;
for ( ; k < 3; ) {
    System.out.println(k);
    k++;
}
```

In theory, you can even omit the *booleanExpression* part. For example, the following **for** statement does not have one, and the loop is only terminated with the **break** statement. See the section, "The break Statement" for more information.

```
int m = 0;
for ( ; ; ) {
    System.out.println(m);
    m++;
    if (m > 4) {
        break;
    }
}
```

If you compare **for** and **while**, you'll see that you can always replace the **while** statement with **for**. This is to say that

```
while (expression) {
    ...
}
```

can always be written as

```
for ( ; expression; ) {
    ...
}
```

Note
In addition, **for** can iterate over an array or a collection. See Chapters 5, "Arrays" for a discussion of the enhanced **for**.

2.6 The break Statement

The **break** statement is used to break from an enclosing **do**, **while**, **for**, or **switch** statement. It is a compile error to use **break** anywhere else.

For example, consider the following code

```
int i = 0;
while (true) {
    System.out.println(i);
    i++;
    if (i > 3) {
        break;
    }
}
```

The result is

```
0
1
2
3
```

Note that **break** breaks the loop without executing the rest of the statements in the block.

Here is another example of break, this time in a **for** loop.

```
int m = 0;
for ( ; ; ) {
    System.out.println(m);
    m++;
    if (m > 4) {
        break;
    }
}
```

The **break** statement can be followed by a label. The presence of a label will transfer control to the start of the code identified by the label. For example, consider this code.

```
start:
for (int i = 0; i < 3; i++) {
    for (int j = 0; j < 4; j++) {
        if (j == 2) {
            break start;
        }
        System.out.println(i + ":" + j);
    }
}
```

The use of label start identifies the first **for** loop. The statement **break start;** therefore breaks from the first loop. The result of running the preceding code is as follows.

```
0:0
0:1
```

Java does not have a goto statement like in C or C++, and labels are meant as a form of goto. However, just as using goto in C/C++ may obscure your code, the use of labels in Java may make your code unstructured. The general advice is to avoid labels if possible and to always use them with caution.

2.7 The continue Statement

The **continue** statement is like **break** but it only stops the execution of the current iteration and causes control to begin with the next iteration.

For example, the following code prints the numbers 0 to 9, except 5.

```
for (int i = 0; i < 10; i++) {
    if (i == 5) {
        continue;
    }
    System.out.println(i);
}
```

When **i** is equals to 5, the expression of the **if** statement evaluates to **true** and causes the **continue** statement to be called. As a result, the statement below it that prints the value of **i** is not executed and control continues with the next loop, i.e. for **i** equal to 6.

As with **break**, **continue** may be followed by a label to identify which enclosing loop to continue to. As with labels with **break**, employ **continue label** with caution and avoid it if you can.

Here is an example of **continue** with a label.

```
start:
for (int i = 0; i < 3; i++) {
    for (int j = 0; j < 4; j++) {
        if (j == 2) {
            continue start;
        }
        System.out.println(i + ":" + j);
    }
}
```

The result of running this code is as follows:

```
0:0
0:1
1:0
1:1
2:0
2:1
```

2.8 The switch Statement

The **switch** statement is an alternative to a series of **else if**. **switch** allows you to choose a block of statements to run from a selection of code, based on the return value of an expression. The expression used in the **switch** statement must return an **int**, a **String**, or an enumerated value.

Note
The **String** class is discussed in Chapter 4, "Core Classes."

The syntax of the **switch** statement is as follows.

```
switch(expression) {
case value_1 :
    statement(s);
    break;
case value_2 :
    statement(s);
    break;
  .
  .
  .
case value_n :
    statement(s);
    break;
default:
    statement(s);
}
```

Failure to add a **break** statement after a case will not generate a compile error but may have more serious consequences because the statements on the next case will be executed.

Here is an example of the **switch** statement. If the value of **i** is 1, "One player is playing this game." is printed. If the value is 2, "Two players are playing this game is printed." If the value is 3, "Three players are playing this game is printed. For any other value, "You did not enter a valid value." will be printed.

```
int i = ...;
switch (i) {
case 1 :
    System.out.println("One player is playing this game.");
    break;
case 2 :
    System.out.println("Two players are playing this game.");
    break;
case 3 :
    System.out.println("Three players are playing this game.");
    break;
default:
    System.out.println("You did not enter a valid value.");
}
```

For examples of switching on a String or an enumerated value, see Chapter 4, "Core Classes."

Self Test

Question 1

Given

```
int j = 0;
for (int i = 0; i < 3; i++) {
    if (i % 2 == 0) j = i;
}
System.out.println(j);
```

What is the output of this code?

A. 0
B. 1
C. 2
D. 3

Question 2

Consider this code snippet:

```
int y = 0;
for (int x = 0; y < 5; ++x) {
    if (x % 2 == 0) continue;
    y += x;
}
System.out.println(y);
```

What is the output of this code?

A. 3
B. 5
C. 7
D. 9

Question 3

Given

```
int y = 0;
for (; ; ) {
    if (y >= 10) break;
    y += ++y;
}
System.out.println(y);
```

What is the output of this code?

A. 14
B. 15
C. 16
D. None of the above

Question 4

Given

```
int y = 0;`
for (; ; ) {
    if (y >= 10) break;
    y += y++;
}
System.out.println(y);
```

What is the output of this code?

A. 14
B. 15
C. 16
D. None of the above

Question 5

Given

```
int i = 1;
switch (i) {
case 1 :
    System.out.println("One player is playing this game.");
case 2 :
    System.out.println("Two players are playing this game.");
    break;
default:
    System.out.println("You did not enter a valid value.");
}
```

What is printed on the console if the code is executed?

A. One player is playing this game.
B. Two players are playing this game.
C. One player is playing this game.
   Two players are playing this game.
D. None of the above.

Question 6

Given

```
int i = 1;
int y = 5;
if (i == 2)
if (i == 1)
    y = 50;
else y = 500;
```

What is the value of y after the code is executed?

A. 5.
B. 50.
C. 500.
D. None of the above.

Question 7

Given this code

```
1.  ...
2.      System.out.print(i + " ");
3.  }
```

and given the following result

```
10 9 8 7 6 5 4 3 2 1
```

What line of code should be inserted into line 1?

A. for (int i = 0; i < 10; i++) {
B. for (int i = 10; i > 0; i--) {
C. while (i < 10) {
D. while (i > 10) {

Question 8

Consider the following code.

```
1.  int x = 0;
2.  while (x < 10) {
3.      x++;
4.      System.out.print(x + " ");
5.  }
```

What is the equivalent for statement that can be used to replace lines 1 to 3?

A. for (int i = 1; i <= 10; i++) {
B. for (int i = 1; i < 11; i++) {
C. for (int i = 1; i < 11; ++i) {
D. for (int i = 1; i <= 10; ++i) {

Question 9

This code prints all odd numbers between 0 and 10.

```
1.  for (int i = 1; i <= 10; i++) {
2.      if (i % 2 == 1)
3.          System.out.print(i + " ");
4.  }
```

Which of the following for statements can be used to replace lines 1 and 2?

A. for (int i = 1; i <= 10; i++) {
B. for (int i = 1; i <= 10; i+=2) {
C. for (int i = 1; i <= 10; i--) {
D. None of the above

Question 10

Given

```
int i = 1;
do {
    System.out.print(i++);
} while (i != 5);
```

What is the output of the program?

A. 012345
B. 01234
C. 1234
D. 12345

Answers to Self Test

Question 1

Given

```
int j = 0;
for (int i = 0; i < 3; i++) {
    if (i % 2 == 0) j = i;
}
System.out.println(j);
```

What is the output of this code?

A. 0
B. 1
C. 2
D. 3

Answer: B

The code in the **if** statement is only executed when **i** is evenly divisible by two, i.e. when i equals 0 or 2. The last statement is j = i where i = 2, therefore the final value of **j** is 2.

Question 2

Consider this code snippet:

```
int y = 0;
for (int x = 0; y < 5; ++x) {
    if (x % 2 == 0) continue;
    y += x;
}
```

```
System.out.println(y);
```

What is the output of this code?

A. 3
B. 5
C. 7
D. 9

Answer: D

y is incremented when **x** is odd (i.e. when **i** equals 1, 3, 5, …). In addition, the for loop will only continue until **y** is equal to or less than 5. Therefore, y = 1 when x = 1, y = 4 when x = 3, and y = 9 when x = 5. When y reaches 9, the loop stops as the condition (**y < 5**) is no longer met.

Question 3

Given

```
int y = 0;
for (; ; ) {
    if (y >= 10) break;
    y += ++y;
}
System.out.println(y);
```

What is the output of this code?

A. 14
B. 15
C. 16
D. None of the above

Answer: B

The **for** statement is an infinite loop that will exit only if **y** is equal to or greater than 10. When the increment operator ++ is used in prefix notation (e.g. ++y), the operand is incremented first and then its value is used in an expression. The statement y += ++y is equivalent to y = y + ++y.

At iteration 1, the value of y at the beginning of the loop is 0. The statement becomes

```
y = 0 + ++y
```

The operand y is incremented and its value used in the expression, thus y = 0 + 1 and y is equal to 1.

At iteration 2, the value of y at the beginning of the loop is 1. The statement becomes y = 1 + ++y = 1 + 2 = 3

At iteration 3, the value of y at the beginning of the loop is 3. The statement becomes

```
y = 3 + ++y = 3 + 4 = 7
```

At iteration 4, the value of y at the beginning of the loop is 7. The statement becomes

```
y = 7 + ++y = 7 + 8 = 15
```

Question 4

Given

```
int y = 0;
for (; ; ) {
    if (y >= 10) break;
    y += y++;
}
System.out.println(y);
```

What is the output of this code?

A. 14
B. 15
C. 16
D. None of the above

Answer: D.

The **for** statement is an infinite loop that will exit only if **y** is equal to or greater than 10. When the increment operator ++ is used in postfix notation (e.g. y++), the value of the operand is used in an expression and then it is incremented. The statement y += y++ is equivalent to y = y + y++.

At iteration 1, the value of **y** at the beginning of the loop is 0. The statement becomes

```
y = 0 + y++
```

The value of y is 0 and is used in the expression 0 + 0. y is then incremented by one but the y on the left of the equal sign is assigned the result of evaluating the expression and its value is therefore 0.

At iteration 2, the value of y is again 0 and the **for** loop goes on indefinitely.

Question 5

Given

```
int i = 1;
switch (i) {
case 1 :
    System.out.println("One player is playing this game.");
case 2 :
    System.out.println("Two players are playing this game.");
    break;
default:
    System.out.println("You did not enter a valid value.");
}
```

What is printed on the console if the code is executed?

A. One player is playing this game.

B. Two players are playing this game.
C. One player is playing this game.
   Two players are playing this game.
D. None of the above.

Answer: C.

Because there is no break statement after the first case, the execution flows through the second case. Hence, C.

Question 6

Given

```
int i = 1;
int y = 5;
if (i == 2)
if (i == 1)
    y = 50;
else y = 500;
```

What is the value of y after the code is executed?

A. 5.
B. 50.
C. 500.
D. None of the above.

Answer: A.

This is the dangling else problem. It is not clear which if statement the else statement is associated with. That's why it is better to use curly brackets with if. In this case, the else statement belongs to the if statement closest to it. The code is the same as this.

```
int i = 1;
int y = 5;
if (i == 2) {
    if (i == 1) {
        y = 50;
    } else {
        y = 500;
    }
}
```

It is now clear that **y** is never re-assigned a new value.

Question 7

Given this code

```
...
        System.out.print(i + " ");
    }
```

and given the following result

```
10 9 8 7 6 5 4 3 2 1
```

What line of code should be inserted into line 1?

A. for (int i = 0; i < 10; i++) {
B. for (int i = 10; i > 0; i--) {
C. while (i < 10) {
D. while (i > 10) {

Answer: A.

Obviously, you need a loop that starts i at 10 and decrements it by one until it reaches 1.

Question 8

Consider the following code.

```
1.  int x = 0;
2.  while (x < 10) {
3.      x++;
4.      System.out.print(x + " ");
5.  }
```

What is the equivalent for statement that can be used to replace lines 1 to 3?

A. for (int i = 1; i <= 10; i++) {
B. for (int i = 1; i < 11; i++) {
C. for (int i = 1; i < 11; ++i) {
D. for (int i = 1; i <= 10; ++i) {

Answer: A, B, C, D.

Any of the for statements can be used to replace the while statement.

Question 9

This code prints all odd numbers between 0 and 10.

```
1.  for (int i = 1; i <= 10; i++) {
2.      if (i % 2 == 1)
3.          System.out.print(i + " ");
4.  }
```

Which of the following for statements can be used to replace lines 1 and 2?

A. for (int i = 1; i <= 10; i++) {
B. for (int i = 1; i <= 10; i+=2) {
C. for (int i = 1; i <= 10; i--) {
D. None of the above

Answer: B.

The update statement **i+=2** in B increments i by 2.

Question 10

Given

```
int i = 1;
do {
    System.out.print(i++);
} while (i != 5);
```

What is the output of the program?

A. 012345
B. 01234
C. 1234
D. 12345

Answer: C.

The **do** block is executed four times, from when i = 1 to i = 4.

Chapter 3
Objects and Classes

Object-oriented programming (OOP) works by modeling applications on real-world objects. The benefits of OOP are real, which explains why OOP is the paradigm of choice today and why OOP languages like Java are popular. This chapter introduces you to objects and classes. If you are new to OOP, you may want to read this chapter carefully. A good understanding of OOP is key to writing quality programs.

This chapter starts by explaining what an object is and what constitutes a class. It then teaches you how to create an object with the **new** keyword, how objects are stored in memory, how classes can be organized into packages, how to use access control to achieve encapsulation, how the Java Virtual Machine (JVM) loads and links objects, and how Java manages unused objects. In addition, method overloading and static class members are explained.

3.1 What Is An Object?

When developing an application in an OOP language, you create a model that resembles a real-life situation to solve your problem. Take for example a payroll application, which calculates an employee's income tax and take home pay. An application like this would have a **Company** object to represent the company using the application, **Employee** objects that represent the employees in the company, **Tax** objects to represent the tax details of each employee, and so on. Before you can start programming such applications, however, you need to understand what Java objects are and how to create them.

Let's begin with a look at objects in life. Objects are everywhere, living (persons, pets, etc) and otherwise (cars, houses, streets, etc); concrete (books, televisions, etc) and abstract (love, knowledge, tax rate, regulations, and so forth). Every object has two features: the attributes and the actions the object can perform. For example, the following are some of a car's attributes:

- color
- number of doors
- plate number

Additionally, a car can perform these actions:

- run
- brake

As another example, a dog has the following attributes: color, age, type, weight, etc. And it can bark, run, urinate, sniff, etc.

A Java object also has attribute(s) and can perform action(s). In Java, attributes are called fields and actions are called methods. In other programming languages these may be known by other names. For example, methods are often called functions.

Both fields and methods are optional, meaning some Java objects may not have fields but have methods and some others may have fields but not methods. Some, of course, have both attributes and methods and some have neither.

How do you create Java objects? This is the same as asking, "How do you make cars?" Cars are expensive objects that need careful design that takes into account many things, such as safety and cost-effectiveness. You need a good blueprint to make good cars. To create Java objects, you need similar blueprints: classes.

3.2 Java Classes

A class is a blueprint or template to create objects of identical type. If you have an **Employee** class, you can create any number of **Employee** objects. To create **Street** objects, you need a **Street** class. A class determines what kind of object you get. For example, if you create an **Employee** class that has **age** and **position** fields, all **Employee** objects created out of this **Employee** class will have **age** and **position** fields as well. No more no less. The class determines the object.

In summary, classes are an OOP tool that enable programmers to create the abstraction of a problem. In OOP, abstraction is the act of using programming objects to represent real-world objects. As such, programming objects do not need to have the details of real-world objects. For instance, if an **Employee** object in a payroll application needs only be able to work and receive a salary, then the **Employee** class would only need two methods, **work** and **receiveSalary**. OOP abstraction ignores the fact that a real-world employee can do many other things including eat, run, kiss and kick.

Classes are the fundamental building blocks of a Java program. All program elements in Java must reside in a class, even if you are writing a simple program that does not require Java's object-oriented features. A Java beginner needs to consider three things when writing a class:

- the class name
- the fields
- the methods

There are other things that can be present in a class, but they will be discussed later.

A class declaration must use the keyword **class** followed by a class name. Also, a class has a body within braces. Here is a general syntax for a class:

```
class className {
    [class body]
}
```

For example, Listing 3.1 shows a Java class named **Employee**, where the lines in bold are the class body.

Listing 3.1: The Employee class

```
class Employee {
```

```
    int age;
    double salary;
}
```

Note

By convention, class names capitalize the initial of each word. For example, here are some names that follow the convention: **Employee**, **Boss**, **DateUtility**, **PostOffice**, **RegularRateCalculator**. This type of naming convention is known as Pascal naming convention. The other convention, the camel naming convention, capitalize the initial of each word, except the first word. Method and field names use the camel naming convention.

A public class definition must be saved in a file that has the same name as the class name, even though this restriction does not apply to non-public classes. The file name must have **java** extension.

Note

In UML class diagrams, a class is represented by a rectangle that consists of three parts: the topmost part is the class name, the middle part is the list of fields, and the bottom part is the list of methods. (See Figure 3.1) The fields and methods can be hidden if showing them is not important.

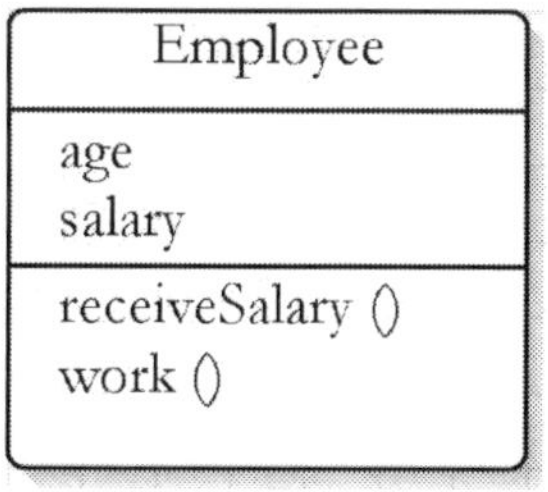

Figure 3.1: The Employee class in the UML class diagram

Fields

Fields are variables. They can be primitives or references to objects. For example, the **Employee** class in Listing 3.1 has two fields, **age** and **salary**. In Chapter 1, "Language Fundamentals" you learned how to declare and initialize variables of primitive types.

However, a field can also refer to another object. For instance, an **Empoyee** class may have an **address** field of type **Address**, which is a class that represents a street address:

```
Address address;
```

In other words, an object can contain other objects, that is if the class of the former contains variables that reference to the latter.

Field names should follow the camel naming convention. The initial of each word in the field, except for the first word, is written with a capital letter. For example, here are some "good" field names: **age**, **maxAge**, **address**, **validAddress**, **numberOfRows**.

Methods

A methods defines an action that a class's objects (or instances) can perform. A method has a declaration part and a body. The declaration part consists of a return value, the method name and a list of arguments. The body contains code that performs the action.

To declare a method, use the following syntax:

```
returnType methodName (listOfArguments)
```

The return type of a method can be a primitive, an object or void. The return type **void** means that the method returns nothing. The declaration part of a method is also called the signature of the method.

For example, here is a method named **getSalary** that returns a **double**.

```
double getSalary()
```

The **getSalary** method does not accept arguments.

As another example, here is a method that returns an **Address** object.

```
Address getAddress()
```

And, here is a method that accepts an argument:

```
int negate(int number)
```

If a method takes more than one argument, two arguments are separated by a comma. For example, the following **add** method takes two **int**s and return an **int**.

```
int add(int a, int b)
```

The Method main

A special method called **main** provides the entry point to an application. An application normally has many classes and only one of the classes needs to have a **main** method. This method allows the containing class to be invoked.

The signature of the **main** method is as follows.

```
public static void main(String[] args)
```

If you wonder why there is "public static void" before **main**, you will get the answer towards the end of this chapter.

You can pass arguments to **main** when using **java** to run a class. To pass arguments, type them after the class name. Two arguments are separated by a space.

```
java className arg1 arg2 arg3 ...
```

All arguments must be passed as strings. For instance, to pass two arguments, "1" and "safeMode" when running a **Test** class, type this:

```
java Test 1 safeMode
```

Strings are discussed in Chapter 4, "Core Classes."

Constructors

Every class must have at least one constructor. Otherwise, no objects could be created out of it and the class would be useless. As such, if your class does not explicitly define a constructor, the compiler adds one for you.

A constructor is used to construct an object. A constructor looks like a method and is sometimes called a constructor method. However, unlike a method, a constructor does not have a return value, not even **void**. Additionally, a constructor must have the same name as the class.

The syntax for a constructor is as follows.

```
constructorName (listOfArguments) {
    [constructor body]
}
```

A constructor may have zero argument, in which case it is called a no-argument (or no-arg, for short) or default constructor. Constructor arguments can be used to initialize the fields in an object.

If the Java compiler adds a no-arg constructor to a class because the class contains no constructor, the addition will be implicit, i.e. it will not be displayed in the source file. However, if there is a constructor in a class definition, regardless of the number of arguments it accepts, no constructor will be added to the class by the compiler.

As an example, Listing 3.2 adds two constructors to the **Employee** class in Listing 3.1.

Listing 3.2: The Employee class with constructors

```
public class Employee {
    public int age;
    public double salary;
    public Employee() {
    }
    public Employee(int ageValue, double salaryValue) {
        age = ageValue;
        salary = salaryValue;
    }
}
```

The second constructor is particularly useful. Without it, to assign values to age and position, you would need to write extra lines of code to initialize the fields:

```
employee.age = 20;
employee.salary = 90000.00;
```

With the second constructor, you can pass the values at the same time you create an object.

```
new Employee(20, 90000.00);
```

The **new** keyword is new to you, but you will learn how to use it later in this chapter.

Varargs

Varargs is a Java feature that allows methods to have a variable length of argument list. Here is an example of a method called **average** that accepts any number of **int**s and calculates their average.

```
public double average(int... args)
```

The ellipsis says that there is zero or more arguments of this type. For example, the following code calls **average** with two and three **int**s.

```
double avg1 = average(100, 1010);
double avg2 = average(10, 100, 1000);
```

If an argument list contains both fixed arguments (arguments that must exist) and variable arguments, the variable arguments must come last.

You should be able to implement methods that accept varargs after you read about arrays in Chapter 5, "Arrays." Basically, you receive a vararg as an array.

Class Members in UML Class Diagrams

Figure 3.1 depicts a class in a UML class diagram. The diagram provides a quick summary of all fields and methods. You could do more in UML. UML allows you to include field types and method signatures. For example, Figure 3.2 presents a **Book** class with five fields and one method.

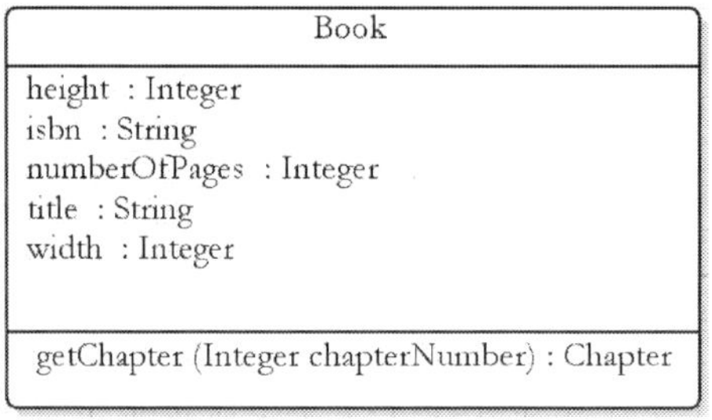

Figure 3.2: Including class member information in a class diagram

Note that in a UML class diagram a field and its type is separated by a colon. A method's argument list is presented in parentheses and its return type is written after a colon.

3.3 Creating An Object

Now that you know how to write a class, it is time to learn how to create an object from a class. An object is also called an instance. The word construct is often used in lieu of create, thus constructing an **Employee** object. Another term commonly used is *instantiate*. Instantiating the **Employee** class is the same as creating an instance of **Employee**.

There are a number of ways to create an object, but the most common one is by using the **new** keyword. **new** is always followed by the constructor of the class to be instantiated. For example, to create an **Employee** object, you write:

```
new Employee();
```

Most of the time, you will want to assign the created object to an object variable (or a reference variable), so that you can manipulate the object later. To achieve this, you need to declare an object reference with the same type as the object. For instance:

```
Employee employee = new Employee();
```

Here, **employee** is an object reference of type **Employee**.

Once you have an object, you can call its methods and access its fields, by using the object reference that was assigned the object. You use a period (.) to call a method or a field. For example:

```
objectReference.methodName
objectReference.fieldName
```

The following code, for instance, creates an **Employee** object and assigns values to its **age** and **salary** fields:

```
Employee employee = new Employee();
employee.age = 24;
employee.salary = 50000;
```

3.4 The null Keyword

A reference variable refers to an object. There are times, however, when a reference variable does not have a value (it is not referencing an object). Such a reference variable is said to have a null value. For example, the following class level reference variable is of type **Book** but has not been assigned a value;

```
Book book; // book is null
```

If you declare a local reference variable within a method but do not assign an object to it, you will need to assign null to it to satisfy the compiler:

```
Book book = null;
```

Class-level reference variables will be initialized when an instance is created, therefore you do not need to assign **null** to them.

Trying to access the field or method of a null variable reference raises an error, such as in the following code:

```
Book book = null;
System.out.println(book.title); // error because book is null
```

You can test if a reference variable is **null** by using the == operator. For instance.

```
if (book == null) {
    book = new Book();
}
```

```
System.out.println(book.title);
```

3.5 Memory Allocation for Objects

When you declare a variable in your class, either in the class level or in the method level, you allocate memory space for data that will be assigned to the variable. For primitives, it is easy to calculate the amount of memory taken. For example, declaring an **int** costs you four bytes and declaring a **long** sets you back eight bytes. However, calculation for reference variables is different.

When a program runs, some memory space is allocated for data. This data space is logically divided into two, the stack and the heap. Primitives are allocated in the stack and Java objects reside in the heap.

When you declare a primitive, several bytes are allocated in the stack. When you declare a reference variable, some bytes are also set aside in the stack, but the memory does not contain the object's data, it contains the address of the object in the heap. In other words, when you declare

```
Book book;
```

Some bytes are set aside for the reference variable **book**. The initial value of **book** is **null** because there is not yet an object assigned to it. When you write

```
Book book = new Book();
```

you create an instance of **Book**, which is stored in the heap, and assign the address of the instance to the reference variable **book**. A Java reference variable is like a C++ pointer except that you cannot manipulate a reference variable. In Java, a reference variable is used to access the member of the object it is referring to. Therefore, if the **Book** class has a public **review** method, you can call the method by using this syntax:

```
book.review();
```

An object can be referenced by more than one reference variable. For example,

```
Book myBook = new Book();
Book yourBook = myBook;
```

The second line copies the value of **myBook** to **yourBook**. As a result, **yourBook** is now referencing the same **Book** object as **myBook**.

Figure 3.3 illustrates memory allocation for a **Book** object referenced by **myBook** and **yourBook**.

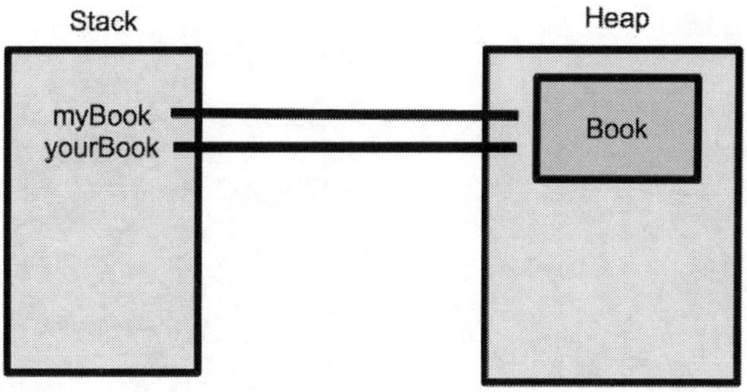

Figure 3.3: An object referenced by two variables

On the other hand, the following code creates two different **Book** objects:

```
Book myBook = new Book();
Book yourBook = new Book();
```

The memory allocation for this code is illustrated in Figure 3.4.

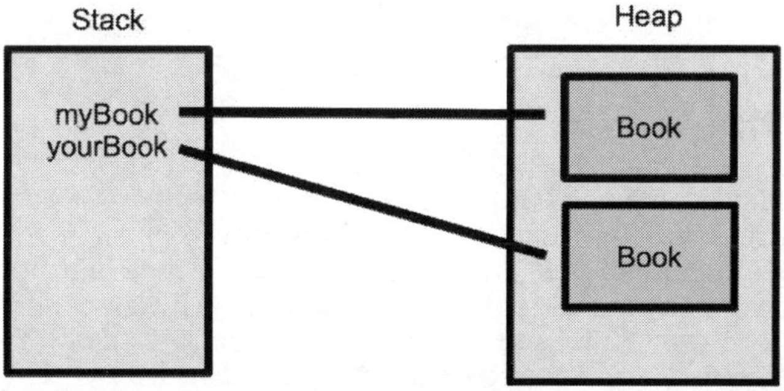

Figure 3.4: Two objects referenced by two variables

Now, how about an object that contains another object? For example, consider the code in Listing 3.3 that shows an **Employee** class that contains an **Address** class.

Listing 3.3: An Employee class that contains another class

```
public class Employee {
    Address address = new Address();
}
```

When you create an **Employee** object using the following code, an **Address** object is also created.

```
Employee employee = new Employee();
```

Figure 3.5 depicts the position of each object in the heap.

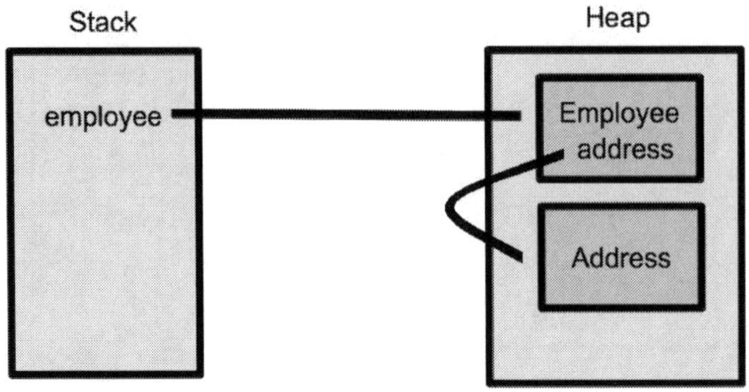

Figure 3.5: An object "within" another object

It turns out that the **Address** object is not really inside the **Employee** object. However, the **address** field within the **Employee** object has a reference to the **Address** object, thus allowing the **Employee** object to manipulate the **Address** object. Because in Java there is no way of accessing an object except through a reference variable assigned the object's address, no one else can access the **Address** object 'within' the **Employee** object.

3.6 Java Packages

If you are developing an application that consists of different parts, you may want to organize your classes to retain maintainability. With Java, you can group related classes or classes with similar functionality in packages. For example, standard Java classes come in packages. Java core classes are in the **java.lang** package. All classes for performing input and output operations are members of the **java.io** package, and so on. If a package needs to be organized in more detail, you can create packages that share part of the name of the former. For example, the Java class library comes with the **java.lang.annotation** and **java.lang.reflect** packages. However, mind you that sharing part of the name does not make two packages related. The **java.lang** package and the **java.lang.reflect** package are different packages.

Package names that start with **java** are reserved for the core libraries. Consequently, you cannot create a package that starts with the word **java**. You can compile classes that belong to such a package, but you cannot run them.

In addition, packages starting with **javax** are meant for extension libraries that accompany the core libraries. You should not create packages that start with **javax** either.

In addition to class organization, packaging can avoid naming conflict. For example, an application may use the **MathUtil** class from company A and an identically named class from another company if both classes belong to different packages. For this purpose, by convention your package names should be based on your domain name in reverse. Therefore, Sun's package names start with **com.sun**. My domain name is **brainysoftware.com**, so it's appropriate for me to start my package name with **com.brainysoftware**. For example, I would place all my applets in a **com.brainysoftware.applet** package and my servlets in **com.brainysoftware.servlet**.

A package is not a physical object, and therefore you do not need to create one. To group a class in a package, use the keyword **package** followed by the package name. For example, the following **MathUtil** class is part of the **com.brainysoftware.common** package:

```
package com.brainysoftware.common;
public class MathUtil {
    ...
}
```

Java also introduces the term *fully qualified name*, which refers to a class name that carries with it its package name. The fully qualified name of a class is its package name followed by a period and the class name. Therefore, the fully qualified name of a **Launcher** class that belongs to package **com.example** is **com.example.Launcher**.

A class that has no package declaration is said to belong to the default package. For example, the **Employee** class in Listing 3.1 belongs to the default package. You should always use a package because types in the default package cannot be used by other types outside the default package (except when using a technique called reflection). It is a bad idea for a class to not have a package.

Even though a package is not a physical object, package names have a bearing on the physical location of their class source files. A package name represents a directory structure in which a period in a package name indicates a subfolder. For example, all Java source files in the **com.brainysoftware.common** package must reside in the **common** directory that is a subdirectory of the **brainysoftware** directory. In turn, the latter must be a subdirectory of the **com** directory. Figure 3.6 depicts the folder structure for a **com.brainysoftware.common.MathUtil** class.

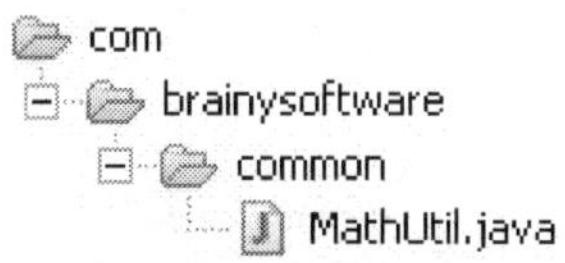

Figure 3.6: The physical location of a class in a package

Compiling a class in a non-default package presents a challenge for beginners. To compile such a class, you need to include the package name, replacing the dot (.) with /. For example, to compile the **com.brainysoftware.common.MathUtil** class, change directory to the working directory (the directory which is the parent directory of **com**) and type

```
javac com/brainysoftware/common/MathUtil.java
```

By default, **javac** will place the result in the same directory structure as the source. In this case, a **MathUtil.class** file will be created in the **com/brainysoftware/common** directory.

Running a class that belongs to a package follows a similar rule: you must include the package name, replacing . with /. For example, to run the **com.brainysoftware.common.MathUtil** class, type the following from your working directory.

```
java com/brainysoftware/common/MathUtil
```

The packaging of your classes also affects the visibility of your classes, as you will witness in the next section.

3.7 Encapsulation and Access Control

An OOP principle, encapsulation is a mechanism that protects parts of an object that need to be secure and exposes only parts that are safe to be exposed. A television is a good example of encapsulation. Inside it are thousands of electronic components that together form the parts that can receive signals and decode them into images and sound. These components are not to be accessible to the user, however, so Sony and other manufacturers wrap them in a strong metallic cover that does not break easily. For a television to be easy to use, it exposes buttons that the user can touch to turn on and off the set, adjust brightness, turn up and down the volume, and so on.

Back to encapsulation in OOP, let's take as an example a class that can encode and decode messages. The class exposes two methods called **encode** and **decode**, that users of the class can access. Internally, there are dozens of variables used to store temporary values and other methods that perform supporting tasks. The author of the class hides these variables and other methods because allowing access to them may compromise the security of the encoding/decoding algorithms. Besides, exposing too many things makes the class harder to use. As you can see later, encapsulation is a powerful feature.

Java supports encapsulation through access control. Access control is governed by access control modifiers. There are four access control modifiers in Java: **public**, **protected**, **private** and the default access level. Access control modifiers can be applied to classes or class members. They are explained in the following subsections.

Class Access Control Modifiers

In an application with many classes, a class may be instantiated and used from another class that is a member of the same package or a different package. You can control from which packages your class can be "seen" by employing an access control modifier at the beginning of the class declaration.

A class can have either the public or the default access control level. You make a class public by using the **public** access control modifier. A class whose declaration bears no access control modifier has default access. A public class is visible from anywhere. Listing 3.4 shows a public class named **Book**.

Listing 3.4: The public class Book

```
package app03;
public class Book {
    String isbn;
    String title;
    int width;
    int height;
    int numberOfPages;
}
```

The **Book** class is a member of the **app03** package and has five fields. Since **Book** is public, it can be instantiated from any other classes. In fact, the majority of the classes in the Java core libraries are public classes. For example, here is the declaration of the **java.lang.Runtime** class:

```
public class Runtime
```

A public class must be saved in a file that has the same name as the class, and the extension must be **java**. The **Book** class in Listing 3.4 must be saved in a **Book.java** file. Also, because **Book** belongs to package **app03**, the **Book.java** file must reside inside an **app03** directory.

Note

A Java source file can only contain one public class. However, it can contain multiple classes that are not public.

When there is no access control modifier preceding a class declaration, the class has the default access level. For example, Listing 3.5 presents the **Chapter** class that has the default access level.

Listing 3.5: The Chapter class, with the default access level

```
package app03;
class Chapter {
    String title;
    int numberOfPages;

    public void review() {
        Page page = new Page();
        int sentenceCount = page.numberOfSentences;
        int pageNumber = page.getPageNumber();
    }
}
```

Classes with the default access level can only be used by other classes that belong to the same package. For instance, the **Chapter** class can be instantiated from inside the **Book** class because **Book** belongs to the same package as **Chapter**. However, **Chapter** is not visible from other packages.

For example, you can add the following **getChapter** method inside the **Book** class:

```
Chapter getChapter() {
    return new Chapter();
}
```

On the other hand, if you try to add the same **getChapter** method to a class that does not belong to the **app03** package, a compile error will be raised.

Class Member Access Control Modifiers

Class members (methods, fields, constructors, etc) can have one of four access control levels: public, protected, private and default access. The access control modifier **public** is used to make a class member public, the **protected** modifier to make a class member protected, and the **private** modifier to make a class member private. Without an access control modifier, a class member will have the default access level.

Table 3.1 shows the visibility of each access level.

Access Level	From classes in other packages	From classes in the same package	From child classes	From the same class
public	yes	yes	yes	yes
protected	no	yes	yes	yes
default	no	yes	no	yes
private	no	no	no	yes

Table 3.1: Class member access levels

Note

The default access is sometimes called package private. To avoid confusion, this book will only use the term default access.

A public class member can be accessed by any other classes that can access the class containing the class member. For example, the **toString** method of the **java.lang.Object** class is public. Here is the method signature:

```
public String toString()
```

Once you construct an **Object** object, you can call its **toString** method because **toString** is public.

```
Object obj = new Object();
obj.toString();
```

Recall that you access a class member by using this syntax:

```
referenceVariable.memberName
```

In the preceding code, **obj** is a reference variable to an instance of **java.lang.Object** and **toString** is the method defined in the **java.lang.Object** class.

A protected class member has a more restricted access level. It can be accessed only from

- any class in the same package as the class containing the member
- a child class of the class containing the member

Note

A child class is a class that extends another class. Chapter 6, "Inheritance" explains this concept.

For instance, consider the public class **Page** in Listing 3.6.

Listing 3.6: The Page class

```
package app03;
public class Page {
    int numberOfSentences = 10;
    private int pageNumber = 5;
    protected int getPageNumber() {
        return pageNumber;
    }
}
```

Page has two fields (**numberOfSentences** and **pageNumber**) and one method (**getPageNumber**). First of all, because **Page** is public, it can be instantiated from any other class. However, even if you can instantiate it, there is no guarantee you can access its members. It depends on from which class you are accessing the **Page** class's members.

Its **getPageNumber** method is protected, so it can be accessed from any classes that belong to **app03**, the package that houses the **Page** class. For example, consider the **review** method in the **Chapter** class (given in Listing 3.5).

```
public void review() {
    Page page = new Page();
    int sentenceCount = page.numberOfSentences;
    int pageNumber = page.getPageNumber();
}
```

The **Chapter** class can access the **getPageNumber** method because **Chapter** belongs to the same package as the **Page** class. Therefore, **Chapter** can access all protected members of the **Page** class.

The default access allows classes in the same package access a class member. For instance, the **Chapter** class can access the **Page** class's **numberOfSentences** field because the **Page** and **Chapter** classes belong to the same package. However, **numberOfSentences** is not accessible from a subclass of **Page** if the subclass belongs to a different package. This differentiates the protected and default access levels and will be explained in detail in Chapter 6, "Inheritance."

The private members of a class can only be accessed from inside the same class. For example, there is no way you can access the **Page** class's private field **pageNumber** from anywhere other than the **Page** class itself. However, look at the following code from the **Page** class definition.

```
private int pageNumber = 5;
protected int getPageNumber() {
    return pageNumber;
}
```

The **pageNumber** field is private, so it can be accessed from the **getPageNumber** method, which is defined in the same class. The return value of **getPageNumber** is **pageNumber**, which is private. Beginners are often confused by this kind of code. If **pageNumber** is private, why use it as a return value of a protected method (**getPageNumber**)? Note that access to **pageNumber** is still private, so other classes cannot modify this field. However, using it as a return value of a non-private method is allowed.

How about constructors? Access levels to constructors are the same as those for fields and methods. Therefore, constructors can have public, protected, default, and private access levels. You may think that all constructors must be public because the intention of having a constructor is to make the class instantiatable. However, to your surprise, this is not the case. Some constructors are made private so that their classes cannot be instantiated from other classes. Private constructors are normally used in singleton classes. If you are interested in this topic, there are articles on this that you can find easily on the Internet.

Note

In a UML class diagram, you can include information on the class member access level. Prefix a public member with a +, a protected member with a # and a private member with a -. Members with no prefix are regarded as having the default access level. Figure 3.7 shows the **Manager** class with members having various access levels.

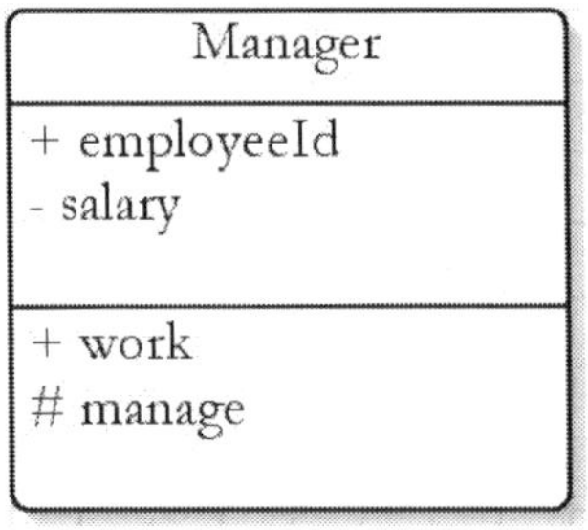

Figure 3.7: Including class member access level in a UML class diagram

3.8 The this Keyword

You use the **this** keyword from any method or constructor to refer to the current object. For example, if you have a class-level field with the same name as a local variable, you can use this syntax to refer to the former:

```
this.field
```

A common use is in the constructor that accepts values used to initialize fields. Consider the **Box** class in Listing 3.7.

Listing 3.7: The Box class

```
package app03;
public class Box {
    int length;
    int width;
    int height;
    public Box(int length, int width, int height) {
        this.length = length;
        this.width = width;
        this.height = height;
    }
}
```

The **Box** class has three fields, **length**, **width**, and **height**. Its constructor accepts three arguments used to initialize the fields. It is very convenient to use **length**, **width**, and **height** as the parameter names because they reflect what they are. Inside the constructor, **length** refers to the **length** argument, not the **length** field. **this.length** refers to the class-level **length** field.

It is of course possible to change the argument names, such as this.

```
public Box (int lengthArg, int widthArg, int heightArg) {
    length = lengthArg;
    width = widthArg;
    height = heightArg;
}
```

This way, the class-level fields are not shadowed by local variables and you do not need to use the **this** keyword to refer to the class-level fields However, using the **this** keyword spares you from having to think of different names for your method or constructor arguments.

3.9 Using Other Classes

It is common to use other classes from the class you are writing. Using classes in the same package as your current class is allowed by default. However, to use classes in other packages, you must first import the packages or the classes you want to use.

Java provides the keyword **import** to indicate that you want to use a package or a class from a package. For example, to use the **java.util.ArrayList** class from your code, you must have the following **import** statement:

```
package app03;
import java.util.ArrayList;

public class Demo {
    ...
}
```

Note that **import** statements must come after the **package** statement but before the class declaration. The **import** keyword can appear multiple times in a class.

```
package app03;
import java.time.Clock;
import java.util.ArrayList;

public class Demo {
    ...
}
```

Sometimes you need many classes in the same package. You can import all classes in the same package by using the wild character *. For example, the following code imports all members of the **java.util** package.

```
package app03;
import java.util.*;
public class Demo {
    ...
}
```

Now, not only can you use the **java.util.ArrayList** class, but you can use other members of the **java.util** package too. However, to make your code more readable, it is recommended that you import a package member one at a time. In other words, if you need to use both the **java.io.PrintWriter** class and the **java.io.FileReader** class, it is better to have two **import** statements like the following than to use the * character.

```
import java.io.PrintWriter;
import java.io.FileReader;
```

Note
Members of the **java.lang** package are imported automatically. Thus, to use the **java.lang.String** class, for example, you do not need to explicitly import the class.

The only way to use classes that belong to other packages without importing them is to use the fully qualified names of the classes in your code. For example, the following code declares the **java.io.File** class using its fully qualified name.

```
java.io.File file = new java.io.File(filename);
```

If you import identically-named classes from different packages, you must use the fully qualified names when declaring the classes. For example, the Java core libraries contain the classes **java.sql.Date** and **java.util.Date**. Importing both upsets the compiler. In this case, you must write the fully qualified names of **java.sql.Date** and **java.util.Date** in your class to use them.

Note
Java classes can be deployed in a jar file. Appendix A details how to compile a class that uses other classes in a jar file. Appendix B shows how to run a Java class in a jar file. Appendix C provides instructions on the **jar** tool, a program that comes with the JDK to package your Java classes and related resources.
A class that uses another class is said to "depend on" the latter. A UML diagram that depicts this dependency is shown in Figure 3.8.

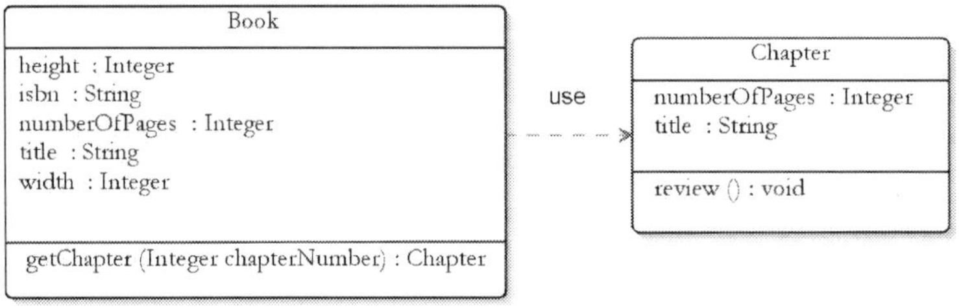

Figure 3.8: Dependency in the UML class diagram

A dependency relationship is represented by a dashed line with an arrow. In Figure 3.8 the **Book** class is dependent on **Chapter** because the **getChapter** method returns a **Chapter** object.

3.10 Final Variables

Java does not reserve the keyword constant to create constants. However, in Java you can prefix a variable declaration with the keyword **final** to make its value unchangeable. You can make both local variables and class fields final.

For example, the number of months in a year never changes, so you can write:

```
final int numberOfMonths = 12;
```

As another example, in a class that performs mathematical calculation, you can declare the variable **pi** whose value is equal to 22/7 (the circumference of a circle divided by its diameter, in math represented by the Greek letter π).

```
final float pi = (float) 22 / 7;
```

Once assigned a value, the value cannot change. Attempting to change it will result in a compile error.

Note that the casting **(float)** after **22 / 7** is needed to convert the value of division to **float**. Otherwise, an **int** will be returned and the **pi** variable will have a value of 3.0, instead of 3.1428.

Also note that since Java uses Unicode characters, you can simply define the variable **pi** as π if you don't think typing it is harder than typing **pi**.

```
final float π = (float) 22 / 7;
```

Note
You can also make a method final, thus prohibiting it from being overridden in a subclass. This will be discussed in Chapter 6, "Inheritance."

3.11 Static Members

You have learned that to access a public field or method of an object, you use a period after the object reference, such as:

```
// Create an instance of Book
Book book = new Book();
// access the review method
book.review();
```

This implies that you must create an object first before you can access its members. However, in previous chapters, there were examples that used **System.out.print** to print values to the console. You may have noticed that you could call the **out** field without first having to construct a **System** object. How come you did not have to do something like this?

```
System ref = new System();
ref.out;
```

Rather, you use a period after the class name:

```
System.out
```

Java (and many OOP languages) supports the notion of static members, which are class members that can be called without first instantiating the class. The **out** field in **java.lang.System** is static, which explains why you can write **System.out**.

Static members are not tied to class instances. Rather, they can be called without having an instance. In fact, the method **main**, which acts as the entry point to a class, is static because it must be called before any object is created.

To create a static member, you use the keyword **static** in front of a field or method declaration. If there is an access modifier, the **static** keyword may come before or after the access modifier. These two are correct:

```
public static int a;
static public int b;
```

However, the first form is more often used.

For example, Listing 3.8 shows the **MathUtil** class with a static method:

Listing 3.8: The MathUtil class

```
package app03;
public class MathUtil {
    public static int add(int a, int b) {
        return a + b;
    }
}
```

To use the **add** method, you can simply call it this way:

```
MathUtil.add(a, b)
```

The term instance methods/fields are used to refer to non-static methods and fields.

From inside a static method, you cannot call instance methods or instance fields because they only exist after you create an object. From a static method, you can access other static methods or static fields, however.

A common confusion that a beginner often encounters is when they cannot compile their class because they are calling instance members from the **main** method. Listing 3.9 shows such a class.

Listing 3.9: Calling non-static members from a static method

```
package app03;
public class StaticDemo {
    public int b = 8;
    public static void main(String[] args) {
        System.out.println(b);
    }
}
```

The line in bold causes a compile error because it attempts to access non-static field **b** from the **main** static method. There are two solutions to this.

1. Make **b** static
2. Create an instance of the class, then access **b** by using the object reference.

Which solution is appropriate depends on the situation. It often takes years of OOP experience to come up with a good decision that you're comfortable with.

Note

You can only declare a static variable in a class level. You cannot declare local static variables even if the method is static.

How about static reference variables? You can declare static reference variables. The variable will contain an address, but the object referenced is stored in the heap. For instance

```
static Book book = new Book();
```

Static reference variables provide a good way of exposing the same object that needs to be shared among other different objects.

Note

In UML class diagrams, static members are underlined. For example, Figure 3.9 shows the **MathUtil** class with the static method **add**.

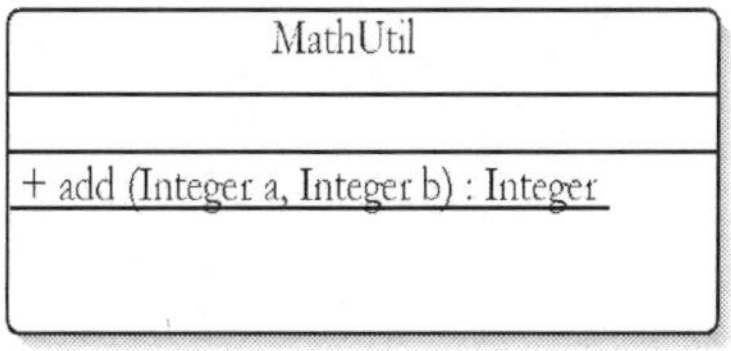

Figure 3.9: Static members in UML class diagrams

3.12 Static Final Variables

In the section "Final Variables" earlier in this chapter, you learned that you could create a final variable by using the keyword **final**. However, final variables at a class level or local variables will always have the same value when the program is run. If you have multiple objects of the same class with final variables, the value of the final variables in those objects will have the same values. It is more common (and also more prudent) to make a final variable static too. This way, all objects share the same value.

The naming convention for static final variables is to have them in upper case and separate two words with an underscore. For example

```
static final int NUMBER_OF_MONTHS = 12;
static final float PI = (float) 22 / 7;
```

The positions of **static** and **final** are interchangeable, but it is more common to use "static final" than "final static."

If you want to make a static final variable accessible from outside the class, you can make it public too:

```
public static final int NUMBER_OF_MONTHS = 12;
public static final float PI = (float) 22 / 7;
```

To better organize your constants, sometimes you want to put all your static final variables in a class. This class most often does not have a method or other fields and is never instantiated.

For example, sometimes you want to represent a month as an **int**, therefore January is 1, February is 2, and so on. Then, you use the word January instead of number 1 because it's more descriptive. Listing 3.10 shows the **Months** class that contains the names of months and its representation.

Listing 3.10: The Months class

```
package app03;
public class Months {
    public static final int JANUARY = 1;
    public static final int FEBRUARY = 2;
    public static final int MARCH = 3;
    public static final int APRIL = 4;
```

```
    public static final int MAY = 5;
    public static final int JUNE = 6;
    public static final int JULY = 7;
    public static final int AUGUST = 8;
    public static final int SEPTEMBER = 9;
    public static final int OCTOBER = 10;
    public static final int NOVEMBER = 11;
    public static final int DECEMBER = 12;
}
```

In your code, you can get the representation of January by writing.

```
int thisMonth = Months.JANUARY;
```

Static final reference variables are also possible. However, note that only the variable is final, which means once it is assigned an address to an instance, it cannot be assigned another object of the same type. The fields in the referenced object itself can be changed.

In the following line of code

```
public static final Book book = new Book();
```

book always refer to this particular instance of **Book**. Reassigning it to another **Book** object raises a compile error:

```
book = new Book(); // compile error
```

However, you can change the **Book** object's field value.

```
book.title = "No Excuses";  // assuming the title field is public
```

3.13 Static import

There are a number of classes in the Java core libraries that contain static final fields. One of them is the **java.util.Calendar** class, that has the static final fields representing days of the week (**MONDAY**, **TUESDAY**, etc). To use a static final field in the **Calendar** class, you must first import the **Calendar** class.

```
import java.util.Calendar;
```

Then, you can use it by using the notation *className.staticField*.

```
if (today == Calendar.SATURDAY)
```

However, you can also import static fields using the **import static** keywords. For example, you can do

```
import static java.util.Calendar.SATURDAY;
```

Then, to use the imported static field, you do not need the class name:

```
if (today == SATURDAY)
```

3.14 Variable Scope

You have seen that you can declare variables in several different places:

- In a class body as class fields. Variables declared here are referred to as class-level variables.
- As parameters of a method or constructor.
- In a method's body or a constructor's body.
- Within a statement block, such as inside a **while** or **for** block.

Now it's time to learn variable scope.

Variable scope refers to the accessibility of a variable. The rule is that variables defined in a block are only accessible from within the block. The scope of the variable is the block in which it is defined. For example, consider the following **for** statement.

```
for (int x = 0; x < 5; x++) {
    System.out.println(x);
}
```

The variable **x** is declared within the **for** statement. As a result, **x** is only available from within this **for** block. It is not accessible or visible from anywhere else. When the JVM executes the **for** statement, it creates **x**. When it is finished executing the **for** block, it destroys **x**. After **x** is destroyed, **x** is said to be out of scope.

Rule number 2 is a nested block can access variables declared in the outer block. Consider this code.

```
for (int x = 0; x < 5; x++) {
    for (int y = 0; y < 3; y++) {
        System.out.println(x);
        System.out.println(y);
    }
}
```

The preceding code is valid because the inner **for** block can access **x**, which is declared in the outer **for** block.

Following the rules, variables declared as method parameters can be accessed from within the method body. Also, class-level variables are accessible from anywhere in the class.

If a method declares a local variable that has the same name as a class-level variable, the former will 'shadow' the latter. To access the class-level variable from inside the method body, use the **this** keyword.

3.15 Method Overloading

Method names are very important and should reflect what the methods do. In many circumstances, you may want to use the same name for multiple methods because they have similar functionality. For instance, the method **printString** may take a **String** argument and prints the string. However, the same class may also provide a method that prints part of a **String** and accepts two arguments, the **String** to be printed and the character position to start printing from. You want to call the latter method **printString** too because it does print a **String**, but that would be the same as the first **printString** method.

Thankfully, it is okay in Java to have multiple methods having the same name, as long as each method accept different sets of argument types. In other words, in our example, it is legal to have these two methods in the same class.

```
public String printString(String string)
public String printString(String string, int offset)
```

This feature is called method overloading.

The return value of the method is not taken into consideration. As such, these two methods must not exist in the same class:

```
public int countRows(int number);
public String countRows(int number);
```

This is because a method can be called without assigning its return value to a variable. In such situations, having the above **countRows** methods would confuse the compiler as it would not know which method is being called when you write

```
System.out.println(countRows(3));.
```

A trickier situation is depicted in the following methods whose signatures are very similar.

```
public int printNumber(int i) {
    return i*2;
}

public long printNumber(long l) {
    return l*3;
}
```

It is legal to have these two methods in the same class. However, you might wonder, which method is being called if you write **printNumber(3)**?

The key is to recall from Chapter 1, "Language Fundamentals" that a numeric literal will be translated into an **int** unless it is suffixed **L** or **l**.. Therefore, **printNumber(3)** will invoke this method:

```
public int printNumber(int i)
```

To call the second, pass a **long**:

```
printNumber(3L);
```

System.out.print() (and **System.out.println()**) is an excellent example of method overloading. You can pass any primitive or object to the method because there are nine overloads of the method. There is an overload that accepts an **int**, one that accepts a **long**, one that accepts a **String**, and so on.

Note
Static methods can also be overloaded.

3.16 Static Factory Methods

You've learned to create an object using **new**. However, there are classes in Java class libraries that cannot be instantiated this way. For example, you cannot create an instance of **java.util.LocalDate** with **new** because its constructor is private. Instead, you would use one of its static methods, such as **now**:

```
LocalDate today = LocalDate.now();
```

Such methods are called static factory methods.

You can design your class to use static factory methods. Listing 3.11 shows a class named **Discount** with a private constructor. It is a simple class that contains an **int** that represents a discount rate. The value is either 10 (for small customers) or 12 (for bigger customers). It has a **getValue** method, which returns the value, and two static factory methods, **createSmallCustomerDiscount** and **createBigCustomerDiscount**. Note that the static factory methods can invoke the private constructor to create an object because they are in the same class. Recall that you can access a class private member from within the class. With this design, you restrict a **Discount** object to contain either 10 or 12. Other values are not possible.

Listing 3.11: The Discount classs

```
package app03;
import java.time.LocalDate;

public class Discount {
    private int value;
    private Discount(int value) {
        this.value = value;
    }

    public int getValue() {
        return this.value;
    }

    public static Discount createSmallCustomerDiscount() {
        return new Discount(10);
    }

    public static Discount createBigCustomerDiscount() {
        return new Discount(12);
    }
}
```

You can construct a **Discount** object by calling one of its static factory methods, for example

```
Discount discount = Discount.createBigCustomerDiscount();
System.out.println(discount.getValue());
```

There are also classes that allow you to create an instance through static factory methods and a constructor. In this case, the constructor must be public. Examples of such classes are **java.lang.Integer** and **java.lang.Boolean**.

With static factory methods, you can control what objects can be created out of your class, like you have seen in **Discount**. Also, you might cache an instance and return the same instance every time an instance is needed. Also, unlike constructors, you can name static factory methods to make clear what kind of object will be created.

3.17 By Value or By Reference?

You can pass primitive variables or reference variables to a method. Primitive variables are passed by value and reference variables are passed by reference. What this means is when you pass a primitive variable, the JVM will copy the value of the passed-in variable to a new local variable. If you change the value of the local variable, the change will not affect the passed in primitive variable.

If you pass a reference variable, the local variable will refer to the same object as the passed in reference variable. If you change the object referenced within your method, the change will also be reflected in the calling code. Listing 3.12 shows the **ReferencePassingTest** class that demonstrates this.

Listing 3.12: The ReferencePassingTest class

```
package app03;
class Point {
    public int x;
    public int y;
}
public class ReferencePassingTest {
    public static void increment(int x) {
        x++;
    }
    public static void reset(Point point) {
        point.x = 0;
        point.y = 0;
    }
    public static void main(String[] args) {
        int a = 9;
        increment(a);
        System.out.println(a); // prints 9
        Point p = new Point();
        p.x = 400;
        p.y = 600;
        reset(p);
        System.out.println(p.x); // prints 0
    }
}
```

There are two methods in **ReferencePassingTest**, **increment** and **reset**. The **increment** method takes an **int** and increments it. The **reset** method accepts a **Point** object and resets its **x** and **y** fields.

Now pay attention to the **main** method. We passed **a** (whose value is 9) to the **increment** method. After the method invocation, we printed the value of **a** and you get 9, which means that the value of **a** did not change.

Afterwards, you create a **Point** object and assign the reference to **p**. You then initialize its fields and pass it to the **reset** method. The changes in the **reset** method affects the **Point** object because objects are passed by reference. As a result, when you print the value of **p.x**, you get 0.

3.18 Loading, Linking, and Initialization

Now that you've learned how to create classes and objects, let's take a look at what happens when the JVM executes a class.

You run a Java program by using the **java** tool. For example, you use the following command to run the **DemoTest** class.

```
java DemoTest
```

After the JVM is loaded into memory, it starts its job by invoking the **DemoTest** class's **main** method. There are three things the JVM will do next in the specified order: loading, linking, and initialization.

Loading

The JVM loads the binary representation of the Java class (in this case, the **DemoTest** class) to memory and may cache it in memory, just in case the class is used again in the future. If the specified class is not found, an error will be thrown and the process stops here.

Linking

There are three things that need to be done in this phase: verification, preparation, and resolution (optional). Verification means the JVM checks that the binary representation complies with the semantic requirements of the Java programming language and the JVM. If, for example, you tamper with a class file created as a result of compilation, the class file may no longer work.

Preparation prepares the specified class for execution. This involves allocating memory space for static variables and other data structured for that class.

Resolution checks if the specified class references other classes/interfaces and if the other classes/interfaces can also be found and loaded. Checks will be done recursively to the referenced classes/interfaces.

For example, if the specified class contains the following code:

```
MathUtil.add(4, 3)
```

the JVM will load, link, and initialize the **MathUtil** class before calling the static **add** method.

Or, if the following code is found in the **DemoTest** class:

```
Book book = new Book();
```

the JVM will load, link, and initialize the **Book** class before an instance of **Book** is created.

Note that a JVM implementation may choose to perform resolution at a later stage, i.e. when the executing code actually requires the use of the referenced class/interface.

Initialization

In this last step, the JVM initializes static variables with assigned or default values and executes static initializers (code in **static** blocks). Initialization occurs just before the **main** method is executed. However, before the specified class can be initialized, its parent class will have to be initialized. If the parent class has not been loaded and linked, the JVM will first load and link the parent class. Again, when the parent class is about to be initialized, the parent's parent will be treated the same. This process occurs recursively until the initialized class is the topmost class in the hierarchy.

For example, if a class contains the following declaration

```
public static int z = 5;
```

the variable **z** will be assigned the value 5. If no initialization code is found, a static variable is given a default value. Table 3.2 lists default values for Java primitives and reference variables.

Type	Default Value
boolean	false
byte	0
short	0
int	0
long	0L
char	\u0000
float	0.0f
double	0.0d
object reference	null

Table 3.2: Default values for primitives and references

In addition, code in **static** blocks will be executed. For example, Listing 3.13 shows the **StaticCodeTest** class with static code that gets executed when the class is loaded. Like static members, you can only access static members from static code.

Listing 3.13: StaticCodeTest

```
package app03;
public class StaticInitializationTest {
    public static int a = 5;
    public static int b = a * 2;
    static {
        System.out.println("static");
        System.out.println(b);
    }
    public static void main(String[] args) {
        System.out.println("main method");
    }
}
```

If you run this class, you will see the following on your console:

```
static
10
main method
```

3.19 Object Creation Initialization

Initialization happens when a class is loaded, as described in the section "Linking, Loading, and Initialization" earlier in this chapter. However, you can also write code that performs initialization every time an instance of a class is created.

When the JVM encounters code that instantiates a class, the JVM does the following.

1. Allocates memory space for a new object, with room for the instance variables declared in the class plus room for instance variables declared in its parent classes.
2. Processes the invoked constructor. If the constructor has parameters, the JVM creates variables for these parameter and assigns them values passed to the constructor.
3. If the invoked constructor begins with a call to another constructor (using the **this** keyword), the JVM processes the called constructor.
4. Performs instance initialization and instance variable initialization for this class. Instance variables that are not assigned a value will be assigned default values (See Table 3.2). Instance initialization applies to code in braces:

```
{
    // code
}
```

5. Executes the rest of the body of the invoked constructor.
6. Returns a reference variable that refers to the new object.

Note that instance initialization is different from static initialization. The latter occurs when a class is loaded and has nothing to do with instantiation. Instance initialization, by contrast, is performed when an object is created. In addition, unlike static initializers, instance initialization may access instance variables.

For example, Listing 3.14 presents a class named **InitTest1** that has the initialization section. There is also some static initialization code to give you the idea of what is being run.

Listing 3.14: The InitTest1 class

```
package app03;

public class InitTest1 {
    int x = 3;
    int y;
    // instance initialization code
    {
        y = x * 2;
        System.out.println(y);
    }
```

```
    // static initialization code
    static {
        System.out.println("Static initialization");
    }
    public static void main(String[] args) {
        InitTest1 test = new InitTest1();
        InitTest1 moreTest = new InitTest1();
    }
}
```

When run, the **InitTest** class prints the following on the console:

```
Static initialization
6
6
```

The static initialization is performed first, before any instantiation takes place. This is where the JVM prints the "Static initialization" message. Afterward, the **InitTest1** class is instantiated twice, explaining why you see "6" twice.

The problem with having instance initialization code is this. As your class grows bigger it becomes harder to notice that there exists initialization code.

Another way to write initialization code is in the constructor. In fact, initialization code in a constructor is more noticeable and hence preferable. Listing 3.15 shows the **InitTest2** class that puts initialization code in the constructor.

Listing 3.15: The InitTest2 class

```
package app03;
public class InitTest2 {
    int x = 3;
    int y;
    // instance initialization code
    public InitTest2() {
        y = x * 2;
        System.out.println(y);
    }
    // static initialization code
    static {
        System.out.println("Static initialization");
    }
    public static void main(String[] args) {
        InitTest2 test = new InitTest2();
        InitTest2 moreTest = new InitTest2();
    }
}
```

The problem with this is when you have more than one constructor and each of them must call the same code. The solution is to wrap the initialization code in a method and let the constructors call them. Listing 3.16 shows this

Listing 3.16: The InitTest3 class

```
package app03;
public class InitTest3 {
    int x = 3;
```

```
    int y;
    // instance initialization code
    public InitTest3() {
        init();
    }
    public InitTest3(int x) {
        this.x = x;
        init();
    }
    private void init() {
        y = x * 2;
        System.out.println(y);
    }
    // static initialization code
    static {
        System.out.println("Static initialization");
    }
    public static void main(String[] args) {
        InitTest3 test = new InitTest3();
        InitTest3 moreTest = new InitTest3();
    }
}
```

Note that the **InitTest3** class is preferable because the calls to the **init** method from the constructors make the initialization code more obvious than if it is in an initialization block.

3.20 The Garbage Collector

In several examples so far, I have shown you how to create objects using the **new** keyword, but you have never seen code that explicitly destroys unused objects to release memory space. If you are a C++ programmer you may have wondered if I had shown flawed code, because in C++ you must destroy objects after use.

Java comes with a garbage collector, which destroys unused objects and frees memory. Unused objects are defined as objects that are no longer referenced or objects whose references are already out of scope.

With this feature, Java becomes much easier than C++ because Java programmers do not need to worry about reclaiming memory space. This, however, does not entail that you may create objects as many as you want because memory is (still) limited and it takes some time for the garbage collector to start. That's right, you can still run out of memory.

Self Test

Question 1

What is the correct syntax for a method?

A. *returnType methodName (listOfArguments)*
B. *methodName (listOfArguments)* { return *returnType* }
C. *returnType methodName [listOfArguments]*
D. None of the above

Question 2

Which of the following are valid components of a Java class?

A. constructors
B. methods
C. fields
D. A return type

Question 3

What keyword indicates that a method returns no value?

A. null
B. nothing
C. void
D. return

Question 4

Which of the following are valid method names? (Choose all that apply)

A. instanceOf
B. $createTempObject
C. return_old_string
D. implements
E. divide-by-two

Question 5

Which of the following methods will make a class executable? (Choose all that apply)

A. protected static void main(String[] args)
B. static public void main(String[] args)
C. void public static main(String[] args)
D. public static void main(String[] args)
E. protected static void main(String args)

Question 6

Which of the following statements about constructors and or methods are true? (Choose all that apply)

A. Constructors are like methods except that constructors have no return value.
B. Constructors with no return value must use void in its signature.
C. Constructors are like methods except that constructors must be public.

D. A method can be private but a constructor cannot.
E. Protected constructors are not allowed.

Question 7

Given

```
package com.example;
public class Descriptor {
    public static void main(String[] args) {
        Object object;
        System.out.println(object);
    }
}
```

Which of the following statements are false?

A. The code prints **null** on the console.
B. The code will not compile because object has not been initialized.
C. The code will not compile because it does not import java.lang.Object.
D. The code will compile but will raise an error when run.

Question 8

Consider the following code fragment with named regions R, S, T, U, V and X.

```
// ------- R --------
for (int m = 0; m < 5; m++) {
  // ------- S --------
    for (int n = 0; n < 3; n++) {
      // ------- T --------
        System.out.println(m);
        System.out.println(n);
      // ------- U --------
    }
  // ------- V --------
}
// ------- X --------
```

Which of the following statements are true?

A. *m* and *n* can be used in region R.
B. *m* and *n* can be used in region T.
C. *m* and *n* can be used in region U.
D. *m* and *n* can be used in region V.
E. *m* can be used in regions S, T, U and V.
F. *m* and *n* are out of scope in Region X.

Question 9

Given the following code

```
class HttpServer {
```

```
    public void service() { ... }
    public void service(int port) { ... }
}

class HttpRequest {
    public int getMethod();
    public String getMethod();
}

class HttpResponse {
    public String getParameter(String name) { ... }
    protected String getParameter(String name, boolean all) { ... }
}
```

Which class(es) feature method overloading?

A. HttpServer
B. HttpRequest
C. HttpResponse
D. None of the above.

Question 10

Given

```
 1.  class Animal {
 2.      public void walk() {
 3.      }
 4.  }
 5.
 6.  public class Printer {
 7.      public static void main(String[] args) {
 8.          Animal animal1 = new Animal();
 9.          Animal animal2 = new Animal();
10.          animal1 = null;
11.          System.out.println(animal1);
12.          animal2 = animal1;
13.          System.out.println(animal2);
14.      }
15.  }
```

Which of the following statements are true?

A. The object referenced by animal1 is eligible for garbage collection on line 11.
B. The object referenced by animal2 is eligible for garbage collection on line 13.
C. Two objects will be garbage collected on line 14.
D. One object will be garbage collected on line 12.

Answers to Self Test

Question 1

What is the correct syntax for a method?

A. *returnType methodName* (*listOfArguments*)
B. *methodName* (*listOfArguments*) { return *returnType* }
C. *returnType methodName* [*listOfArguments*]
D. None of the above

Answer: A.

The signature of a method has a return type followed by the method name and the list of arguments.

Question 2

Which of the following are valid components of a Java class?

A. constructors
B. methods
C. fields
D. A return type

Answer: A, B, C.

A class may contain one or more constructors, zero or more methods and zero or more fields. It does not need a return type.

Question 3

What keyword indicates that a method returns no value?

A. null
B. nothing
C. void
D. return

Answer: C.

The keyword **void** indicates a method has no return value.

Question 4

Which of the following are valid method names? (Choose all that apply)

A. instanceOf
B. $createTempObject
C. return_old_string

D. implements
E. divide-by-two

Answer: A, B, C.

instanceof is a reserved keyword and cannot be used as a method name, but instanceOf is valid. B and C are legal because a method name may contain $ and _ characters. D is invalid because **implements** is a reserved keyword in Java. E is illegal because it contains hyphens.

Question 5

Which of the following methods will make a class executable? (Choose all that apply)

A. protected static void main(String[] args)
B. static public void main(String[] args)
C. void public static main(String[] args)
D. public static void main(String[] args)
E. protected static void main(String args)

Answer: B, D.

The **main** method must be public and static, return no value and take a String array argument. The public and static modifiers are interchangeable.

Question 6

Which of the following statements about constructors and or methods are true? (Choose all that apply)

A. Constructors are like methods except that constructors have no return value.
B. Constructors with no return value must use void in its signature.
C. Constructors are like methods except that constructors must be public.
D. A method can be private but a constructor cannot.
E. Protected constructors are not allowed.

Answer: A.

Constructors cannot have a return value, not even void. Constructors can be public, protected or private.

Question 7

Given

```
package com.example;
public class Descriptor {
    public static void main(String[] args) {
        Object object;
        System.out.println(object);
    }
}
```

Which of the following statements are false?

A. The code prints **null** on the console.
B. The code will not compile because object has not been initialized.
C. The code will not compile because it does not import java.lang.Object.
D. The code will compile but will raise an error when run.

Answer: A, C, D.

The class will not compile as object has not been initialized. As a result, nothing can be executed. You can use members of the **java.lang** package without explicitly importing them.

Question 8

Consider the following code fragment with named regions R, S, T, U, V and X.

```
// ------- R --------
for (int m = 0; m < 5; m++) {
  // ------- S --------
    for (int n = 0; n < 3; n++) {
      // ------- T --------
        System.out.println(m);
        System.out.println(n);
      // ------- U --------
    }
  // ------- V --------
}
// ------- X --------
```

Which of the following statements are true?

A. *m* and *n* can be used in region R.
B. *m* and *n* can be used in region T.
C. *m* and *n* can be used in region U.
D. *m* and *n* can be used in region V.
E. *m* can be used in regions S, T, U and V.
F. *m* and *n* are out of scope in Region X.

Answer: B, C, E, F.

m is visible in Regions S, T, U and V. *n* is visible in Regions T and U.

Question 9

Given the following code

```
class HttpServer {
    public void service() { ... }
    public void service(int port) { ... }
}

class HttpRequest {
    public int getMethod();
    public String getMethod();
```

```
}

class HttpResponse {
    public String getParameter(String name) { ... }
    protected String getParameter(String name, boolean all) { ... }
}
```

Which class(es) feature method overloading?

A. HttpServer
B. HttpRequest
C. HttpResponse
D. None of the above.

Answer: A, C.

Method overloading refers to multiple methods having the same name and different sets of arguments. In HttpRequest, both methods have the same argument set and generate a compile error.

Question 10

Given

```
 1.  class Animal {
 2.      public void walk() {
 3.      }
 4.  }
 5.
 6.  public class Printer {
 7.      public static void main(String[] args) {
 8.          Animal animal1 = new Animal();
 9.          Animal animal2 = new Animal();
10.          animal1 = null;
11.          System.out.println(animal1);
12.          animal2 = animal1;
13.          System.out.println(animal2);
14.      }
15.  }
```

Which of the following statements are true?

A. The object referenced by animal1 is eligible for garbage collection on line 11.
B. The object referenced by animal2 is eligible for garbage collection on line 13.
C. Two objects will be garbage collected on line 14.
D. One object will be garbage collected on line 12.

Answer: A, B.

An object is eligible for garbage collection if it is no longer referenced by any variable. Assigning null to an reference variable decrements the number of references to the object. Therefore, A and B are correct.

C and D are incorrect because there is no guarantee when or if an object will be garbage-collected. The garbage collector runs on a low-priority thread and an intelligent garbage collector will not start destroying objects unless the heap is close to full.

Chapter 4
Core Classes

Before discussing other features of object-oriented programming (OOP), let's examine several important classes that are commonly used in Java. These classes are included in the Java core libraries that come with the JDK. Mastering them will help you understand the examples that accompany the next OOP lessons.

The most prominent class of all is definitely **java.lang.Object**. However, it is hard to talk about this class without first covering inheritance, which I will do in Chapter 6, "Inheritance." Therefore, **java.lang.Object** is only discussed briefly in this chapter. Right now I will concentrate on classes that you can use in your programs. I will start with **java.lang.String** and other types of strings: **java.lang.StringBuffer** and **java.lang.StringBuilder**. Then, I will discuss the **java.lang.System** class.

Note

When describing a method in a Java class, presenting the method signature always helps. A method often takes as parameters objects whose classes belong to different packages than the method's class. Or, it may return a type from a different package than its class. For clarity, fully qualified names will be used for classes from different packages. For example, here is the signature of the **toString** method of **java.lang.Object**:

```
public String toString()
```

A fully qualified name for the return type is not necessary because the return type **String** is part of the same package as **java.lang.Object**. On the other hand, the signature of the **toString** method in **java.util.Scanner** uses a fully qualified name because the **Scanner** class is part of a different package (**java.util**).

```
public java.lang.String toString()
```

4.1 java.lang.Object

The **java.lang.Object** class represents a Java object. In fact, all classes are direct or indirect descendants of this class. Since we have not learned inheritance (which is only given in Chapter 6, "Inheritance"), the word descendant probably makes no sense to you. Therefore, we will briefly discuss the method in this class and revisit this class in Chapter 6.

Table 4.1 shows the methods in the **Object** class.

Method	Description
clone	Creates and returns a copy of this object. A class implements this method to support object cloning.
equals	Compares this object with the passed-in object. A class must implement this method to provide a means to compare the contents of its instances.
finalize	Called by the garbage collector on an object that is about to be garbage-collected. In theory a subclass can override this method to dispose of system resources or to perform other cleanup. However, performing the aforesaid operations should be done somewhere else and you should not touch this method.
getClass	Returns a **java.lang.Class** object of this object. See the section "java.lang.Class" for more information on the **Class** class.
hashCode	Returns a hash code value for this object.
toString	Returns the description of this object.
wait, notify, notifyAll	Used in multithreaded programming in pre-5 Java. Should not be used directly in Java 5 or later. Instead, use the Java concurrency utilities.

Table 4.1: java.lang.Object methods

4.2 java.lang.String

I have not seen a serious Java program that does not use the **java.lang.String** class. It is one of the most often used classes and definitely one of the most important.

A **String** object represents a string, i.e. a piece of text. You can also think of a **String** as a sequence of Unicode characters. A **String** object can consists of any number of characters. A **String** that has zero character is called an empty **String**. **String** objects are constant. Once they are created, their values cannot be changed. Because of this, **String** instances are said to be immutable. And, because they are immutable, they can be safely shared.

You could construct a **String** object using the **new** keyword, but this is not a common way to create a **String**. Most often, you assign a string literal to a **String** reference variable. Here is an example:

```
String s = "Java is cool";
```

This produces a **String** object containing "Java is cool" and assigns a reference to it to **s**. It is the same as the following.

```
String message = new String("Java is cool");
```

However, assigning a string literal to a reference variable works differently from using the **new** keyword. If you use the **new** keyword, the JVM will always create a new instance of **String**. With a string literal, you get an identical **String** object, but the object is not always new. It may come from a pool if the string "Java is cool" has been created before.

Thus, using a string literal is better because the JVM can save some CPU cycles spent on constructing a new instance. Because of this, you seldom use the **new** keyword when creating a **String** object. The **String** class's constructors can be used if you have specific needs, such as converting a character array into a **String**.

Comparing Two Strings

String comparison is one of the most useful operations in Java programming. Consider the following code.

```
String s1 = "Java";
String s2 = "Java";
if (s1 == s2) {
    ...
}
```

Here, **(s1 == s2)** evaluates to **true** because **s1** and **s2** reference the same instance. On the other hand, in the following code **(s1 == s2)** evaluates to **false** because **s1** and **s2** reference different instances:

```
String s1 = new String("Java");
String s2 = new String("Java");
if (s1 == s2) {
    ...
}
```

This shows the difference between creating **String** objects by writing a string literal and by using the **new** keyword.

Comparing two **String** objects using the == operator is of little use because you are comparing the addresses referenced by two variables. Most of the time, when comparing two **String** objects, you want to know whether the values of the two objects are the same. In this case, you need to use the **String** class's **equals** method.

```
String s1 = "Java";
if (s1.equals("Java")) // returns true.
```

And, sometimes you see this style.

```
if ("Java".equals(s1))
```

In **(s1.equals("Java"))**, the **equals** method on **s1** is called. If **s1** is null, the expression will generate a runtime error. To be safe, you have to make sure that **s1** is not null, by first checking if the reference variable is null.

```
if (s1 != null && s1.equals("Java"))
```

If **s1** is null, the **if** statement will return **false** without evaluating the second expression because the AND operator **&&** will not try to evaluate the right hand operand if the left hand operand evaluates to **false**.

In **("Java".equals(s1))**, the JVM creates or takes from the pool a **String** object containing "Java" and calls its **equals** method. No nullity checking is required here because "Java" is obviously not null. If **s1** is null, the expression simply returns **false**. Therefore, these two lines of code have the same effect.

```
if (s1 != null && s1.equals("Java"))

if ("Java".equals(s1))
```

String Literals

Because you always work with **String** objects, it is important to understand the rules for working with string literals.

First of all, a string literal starts and ends with a double quote ("). Second, it is a compile error to change line before the closing double quote. For example, this code snippet will raise a compile error.

```
String s2 = "This is an important
        point to note";
```

You can compose long string literals by using the plus sign to concatenate two string literals.

```
String s1 = "Java strings " + "are important";
String s2 = "This is an important " +
        "point to note";
```

You can concatenate a String with a primitive or another object. For instance, this line of code concatenates a **String** and an integer.

```
String s3 = "String number " + 3;
```

If an object is concatenated with a String, the **toString** method of the former will be called and the result used in the concatenation.

Escaping Certain Characters

You sometimes need to use special characters in your strings such as carriage return (CR) and linefeed (LF). In other occasions, you may want to have a double quote character in your string. In the case of CR and LF, it is not possible to input these characters because pressing Enter changes lines. A way to include special characters is to escape them, i.e. use the character replacement for them.

Here are some escape sequences:

```
\u          /* a Unicode character
\b          /* \u0008: backspace BS */
\t          /* \u0009: horizontal tab HT */
\n          /* \u000a: linefeed LF */
\f          /* \u000c: form feed FF */
\r          /* \u000d: carriage return CR */
\"          /* \u0022: double quote " */
\'          /* \u0027: single quote ' */
\\          /* \u005c: backslash \ */
```

For example, the following code includes the Unicode character 0122 at the end of the string.

```
String s = "Please type this character \u0122";
```

To obtain a **String** object whose value is John "The Great" Monroe, you escape the double quotes:

```
String s = "John \"The Great\" Monroe";
```

Switching on A String

Starting from Java 7 you can use the **switch** statement with a String. Recall the syntax of the **switch** statement given in Chapter 2, “Statements.”

```
switch(expression) {
case value_1 :
    statement(s);
    break;
case value_2 :
    statement(s);
    break;
  .
  .
  .
case value_n :
    statement(s);
    break;
default:
    statement(s);
}
```

Here is an example of using the **switch** statement on a String.

```
String input = ...;
switch (input) {
case "one" :
    System.out.println("You entered 1.");
    break;
case "two" :
    System.out.println("You entered 2.");
    break;
default:
    System.out.println("Invalid value.");
}
```

The String Class’s Constructors

The **String** class provides a number of constructors. These constructors allow you to create an empty string, a copy of another string, and a **String** from an array of chars or bytes. Use the constructors with caution as they always create a new instance of **String**.

> **Note**
> Arrays are discussed in Chapter 5, “Arrays.”

`public String()`

Creates an empty string.

`public String(String original)`

Creates a copy of the original string.

`public String(char[] value)`

Creates a **String** object from an array of chars.

`public String(byte[] bytes)`

Creates a **String** object by decoding the bytes in the array using the computer's default encoding.

`public String(byte[] bytes, String encoding)`

Creates a **String** object by decoding the bytes in the array using the specified encoding.

The String Class's Methods

The **String** class provides methods for manipulating the value of a **String**. However, since **String** objects are immutable, the result of the manipulation is always a new **String** object.

Here are some of the more useful methods.

`public char charAt(int index)`

Returns the char at the specified index. For example, the following code returns 'J'.

```
"Java is cool".charAt(0)
```

`public String concat(String s)`

Concatenates the specified string to the end of this **String** and return the result. For example, **"Java ".concat("is cool")** returns "Java is cool".

`public boolean equals(String anotherString)`

Compares the value of this **String** and *anotherString* and returns **true** if the values match.

`public boolean endsWith(String suffix)`

Tests if this **String** ends with the specified suffix.

`public int indexOf(String substring)`

Returns the index of the first occurrence of the specified substring. If no match is found, returns -1. For instance, the following code returns 8.

```
"Java is cool".indexOf("cool")
```

`public int indexOf(String substring, int fromIndex)`

Returns the index of the first occurrence of the specified substring starting from the specified index. If no match is found, returns -1.

`public int lastIndexOf(String substring)`

Returns the index of the last occurrence of the specified substring. If no match is found, returns -1.

`public int lastIndexOf(String substring, int fromIndex)`

Returns the index of the last occurrence of the specified substring starting from the specified index. If no match is found, returns -1. For example, the following expression returns 3.

```
"Java is cool".lastIndexOf("a")
```

`public String substring(int beginIndex)`

Returns a substring of the current string starting from the specified index. For instance, **"Java is cool".substring(8)** returns "cool".

`public String substring(int beginIndex, int endIndex)`

Returns a substring of the current string starting from *beginIndex* to *endIndex*. For example, the following code returns “is”:

```
"Java is cool".substring(5, 7)
```

`public String replace(char oldChar, char newChar)`

Replaces every occurrence of *oldChar* with *newChar* in the current string and returns the new **String**. **"dingdong".replace('d', 'k')** returns “kingkong”.

`public int length()`

Returns the number of characters in this **String**. For example, **"Java is cool".length()** returns 12. Prior to Java 6, this method was often used to test if a **String** was empty. However, the **isEmpty** method is preferred because it's more descriptive.

`public boolean isEmpty()`

Returns true is the string is empty (contains no characters).

`public String[] split(String regEx)`

Splits this **String** around matches of the specified regular expression. For example, **"Java is cool".split(" ")** returns an array of three **String**s. The first array element is “Java”, the second “is”, and the third “cool”.

`public boolean startsWith(String prefix)`

Tests if the current string starts with the specified prefix.

`public char[] toCharArray()`

Converts this string to an array of chars.

`public String toLowerCase()`

Converts all the characters in the current string to lower case. For instance, **"Java is cool".toLowerCase()** returns “java is cool”.

`public String toUpperCase()`

Converts all the characters in the current string to upper case. For instance, **"Java is cool".toUpperCase()** returns “JAVA IS COOL”.

`public String trim()`

Trims the trailing and leading white spaces and returns a new string. For example, **" Java ".trim()** returns “Java”.

In addition, there are static methods such as **valueOf** and **format**. The **valueOf** method converts a primitive, a char array, or an instance of **Object** into a string representation and there are nine overloads of this method.

```
public static String valueOf(boolean value)
public static String valueOf(char value)
public static String valueOf(char[] value)
public static String valueOf(char[] value, int offset, int length)
public static String valueOf(double value)
public static String valueOf(float value)
public static String valueOf(int value)
public static String valueOf(long value)
public static String valueOf(Object value)
```

For example, the following code returns the string “23”

```
String.valueOf(23);
```

The **format** method allows you to pass an arbitrary number of parameters. Here is its signature.

```
public static String format(String format, Object... args)
```

This method returns a **String** formatted using the specified format string and arguments. The format pattern must follow the rules specified in the **java.util.Formatter** class and you can read them in the JavaDoc for the **Formatter** class. A brief description of these rules are as follows.

To specify an argument, use the notation **%s**, which denotes the next argument in the array. For example, the following is a method call to the **printf** method.

```
String firstName = "John";
String lastName = "Adams";
System.out.format("First name: %s. Last name: %s",
        firstName, lastName);
```

This prints the following string to the console:

```
First name: John. Last name: Adams
```

Without varargs, you have to do it in a more cumbersome way.

```
String firstName = "John";
String lastName = "Adams";
System.out.println("First name: " + firstName +
        ". Last name: " + lastName);
```

Note
The **printf** method in **java.io.PrintStream** is an alias for **format**.

The formatting example described here is only the tip of the iceberg. The formatting feature is much more powerful than that and you are encouraged to explore it by reading the Javadoc for the **Formatter** class.

4.3 java.lang.StringBuffer and java.lang.StringBuilder

String objects are immutable and are not suitable to use if you need to append or insert characters into them because string operations on **String** always create a new **String** object. For append and insert, you'd be better off using the **java.lang.StringBuffer** or **java.lang.StringBuilder** class. Once you're finished manipulating the string, you can convert a **StringBuffer** or **StringBuilder** object to a **String**.

Until JDK 1.4, the **StringBuffer** class was solely used for mutable strings. Methods in **StringBuffer** are synchronized, making **StringBuffer** suitable for use in multithreaded environments. However, the price for synchronization is performance. JDK 5 added the **StringBuilder** class, which is the unsynchronized version of **StringBuffer**. **StringBuilder** should be chosen over **StringBuffer** if you do not need synchronization.

The rest of this section will use **StringBuilder**. However, the discussion is also applicable to **StringBuffer** as both **StringBuilder** and **StringBuffer** shares similar constructors and methods.

StringBuilder Class's Constructors

The **StringBuilder** class has four constructors. You can pass a **java.lang.CharSequence**, a **String**, or an **int**.

```
public StringBuilder()
public StringBuilder(CharSequence seq)
public StringBuilder(int capacity)
public StringBuilder(String string)
```

If you create a **StringBuilder** object without specifying the capacity, the object will have a capacity of 16 characters. If its content exceeds 16 characters, it will grow automatically. If you know that your string will be longer than 16 characters, it is a good idea to allocate enough capacity as it takes time to increase a **StringBuilder**'s capacity.

StringBuilder Class's Methods

The **StringBuilder** class has several methods. The main ones are **capacity**, **length**, **append**, and **insert**.

`public int capacity()`

Returns the capacity of the **StringBuilder** object.

`public int length()`

Returns the length of the string the **StringBuilder** object stores. The value is less than or equal to the capacity of the **StringBuilder**.

`public StringBuilder append(String string)`

Appends the specified **String** to the end of the contained string. In addition, **append** has various overloads that allow you to pass a primitive, a char array, and an **java.lang.Object** instance.
For example, examine the following code.

```
StringBuilder sb = new StringBuilder(100);
sb.append("Matrix ");
sb.append(2);
```

After the last line, the content of **sb** is "Matrix 2".
An important point to note is that the **append** methods return the **StringBuilder** object itself, the same object on which **append** is invoked. As a result, you can chain calls to **append**.

```
sb.append("Matrix ").append(2);
```

`public StringBuilder insert(int offset, String string)`

Inserts the specified string at the position indicated by *offset*. In addition, **insert** has various overloads that allow you to pass primitives and a **java.lang.Object** instance. For example,

```
StringBuilder sb2 = new StringBuilder(100);
sb2.append("night");
```

```
sb2.insert(0, 'k'); // value = "knight"
```

Like **append**, **insert** also returns the current **StringBuilder** object, so chaining **insert** is also permitted.

```
public String toString()
```

Returns a **String** object representing the value of the **StringBuilder**.

4.4 Primitive Wrappers

For the sake of performance, not everything in Java is an object. There are also primitives, such as **int**, **long**, **float**, **double**, etc. When working with both primitives and objects, there are often circumstances that necessitate primitive to object conversions and vice versa. For example, a **java.util.Collection** object can be used to store objects, not primitives. If you want to store primitive values in a **Collection**, they must be converted to objects first.

The **java.lang** package has several classes that function as primitive wrappers. They are **Boolean**, **Character**, **Byte**, **Double**, **Float**, **Integer**, **Long**, and **Short**. **Byte**, **Double**, **Float**, **Integer**, **Long**, and **Short** share similar methods, therefore only **Integer** will be discussed here. You should consult the Javadoc for information on the others.

The following sections discuss the wrapper classes in detail.

java.lang.Integer

The **java.lang.Integer** class wraps an **int**. The **Integer** class has two static final fields of type **int**: **MIN_VALUE** and **MAX_VALUE**. **MIN_VALUE** contains the minimum possible value for an **int** (-2^{31}) and **MAX_VALUE** the maximum possible value for an **int** ($2^{31} - 1$).

The **Integer** class has two constructors:

```
public Integer(int value)
public Integer(String value)
```

For example, this code constructs two **Integer** objects.

```
Integer i1 = new Integer(12);
Integer i2 = new Integer("123");
```

Integer has the no-arg **byteValue**, **doubleValue**, **floatValue**, **intValue**, **longValue**, and **shortValue** methods that convert the wrapped value to a **byte**, **double**, **float**, **int**, **long**, and **short**, respectively. In addition, the **toString** method converts the value to a **String**.

There are also static methods that you can use to parse a **String** to an **int** (**parseInt**) and convert an **int** to a **String** (**toString**). The signatures of the methods are as follows.

```
public static int parseInt(String string)
public static String toString(int i)
```

java.lang.Boolean

The **java.lang.Boolean** class wraps a **boolean**. Its static final fields **FALSE** and **TRUE** represents a **Boolean** object that wraps the primitive value **false** and a **Boolean** object wrapping the primitive value **true**, respectively.

You can construct a **Boolean** object from a **boolean** or a **String**, using one of these constructors.

```
public Boolean(boolean value)
public Boolean(String value)
```

For example:

```
Boolean b1 = new Boolean(false);
Boolean b2 = new Boolean("true");
```

To convert a **Boolean** to a **boolean**, use its **booleanValue** method:

```
public boolean booleanValue()
```

In addition, the static method **valueOf** parses a **String** to a **Boolean** object.

```
public static Boolean valueOf(String string)
```

And, the static method **toString** returns the string representation of a **boolean**.

```
public static String toString(boolean boolean)
```

java.lang.Character

The **Character** class wraps a **char**. There is only one constructor in this class:

```
public Character(char value)
```

To convert a **Character** object to a **char**, use its **charValue** method.

```
public char charValue()
```

There are also a number of static methods that can be used to manipulate characters.

`public static boolean isDigit(char ch)`
Determines if the specified argument is one of these: ‘1’, ‘2’, ‘3’, ‘4’, ‘5’, ‘6’, ‘7’, ‘8’, ‘9’, ‘0’.

`public static char toLowerCase(char ch)`
Converts the specified char argument to its lower case.

`public static char toUpperCase(char ch)`
Converts the specified char argument to its upper case.

4.5 java.lang.Class

One of the members of the **java.lang** package is a class named **Class**. Every time the JVM creates an object, it also creates a **java.lang.Class** object that describes the type of the object. All instances of the same class share the same **Class** object. You can obtain the **Class** object by calling the **getClass** method of the object. This method is inherited from **java.lang.Object**.

For example, the following code creates a **String** object, invokes the **getClass** method on the **String** instance, and then invokes the **getName** method on the **Class** object.

```
String country = "Fiji";
Class myClass = country.getClass();
System.out.println(myClass.getName()); // prints java.lang.String
```

As it turns out, the **getName** method returns the fully qualified name of the class represented by a **Class** object.

The **Class** class also brings the possibility of creating an object without using the **new** keyword. You achieve this by using the two methods of the **Class** class, **forName** and **newInstance**.

```
public static Class forName(String className)
public Object newInstance()
```

The static **forName** method creates a **Class** object of the given class name. The **newInstance** method creates a new instance of a class.

The **ClassDemo** in Listing 4.1 uses **forName** to create a **Class** object of the **app04.Test** class and create an instance of the **Test** class. Since **newInstance** returns a **java.lang.Object** object, you need to downcast it to its original type.

Listing 4.1: The ClassDemo class

```
package app04;
public class ClassDemo {
    public static void main(String[] args) {
        String country = "Fiji";
        Class myClass = country.getClass();
        System.out.println(myClass.getName());
        Class klass = null;
        try {
            klass = Class.forName("app04.Test");
        } catch (ClassNotFoundException e) {
        }

        if (klass != null) {
            try {
                Test test = (Test) klass.newInstance();
                test.print();
            } catch (IllegalAccessException e) {
            } catch (InstantiationException e) {
            }
```

```
        }
    }
}
```

Do not worry about the **try ... catch** blocks as they will be explained in Chapter 8, "Error Handling."

You might want to ask this question, though. Why would you want to create an instance of a class using **forName** and **newInstance**, when using the **new** keyword is shorter and easier? The answer is because there are circumstances whereby the name of the class is not known when you are writing the program.

4.6 java.lang.System

The **System** class is a final class that exposes useful static fields and static methods that can help you with common tasks.

The three fields of the **System** class are **out**, **in**, and **err**:

```
public static final java.io.PrintStream out;
public static final java.io.InputStream in;
public static final java.io.PrintStream err;
```

The **out** field represents the standard output stream which by default is the same console used to run the running Java application. Note that you can use the **out** field to write messages to the console. You will often write the following line of code:

```
System.out.print(message);
```

where *message* is a **String** object. However, **PrintStream** has many **print** method overloads that accept different types, so you can pass any primitive type to the **print** method:

```
System.out.print(12);
System.out.print('g');
```

In addition, there are **println** methods that are equivalent to **print**, except that **println** adds a line terminator at the end of the argument.

Note also that because **out** is static, you can access it by using this notation: **System.out**, which returns a **java.io.PrintStream** object. You can then access the many methods on the **PrintStream** object as you would methods of other objects: **System.out.print**, **System.out.format**, etc.

The **err** field also represents a **PrintStream** object, and by default the output is channeled to the console from where the current Java program was invoked. However, its purpose is to display error messages that should get immediate attention of the user.

For example, here is how you can use **err**:

```
System.err.println("You have a runtime error.");
```

The **in** field represents the standard input stream. You can use it to accept keyboard input. For example, the **getUserInput** method in Listing 4.2 accepts the user input and returns it as a String:

Listing 4.2: The InputDemo class

```
package app04;
import java.io.IOException;

public class InputDemo {
    public String getUserInput() {
        StringBuilder sb = new StringBuilder();
        try {
            char c = (char) System.in.read();
            while (c != '\r' && c != '\n') {
                sb.append(c);
                c = (char) System.in.read();
            }
        } catch (IOException e) {
        }
        return sb.toString();
    }

    public static void main(String[] args) {
        InputDemo demo = new InputDemo();
        String input = demo.getUserInput();
        System.out.println(input);
    }
}
```

However, an easier way to receive keyboard input is to use the **java.util.Scanner** class.

The **System** class has many useful methods, all of which are static. Some of the more important ones are listed here.

`public static void arraycopy(Object source, int sourcePos, Object destination, int destPos, int length)`

This method copies the content of an array (*source*) to another array (*destination*), beginning at the specified position, to the specified position of the destination array. For example, the following code uses **arraycopy** to copy the contents of **array1** to **array2**.

```
int[] array1 = {1, 2, 3, 4};
int[] array2 = new int[array1.length];
System.arraycopy(array1, 0, array2, 0, array1.length);
```

`public static void exit(int status)`

Terminates the running program and the current JVM. You normally pass 0 to indicate that a normal exit and a nonzero to indicate there has been an error in the program prior to calling this method.

`public static long currentTimeMillis()`

Returns the computer time in milliseconds. The value represents the number of milliseconds that has elapsed since January 1, 1970 UTC.
Prior to Java 8, **currentTimeMillis** was used to time an operation. In Java 8 and later, you can use the **java.time.Instant** class, instead.

`public static long nanoTime()`

This method is similar to **currentTimeMillis**, but with nanosecond precision.

```
public static String getProperty(String key)
```

This method returns the value of the specified property. It returns **null** if the specified property does not exist. There are system properties and there are user-defined properties. When a Java program runs, the JVM provides values that may be used by the program as properties.

Each property comes as a key/value pair. For example, the **os.name** system property provides the name of the operating system running the JVM. Also, the directory name from which the application was invoked is provided by the JVM as a property named **user.dir**. To get the value of the **user.dir** property, you use:

```
System.getProperty("user.dir");
```

Table 4.2 lists the system properties.

System property	Description
java.version	Java Runtime Environment version
java.vendor	Java Runtime Environment vendor
java.vendor.url	Java vendor URL
java.home	Java installation directory
java.vm.specification.version	Java Virtual Machine specification version
java.vm.specification.vendor	Java Virtual Machine specification vendor
java.vm.specification.name	Java Virtual Machine specification name
java.vm.version	Java Virtual Machine implementation version
java.vm.vendor	Java Virtual Machine implementation vendor
java.vm.name	Java Virtual Machine implementation name
java.specification.version	Java Runtime Environment specification version
java.specification.vendor	Java Runtime Environment specification vendor
java.specification.name	Java Runtime Environment specification name
java.class.version	Java class format version number
java.class.path	Java class path
java.library.path	List of paths to search when loading libraries
java.io.tmpdir	Default temp file path
java.compiler	Name of JIT compiler to use
java.ext.dirs	Path of extension directory or directories
os.name	Operating system name
os.arch	Operating system architecture
os.version	Operating system version
file.separator	File separator ("/" on UNIX)
path.separator	Path separator (":" on UNIX)
line.separator	Line separator ("\n" on UNIX)
user.name	User's account name
user.home	User's home directory
user.dir	User's current working directory

Table 4.2: Java system properties

```
public static void setProperty(String property, String newValue)
```

You use **setProperty** to create a user-defined property or change the value of the current property. For instance, you can use this code to create a property named **password**:

```
System.setProperty("password", "tarzan");
```

And, you can retrieve it by using **getProperty**:

```
System.getProperty("password")
```

For instance, here is how you change the **user.name** property.

```
System.setProperty("user.name", "tarzan");
```

`public static String getProperty(String key, String default)`
This method is similar to the single argument **getProperty** method, but returns a default value if the specified property does not exist.

`public static java.util.Properties getProperties()`
This method returns all system properties. The return value is a **java.util.Properties** object. The **Properties** class is a subclass of **java.util.Hashtable**.
For example, the following code uses the **list** method of the **Properties** class to iterate and display all system properties on the console.

```
java.util.Properties properties = System.getProperties();
properties.list(System.out);
```

Self Test

Question 1

Consider the following code snippet.

```
public static void main(String[] args) {
    String s1 = "start";
    String s2 = "start";
    System.out.print(s1 == s2);
    System.out.print(" ... ");

    String s3 = new String("finish");
    String s4 = new String("finish");
    System.out.println(s3 == s4);
}
```

What is printed on the console when the **main** method is invoked?

A. true … false
B. true … true
C. false … false
D. false … true

Question 2

The following code showcases two different ways of splitting a string.

```
String input = "Windows,Linux,,Mac OSX";
StringTokenizer tokenizer = new StringTokenizer(input, ",");
System.out.print(tokenizer.countTokens() + " ");
String[] tokens = input.split(",");
```

```
System.out.print(tokens.length);
```

What does this code print on the console?

A. 3 4
B. 4 4
C. 3 3
D. 4 3

Question 3

Given

```
String input = "\tContango  ";
System.out.println(input.trim().length());
```

What does this code print on the console?

A. 8
B. 9
C. 10
D. 11

Question 4

Given

```
class FileUtil {
    public static String getFileExtension(String fileName) {
        int index = fileName.lastIndexOf(".");
        return fileName.substring(index);
    }
    public static void main(String[] args) {
        String fileName = "market.pdf";
        System.out.println(getFileExtension(fileName));
    }
}
```

What does the code print?

A. pdf
B. .pdf
C. market
D. market.

Question 5

Consider this code snippet:

```
StringBuilder sb = new StringBuilder("Storage ");
sb.insert(0, "File");
sb.append("almost full");
System.out.print(sb);
```

What will be printed if the code is executed?

A. File Storage almost full
B. FileStorage almost full
C. java.lang.StringBuilder
D. The fully-qualified class name for StringBuilder followed by a random string.

Question 6

Given

```
1.   public class Calculator {
2.       public static void main(String[] args) {
3.           Integer radius = (Integer) 123;
4.           Integer height = 234;
5.           System.out.println(radius + ", " + height);
6.       }
7.   }
```

What happens if you try to compile and run the code?

A. It will not compile because of a compile error on line 3
B. It will not compile because you are trying to convert an int to an Integer on line 4.
C. It will compile and print 123, 234
D. It will compile but it will throw a runtime exception when executed

Question 7

Given

```
public class VideoGame {
    public static void main(String[] args) {
        switch (args[1]) {
        case "1":
            System.out.println("One player");
            break;
        case "2":
            System.out.println("Two players");
            break;
        default:
            System.out.println("Unknown");
        }
    }
}
```

What will happen if the VideoGame class is invoked using this command:

```
java VideoGame 1 2
```

A. “One player” will be printed on the console
B. “Two players” will be printed on the console
C. An ArrayIndexOutOfBoundsException will be thrown
D. “Unknown” will be printed on the console

Question 8

The code below is an incomplete method named **digitsOnly** that returns true if the string argument contains only digits.

```
1. public static boolean digitsOnly(String s) {
2.     String reference = "0123456789";
3.     for (int i = 0; i < s.length(); i++) {
4.         ...
5.             return false;
6.         }
7.     }
8.     return true;
9. }
```

Which line of code needs to be inserted into line 4 for the method to work correctly? (Choose all that apply)

A. if (s.charAt(i) < 48 || s.charAt(i) > 57) {
B. if (!reference.contains(s.charAt(i))) {
C. if (!reference.contains("" + s.charAt(i))) {
D. if (s.charAt(i) <= 48 || s.charAt(i) >= 57) {

Question 9

Given

```
public class SalaryCalculator {
    public static void main(String[] args) {
        Long i = new Long(100L);
        Boolean b = null;
        String s = "1000" + i + (b? 1 : 0);
        System.out.println(s);
    }
}
```

What happens if you try to compile and run the code?

A. It will compile and "10001000" will be printed on the console
B. It will compile and "10001001" will be printed on the console
C. It will compile and a NullPointerException will be thrown when the code is executed.
D. It will not compile because you are trying to concatenate a String with an long and a boolean.

Question 10

Given the code below

```
String s = "kingkong";
System.out.println(s.replace("d", "k"));
```

What will be printed on the console if the code is executed?

A. dingdong
B. dingkong
C. kingkong
D. kingdong

Answers to Self Test

Question 1

Consider the following code snippet.

```
public static void main(String[] args) {
    String s1 = "start";
    String s2 = "start";
    System.out.print(s1 == s2);
    System.out.print(" ... ");

    String s3 = new String("finish");
    String s4 = new String("finish");
    System.out.println(s3 == s4);
}
```

What is printed on the console when the **main** method is invoked?

A. true ... false
B. true ... true
C. false ... false
D. false ... true

Answer: A.

String objects created using the same string literal are shared. Thus, s1 and s2 reference the same object and s1==s2 evaluates to true. String objects containing the same string but created using the String constructor are different objects. Therefore, s3 and s4 point to two different objects and s3==s4 evaluates to false.

Question 2

The following code showcases two different ways of splitting a string.

```
String input = "Windows,Linux,,Mac OSX";
StringTokenizer tokenizer = new StringTokenizer(input, ",");
System.out.print(tokenizer.countTokens() + " ");
String[] tokens = input.split(",");
System.out.print(tokens.length);
```

What does this code print on the console?

A. 3 4
B. 4 4
C. 3 3

D. 4 3

Answer: A.

Using **StringTokenizer** is an old technique for splitting a string. It does not consider an empty string a token. By contrast, the **split** method returns an empty string as a token so you know if there are empty tokens in a string. Use **split** instead of **StringTokenizer**.

Question 3

Given

```
String input = "\tContango  ";
System.out.println(input.trim().length());
```

What does this code print on the console?

A. 8
B. 9
C. 10
D. 11

Answer: A.

The **trim** method removes all white spaces, including tabs.

Question 4

Given

```
class FileUtil {
    public static String getFileExtension(String fileName) {
        int index = fileName.lastIndexOf(".");
        return fileName.substring(index);
    }
    public static void main(String[] args) {
        String fileName = "market.pdf";
        System.out.println(getFileExtension(fileName));
    }
}
```

What does the code print?

A. pdf
B. .pdf
C. market
D. market.

Answer: B.

The **lastIndexOf** method return the last occurrence of the given substring, which in this case is a dot. The **substring** method returns a substring starting from the given index.

Question 5

Consider this code snippet:

```
StringBuilder sb = new StringBuilder("Storage ");
sb.insert(0, "File");
sb.append("almost full");
System.out.print(sb);
```

What will be printed if the code is executed?

A. File Storage almost full
B. FileStorage almost full
C. java.lang.StringBuilder
D. The fully-qualified class name for StringBuilder followed by a random string.

Answer: B.

Passing an object to **System.out.print** will call the object's **toString** method and print the returned String.

Question 6

Given

```
1.   public class Calculator {
2.       public static void main(String[] args) {
3.           Integer radius = (Integer) 123;
4.           Integer height = 234;
5.           System.out.println(radius + ", " + height);
6.       }
7.   }
```

What happens if you try to compile and run the code?

A. It will not compile because of a compile error on line 3
B. It will not compile because you are trying to convert an int to an Integer on line 4.
C. It will compile and print 123, 234
D. It will compile but it will throw a runtime exception when executed

Answer: C.

Thanks to boxing and unboxing, conversion from a primitive to a wrapper class and vice versa happen automatically. In this case, an int will be converted to Integer with or without type casting.

Question 7

Given

```
public class VideoGame {
    public static void main(String[] args) {
        switch (args[1]) {
```

```
            case "1":
                System.out.println("One player");
                break;
            case "2":
                System.out.println("Two players");
                break;
            default:
                System.out.println("Unknown");
            }
        }
    }
```

What will happen if the VideoGame class is invoked using this command:

```
java VideoGame 1 2
```

A. "One player" will be printed on the console
B. "Two players" will be printed on the console
C. An ArrayIndexOutOfBoundsException will be thrown
D. "Unknown" will be printed on the console

Answer: B.

args[1] refers to the second argument, so "Two Players" will be printed on the console.

Question 8

The code below is an incomplete method named **digitsOnly** that returns true if the string argument contains only digits.

```
1. public static boolean digitsOnly(String s) {
2.     String reference = "0123456789";
3.     for (int i = 0; i < s.length(); i++) {
4.         ...
5.             return false;
6.         }
7.     }
8.     return true;
9. }
```

Which line of code needs to be inserted into line 4 for the method to work correctly? (Choose all that apply)

A. if (s.charAt(i) < 48 || s.charAt(i) > 57) {
B. if (!reference.contains(s.charAt(i))) {
C. if (!reference.contains("" + s.charAt(i))) {
D. if (s.charAt(i) <= 48 || s.charAt(i) >= 57) {

Answer: A, C.

A is correct because the ASCII code for 0 is 48 and the ASCII code for 9 is 57. B causes a compile error because the contains method expects a String and charAt returns a char. C is correct because the argument is implicitly converted to a String by appending the returned char with an empty string. D is incorrect since this means characters 0 and 9 will be rejected.

Question 9

Given

```
public class SalaryCalculator {
    public static void main(String[] args) {
        Long i = new Long(100L);
        Boolean b = null;
        String s = "1000" + i + (b? 1 : 0);
        System.out.println(s);
    }
}
```

What happens if you try to compile and run the code?

A. It will compile and "10001000" will be printed on the console
B. It will compile and "10001001" will be printed on the console
C. It will compile and a NullPointerException will be thrown when the code is executed.
D. It will not compile because you are trying to concatenate a String with an long and a boolean.

Answer: C.

Inquiring the value of a **Boolean** is equivalent to calling its **booleanValue** method. Since **b** is null, this will thrown a **NullPointerException**.

Question 10

Given the code below

```
String s = "kingkong";
System.out.println(s.replace("d", "k"));
```

What will be printed on the console if the code is executed?

A. dingdong
B. dingkong
C. kingkong
D. kingdong

Answer: C.

The **replace** method replaces all occurrences of the first argument with the second argument.

Chapter 5
Arrays

In Java you can use an array to group primitives or objects of the same type. The entities belonging to an array is called the elements or components of the array. In this chapter you will learn how to create, initialize and iterate over an array as well as manipulate its elements. This chapter also features the **java.util.Arrays** and **java.util.ArrayList** classes.

5.1 Array Overview

In the background, every time you create an array, the compiler creates an object which allows you to:

- get the number of elements in the array through the **length** field. The length or size of an array is the number of elements in it.
- access each element by specifying an index. This indexing is zero-based. Index 0 refers to the first element, 1 to the second element, etc.

All the elements of an array have the same type, called the element type of the array. An array is not resizable and an array with zero element is called an empty array.

An array is a Java object. Therefore, an array variable behaves like other reference variables. For example, you can compare an array variable with **null**.

```
String[] names;
if (names == null)   // evaluates to true
```

If an array is a Java object, shouldn't there be a class that gets instantiated when you create an array? May be something like **java.lang.Array**? The truth is, no. Arrays are indeed special Java objects whose class is not documented and is not meant to be extended.

To use an array, first you need to declare one. You can use this syntax to declare an array:

```
type[] arrayName;
```

or

```
type arrayName[]
```

For example, the following declares an array of **long**s named **numbers**:

```
long[] numbers;
```

Declaring an array does not create an array or allocate space for its elements, the compiler simply creates an object reference. One way to create an array is by using the **new** keyword. You must specify the size of the array you are creating.

```
new type[size]
```

As an example, the following code creates an array of four **int**s:

```
new int[4]
```

Alternatively, you can declare and create an array in the same line.

```
int[] ints = new int[4];
```

After an array is created, its elements are either **null** (if the element type is a reference type) or the default value of the element type (if the array contains primitives). For example, an array of **int**s contain zeros by default.

To reference an array element, use an index. If the size of an array is *n*, then the valid indexes are all integers between 0 and *n*-1. For example, if an array has four elements, the valid indexes are 0, 1, 2 and 3. The following snippet creates an array of four **String** objects and assigns a value to its first element.

```
String[] names = new String[4];
names[0] = "Hello World";
```

Using a negative index or a positive integer equal to or greater than the array size will throw a **java.lang.ArrayIndexOutOfBoundsException**. See Chapter 8, "Error Handling" for information about exceptions.

Since an array is an object, you can call the **getClass** method on an array. The string representation of the **Class** object of an array has the following format:

```
[type
```

where *type* is the object type. Calling **getClass().getName()** on a **String** array returns **[Ljava.lang.String**. The class name of a primitive array, however, is harder to decipher. Calling **getClass().getName()** on an **int** array returns **[I** and on a long array returns **[J**.

You can create and initialize an array without using the **new** keyword. Java allows you to create an array by grouping values within a pair of braces. For example, the following code creates an array of three **String** objects.

```
String[] names = { "John", "Mary", "Paul" };
```

The following code creates an array of four **int**s and assign the array to the variable **matrix**.

```
int[] matrix = { 1, 2, 3, 10 };
```

Be careful when passing an array to a method because the following is illegal even though the method **average** takes an array of **int**s.

```
int avg = average( { 1, 2, 3, 10 } ); // illegal
```

Instead, you have to instantiate the array separately.

```
int[] numbers = { 1, 2, 3, 10 };
```

```
int avg = average(numbers);
```

or you can do this

```
int avg = average(new int[] { 1, 2, 3, 10 });
```

5.2 Iterating over an Array

Prior to Java 5, the only way to iterate the members of an array was to use a **for** loop and the array's indexes. For example, the following code iterates over a **String** array referenced by the variable **names**:

```
for (int i = 0; i < 3; i++) {
    System.out.println("\t- " + names[i]);
}
```

Java 5 enhanced the **for** statement. You can now use it to iterate over an array or a collection without the index. Use this syntax to iterate over an array:

```
for (elementType variable : arrayName)
```

Where *arrayName* is the reference to the array, *elementType* is the element type of the array, and *variable* is a variable that references each element of the array.

For example, the following code iterates over an array of **Strings**.

```
String[] names = { "John", "Mary", "Paul" };
for (String name : names) {
    System.out.println(name);
}
```

The code prints this on the console.

```
John
Mary
Paul
```

5.3 The java.util.Arrays Class

The **Arrays** class provides static methods to manipulate arrays. Table 5.1 shows some of its methods.

Method	Description
asList	Returns a fixed-size **List** backed by the array. No other elements can be added to the **List**.
binarySearch	Searches an array for the specified key. If the key is found, returns the index of the element. If there is no match, returns the negative value of the insertion point minus one. See the section "Searching An Array" for details.
copyOf	Creates a new array having the specified length. The new array will have the same elements as the original array. If the new length is not the same as the length of the original array, it pads the new array with null or default values or truncates the original array.
copyOfRange	Creates a new array based on the specified range of the original array.
equals	Compares the contents of two arrays.
fill	Assigns the specified value to each element of the specified array.
sort	Sorts the elements of the specified array.
parallelSort	Parallel sorts the elements of the specified array.
toString	Returns the string representation of the specified array.

Table 5.1: More important methods of java.util.Arrays

Some of these methods are explained further in the next sections.

5.4 Changing an Array Size

Once an array is created, its size cannot be changed. If you want to change the size, you must create a new array and populates it using the values of the old array. For instance, the following code increases the size of **numbers**, an array of three **int**s, to 4.

```
int[] numbers = { 1, 2, 3 };
int[] temp = new int[4];
int length = numbers.length;
for (int j = 0; j < length; j++) {
    temp[j] = numbers[j];
}
numbers = temp;
```

A shorter way of doing this is by using the **copyOf** method of **java.util.Arrays**. For instance, this code creates a four-element array and copies the content of **numbers** to its first three elements.

```
int[] numbers = { 1, 2, 3 };
int[] newArray = Arrays.copyOf(numbers, 4);
```

Of course you can reassign the new array to the original variable:

```
numbers = Arrays.copyOf(numbers, 4);
```

The **copyOf** method comes with ten overloads, eight for each type of Java primitives and two for objects. Here are their signatures:

```
public static boolean[] copyOf(boolean[] original, int newLength)

public static byte[] copyOf(byte[] original, int newLength)

public static char[] copyOf(char[] original, int newLength)

public static double[] copyOf(double[] original, int newLength)

public static float[] copyOf(float[] original, int newLength)

public static int[] copyOf(int[] original, int newLength)

public static long[] copyOf(long[] original, int newLength)

public static short[] copyOf(short[] original, int newLength)

public static <T> T[] copyOf(T[] original, int newLength)

public static <T,U> T[] copyOf(U[] original, int newLength,
        java.lang.Class<? extends T[]> newType)
```

Each of these overloads may throw a **java.lang.NullPointerException** if *original* is null and a **java.lang.NegativeArraySizeException** if *newLength* is negative.

The *newLength* argument can be smaller, equal to, or larger than the length of the original array. If it is smaller, then only the first *newLength* elements will be included in the copy. If it is larger, the last few elements will have default values, i.e. 0 if it is an array of integers or **null** if it is an array of objects.

Another method similar to **copyOf** is **copyOfRange**. **copyOfRange** copies a range of elements to a new array. Like **copyOf**, **copyOfRange** also provides overrides for each Java data type. Here are their signatures:

```
public static boolean[] copyOfRange(boolean[] original,
        int from, int to)

public static byte[] copyOfRange(byte[] original,
        int from, int to)

public static char[] copyOfRange(char[] original,
        int from, int to)

public static double[] copyOfRange(double[] original,
        int from, int to)

public static float[] copyOfRange(float[] original,
        int from, int to)

public static int[] copyOfRange(int[] original, int from, int to)

public static long[] copyOfRange(long[] original, int from, int to)

public static short[] copyOfRange(short[] original, int from,
        int to)

public static <T> T[] copyOfRange(T[] original, int from, int to)

public static <T,U> T[] copyOfRange(U[] original, int from,
        int to, java.lang.Class<? extends T[]> newType)
```

You can also use **System.arraycopy()** to copy an array. However, **Arrays.copyOf()** is easier to use and internally it calls **System.arraycopy()**.

5.5 Searching An Array

You can use the **binarySearch** method of the **Arrays** class to search an array. This method comes with twenty overloads. Here are two of its overloads:

```
public static int binarySearch(int[] array, int key)

public static int binarySearch(java.lang.Object[] array,
        java.lang.Object key)
```

There are also overloads that restrict the search area.

```
public static int binarySearch(int[] array, int fromIndex,
        int toIndex, int key)

public static int binarySearch(java.lang.Object[] array,
        int fromIndex, int toIndex, java.lang.Object key)
```

The **binarySearch** method employs a binary search algorithm to do the search. Using this algorithm, the array is first sorted in ascending or descending order. It then compares the search key with the middle element of the array. If there is a match, the element index is returned. If there is no match, depending whether the search key is lower or higher than the index, the search continues in the first or second half of the array, repeating the same procedure until there is no or only one element left. If at the end of the search no match is found, the **binarySearch** method returns the negative value of the insertion point minus one. The example in Listing 5.1 will make this point clearer.

Listing 5.1: A binary search example

```
package app05;
import java.util.Arrays;

public class BinarySearchDemo {
    public static void main(String[] args) {
        int[] primes = { 2, 3, 5, 7, 11, 13, 17, 19 };
        int index = Arrays.binarySearch(primes, 13);
        System.out.println(index); // prints 5
        index = Arrays.binarySearch(primes, 4);
        System.out.println(index); // prints -3
    }
}
```

The **BinarySearchDemo** class in Listing 5.1 uses an **int** array containing the first eight prime numbers. Passing 13 as the search key returns 5 because 13 is the sixth element in the array, i.e. with index 5. Passing 4 does not find a match and the method returns -3, which is -2 minus one. If the key were to be inserted to the array, it would have the index 2.

5.6 Passing a String Array to main

The public static void method **main** that you use to invoke a Java class takes an array of **Strings**. Here is the signature of **main**:

```
public static void main(String[] args)
```

You can pass arguments to **main** by typing them as arguments to the **java** program. The arguments should appear after the class name and two arguments are separated by a space. You use the following syntax:

```
java className arg1 arg2 arg3 ... arg-n
```

Listing 5.2 shows a class that iterates over the **main** method's **String** array argument.

Listing 5.2.: Accessing the main method's arguments

```
package app05;
public class MainMethodTest {
    public static void main(String[] args) {
        for (String arg : args) {
            System.out.println(arg);
        }
    }
}
```

The following command invokes the class and passes two arguments to the **main** method.

```
java app05/MainMethodTest john mary
```

The **main** method will then print the arguments to the console.

```
john
mary
```

If no argument is passed to **main**, the **String** array **args** will be empty and not null.

5.7 Multidimensional Arrays

In Java a multidimensional array is an array whose elements are also arrays. As such, the rows can have different lengths, unlike multidimensional arrays in C language.

To declare a two dimensional array, use two pairs of brackets after the type:

```
int[][] numbers;
```

To create an array, pass the sizes for both dimensions:

```
int[][] numbers = new int[3][2];
```

Listing 5.3 shows a multidimensional array of **int**s.

Listing 5.3: A multidimensional array.

```
package app05;
import java.util.Arrays;

public class MultidimensionalDemo1 {
    public static void main(String[] args) {
        int[][] matrix = new int[2][3];
        for (int i = 0; i < 2; i++) {
```

```
            for (int j = 0; j < 3; j++) {
                matrix[i][j] = j + i;
            }
        }

        for (int i = 0; i < 2; i++) {
            System.out.println(Arrays.toString(matrix[i]));
        }
    }
}
```

The following will be printed on the console if you run the class.

```
[0, 1, 2]

[1, 2, 3]
```

5.8 ArrayList

As mentioned previously, arrays cannot be resized. Oftentimes, however, you need the flexibility to be able to add elements to a container without constantly worrying about the size of the container. For this, you can use **ArrayList**.

A member of the **java.util** package, **ArrayList** is an ordered collection. You can access its elements by using indices and you can insert an element into an exact location. Index 0 of an **ArrayList** references the first element, index 1 the second element, and so on.

The **add** method appends the specified element to the end of the list. Here is its signature.

```
public boolean add(java.lang.Object element)
```

This method returns **true** if the addition is successful. Otherwise, it returns **false**. **ArrayList** allows you to add null.

ArrayList also has another **add** method with the following signature:

```
public void add(int index, java.lang.Object element)
```

With this **add** method you can insert an element at any position.

In addition, you can replace and remove an element by using the **set** and **remove** methods, respectively.

```
public java.lang.Object set(int index, java.lang.Object element)

public java.lang.Object remove(int index)
```

The **set** method replaces the element at the position specified by *index* with *element* and returns the reference to the element inserted. The **remove** method removes the element at the specified position and returns a reference to the removed element.

To create an **ArrayList**, you specify the type of objects that it can contain. For example, to create an **ArrayList** that can store String object, you would write one of these:

```
ArrayList<String> myArrayList = new ArrayList<String>();
```

```
ArrayList<String> myArrayList = new ArrayList<>();
```

The no-argument constructor of **ArrayList** creates an **ArrayList** object with an initial capacity of ten elements. The size will grow automatically as you add more elements than its capacity. If you know that the number of elements in your **ArrayList** will be more than its capacity, you can use the second constructor:

```
public ArrayList(int initialCapacity)
```

This will result in a slightly faster **ArrayList** because the instance does not have to grow in capacity.

Listing 5.4 demonstrates the use of **ArrayList** and some of its methods.

Listing 5.4: Using ArrayList

```
package app05;
import java.util.ArrayList;

public class ArrayListDemo1 {
    public static void main(String[] args) {
        ArrayList<String> myList = new ArrayList<>();
        myList.add("Hello");
        myList.add(1, "World");
        myList.add(null);
        System.out.println("Size: " + myList.size());
        for (String word: myList) {
            System.out.println(word);
        }
    }
}
```

When run, here is the result on the console.

```
Size: 3
Hello
World
null
```

Self Test

Question 1

Which of the following statements about arrays is (are) true?

A. An array is an object
B. Only an array of objects is an object
C. An array of primitives is not an object
D. An array cannot be resized

Question 2

Here is an intriguing piece of code.

```
... numbers = {{1, 2, 3}, {4}};
```

What Java type can be used for **numbers**? (Choose all that apply)

A. int[][]
B. byte[][]
C. float[][]
D. Integer[][]
E. Object[][]
F. It is an attempt to declare a two-dimensional array, but the statement is invalid because each row in a two-dimensional array must have the same number of elements.

Question 3

Consider the following code snippet.

```
public class Container {
    public static void main(String[] args) {
        for (String arg : args) {
            System.out.println(arg);
        }
    }
}
```

What can be said about iterating the arguments in an enhanced for?

A. It will throw a NullPointerException if the class is invoked without an argument
B. It will throw a ArrayIndexOutOfBoundsException if the class is invoked without an argument
C. The code will not throw an exception
D. The code will print the arguments passed to the class

Question 4

Given

```
public class ArrayTest {
    public static void main(String[] args) {
        int[] numbers = new int[5];
        numbers[0] = 100;
        for (int i = 1; i < 5; i++) {
            numbers[i] = i + numbers[i - 1];
        }
        System.out.println(numbers[4]);
    }
}
```

What is the output of the program?

A. 108
B. 109
C. 110
D. 120

Question 5

Given

```
package com.brainysoftware.oca;
import java.util.ArrayList;
public class EmployeeRecord {
    public static void main(String[] args) {
        ArrayList<String> employees = new ArrayList<>();
        employees.add("Henry Higgins");
        employees.add("William Murdoch");
        employees.add(0, "Craig Thomas");
        for (int i = 0; i < 3; i++) {
            System.out.print(employees.get(i));
            if (i < 2) {
                System.out.print(", ");
            }
        }
    }
}
```

What is the output of this program?

A. Henry Higgins, William Murdoch, Craig Thomas
B. Craig Thomas, William Murdoch, Craig Thomas
C. Craig Thomas, Henry Higgins, William Murdoch
D. Henry Higgins, Craig Thomas, William Murdoch

Question 6

Which statement(s) creates an **ArrayList** of **Employee** object with an initial capacity of 10? (Choose all that apply)

A. ArrayList<Employee> list = new ArrayList<>();
B. ArrayList<Employee> list = new ArrayList<>(10);
C. ArrayList<Employee> list = new ArrayList<Employee>();
D. ArrayList<Employee> list = new ArrayList<Employee>(10);

Question 7

This code fragment attempts to convert an **ArrayList** to an array:

```
ArrayList<String> list = new ArrayList<>();
list.add("Benson");
String[] names = list.toArray(new String[0]);
for (String name : names) {
    System.out.println(name);
```

```
}
```

What is the output of this code fragment?

A. No output because the **toArray** method returns an empty String array
B. A runtime error because there is no place in the array to move the element in the **ArrayList** to.
C. Benson
D. null because the String array has not been initialized

Question 8

Given this class:

```
1. public class MyDB {
2.     public static void main(String[] args) {
3.         String name1 = "John Troy";
4.         String name2 = "Simba";
5.         String[] names = {name1, name2};
6.         name1 = null;
7.         name2 = null;
8.     }
9. }
```

Which of the following statements are correct?

A. One object is eligible for garbage collection at line 7
B. Two objects are eligible for garbage collection at line 8
C. No object is eligible for garbage collection at line 7
D. No object is eligible for garbage collection at line 8

Question 9

Given the following code snippet:

```
public class FriendManager {
    public static void main(String[] args) {
        String[][] friends = {{"James", "Gillis"}, {"Tony", "Bubba"},
                {"Alexis"}};
        System.out.println(friends[0][1]);
    }
}
```

What is the output of this program?

A. James
B. Gillis
C. null
D. Alexis

Question 10

Given the following class:

```
package test;
import java.util.ArrayList;
public class Entertainer {
    public static void main(String[] args) {
        ArrayList<int> cards = new ArrayList<>();
        cards.add(1);
        cards.add(2);
        cards.add(3);
        for (int i : cards) {
            System.out.print(i);
        }
    }
}
```

What is the output of this class?

A. 123
B. 1 2 3
C. The class will not compile.
D. The program will throw a NullPointerException

Answers to Self Test

Question 1

Which of the following statements about arrays is (are) true?

A. An array is an object
B. Only an array of objects is an object
C. An array of primitives is not an object
D. An array cannot be resized

Answer: A, D.

An array is always an object, regardless of the type of the data it contains. Once created, an array cannot be resized.

Question 2

Here is an intriguing piece of code.

```
... numbers = {{1, 2, 3}, {4}};
```

What Java type can be used for **numbers**? (Choose all that apply)

A. int[][]
B. byte[][]
C. float[][]
D. Integer[][]
E. Object[][]

F. It is an attempt to declare a two-dimensional array, but the statement is invalid because each row in a two-dimensional array must have the same number of elements.

Answer: A, B, C, D, E.

A and B are the most likely, but C, D and E are also valid. With regard to D, the array elements will be converted to Integer objects automatically. F is incorrect as each dimension in a multidimensional array may have a different number of elements in each of its rows.

Question 3

Consider the following code snippet.

```
public class Container {
    public static void main(String[] args) {
        for (String arg : args) {
            System.out.println(arg);
        }
    }
}
```

What can be said about iterating the arguments in an enhanced for?

A. It will throw a NullPointerException if the class is invoked without an argument
B. It will throw a ArrayIndexOutOfBoundsException if the class is invoked without an argument
C. The code will not throw an exception
D. The code will print the arguments passed to the class

Answer: C, D.

The String array passed to the **main** method will never be null. In the event the class is invoked without an argument, the JVM will create an empty array.

Question 4

Given

```
public class ArrayTest {
    public static void main(String[] args) {
        int[] numbers = new int[5];
        numbers[0] = 100;
        for (int i = 1; i < 5; i++) {
            numbers[i] = i + numbers[i - 1];
        }
        System.out.println(numbers[4]);
    }
}
```

What is the output of the program?

A. 108

B. 109
C. 110
D. 120

Answer: C.

Focus on the loop. There are four iterations, from i = 1 to i = 4.

numbers[1] = 1 + numbers[0] = 1 + 100 = 101

numbers[2] = 2 + numbers[1] = 2 + 101 = 103

numbers[3] = 3 + numbers[2] = 3 + 103 = 106

numbers[4] = 4 + numbers[3] = 4 + 106 = 110

Question 5

Given

```
package com.brainysoftware.oca;
import java.util.ArrayList;
public class EmployeeRecord {
    public static void main(String[] args) {
        ArrayList<String> employees = new ArrayList<>();
        employees.add("Henry Higgins");
        employees.add("William Murdoch");
        employees.add(0, "Craig Thomas");
        for (int i = 0; i < 3; i++) {
            System.out.print(employees.get(i));
            if (i < 2) {
                System.out.print(", ");
            }
        }
    }
}
```

What is the output of this program?

A. Henry Higgins, William Murdoch, Craig Thomas
B. Craig Thomas, William Murdoch, Craig Thomas
C. Craig Thomas, Henry Higgins, William Murdoch
D. Henry Higgins, Craig Thomas, William Murdoch

Answer: C.

The code added "Henry Higgins" and "William Murdoch" as the first and second elements of the ArrayList, respectively. Then, it inserted "Craig Thomas" at position 1, pushing the previous elements to positions 2 and 3, respectively.

Question 6

Which statement(s) creates an **ArrayList** of **Employee** object with an initial capacity of 10? (Choose all that apply)

A. ArrayList<Employee> list = new ArrayList<>();
B. ArrayList<Employee> list = new ArrayList<>(10);
C. ArrayList<Employee> list = new ArrayList<Employee>();
D. ArrayList<Employee> list = new ArrayList<Employee>(10);

Answer: A, B, C, D.

All of them. By default, an **ArrayList** is created with an initial capacity of 10 elements.

Question 7

This code fragment attempts to convert an **ArrayList** to an array:

```
ArrayList<String> list = new ArrayList<>();
list.add("Benson");
String[] names = list.toArray(new String[0]);
for (String name : names) {
    System.out.println(name);
}
```

What is the output of this code fragment?

A. No output because the **toArray** method returns an empty String array
B. A runtime error because there is no place in the array to move the element in the **ArrayList** to.
C. Benson
D. null because the String array has not been initialized

Answer: C.

The **toArray** method returns an array and copies all the elements of the **ArrayList** to the array. The array will have the same size as the **ArrayList**.

Question 8

Given this class:

```
1. public class MyDB {
2.     public static void main(String[] args) {
3.         String name1 = "John Troy";
4.         String name2 = "Simba";
5.         String[] names = {name1, name2};
6.         name1 = null;
7.         name2 = null;
8.     }
9. }
```

Which of the following statements are correct?

A. One object is eligible for garbage collection at line 7
B. Two objects are eligible for garbage collection at line 8
C. No object is eligible for garbage collection at line 7
D. No object is eligible for garbage collection at line 8

Answer: C, D.

The array holds references two the two String objects even after the reference variables name1 and name2 are set to null. Therefore, no object is eligible for garbage collection on line 7 and line 8.

Question 9

Given the following code snippet:

```
public class FriendManager {
    public static void main(String[] args) {
        String[][] friends = {{"James", "Gillis"}, {"Tony", "Bubba"},
                {"Alexis"}};
        System.out.println(friends[0][1]);
    }
}
```

What is the output of this program?

A. James
B. Gillis
C. null
D. Alexis

Answer: B.

friends[0] refers to the first array in the two-dimensional array, which is {"James", "Gillis"}. **friends[0][1]** references the second element in the first array.

Question 10

Given the following class:

```
package test;
import java.util.ArrayList;
public class Entertainer {
    public static void main(String[] args) {
        ArrayList<int> cards = new ArrayList<>();
        cards.add(1);
        cards.add(2);
        cards.add(3);
        for (int i : cards) {
            System.out.print(i);
        }
    }
}
```

What is the output of this class?

A. 123
B. 1 2 3
C. The class will not compile.
D. The program will throw a NullPointerException

Answer: C.

An **ArrayList** may only contain objects and not primitives.

Chapter 6
Inheritance

Inheritance is a very important object-oriented programming (OOP) feature. It is what makes code extensible in an OOP language. Extending a class is also called inheriting or subclassing. In Java, by default all classes are extendible, but you can use the **final** keyword to prevent classes from being subclassed. This chapter explains inheritance in Java.

6.1 Inheritance Overview

You extend a class by creating a new class. The former and the latter will then have a parent-child relationship. The original class is the parent class or the base class or the superclass. The new class is the child class or the subclass or the derived class of the parent. The process of extending a class in OOP is called inheritance. In a subclass you can add new methods and new fields as well as override existing methods to change their behaviors.

Figure 6.1 presents a UML class diagram that depicts a parent-child relationship between a class and a child class.

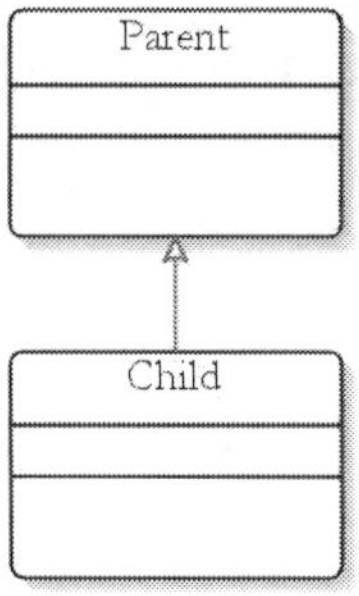

Figure 6.1: The UML class diagram for a parent class and a child class

Note that a line with an arrow is used to depict generalization, e.g. the parent-child relationship.

A child class in turn can be extended, unless you specifically make it inextensible by declaring it final. Final classes are discussed in the section "Final Classes" later in this chapter.

The benefits of inheritance are obvious. Inheritance gives you the opportunity to add some functionality that does not exist in the original class. It also gives you the chance to change the behaviors of the existing class to better suit your needs.

The extends Keyword

You extend a class by using the **extends** keyword in a class declaration, after the class name and before the parent class. Listing 6.1 presents a class named **Parent** and Listing 6.2 a class named **Child** that extends **Parent**.

Listing 6.1: The Parent class

```
public class Parent {
}
```

Listing 6.2: The Child class

```
public class Child extends Parent {
}
```

Extending a class is as simple as that.

> **Note**
> All Java classes that do not explicitly extend a parent class automatically extend the **java.lang.Object** class. **Object** is the ultimate superclass in Java. **Parent** in Listing 6.1 by default is a subclass of **Object**.

> **Note**
> In Java a class can only extend one class. This is unlike C++ where multiple inheritance is allowed. However, the notion of multiple inheritance can be achieved by using interfaces in Java, as discussed in Chapter 7, "Interfaces, Abstract Classes and Polymorphism."

The Is-A Relationship

There is a special relationship that is formed when you create a new class by inheritance. The subclass and the superclass has an "is-a" relationship.

For example, **Animal** is a class that represents animals. There are many types of animals, including birds, fish and dogs, so you can create subclasses of **Animal** that model specific types of animals. Figure 6.2 features the **Animal** class with three subclasses, **Bird**, **Fish** and **Dog**.

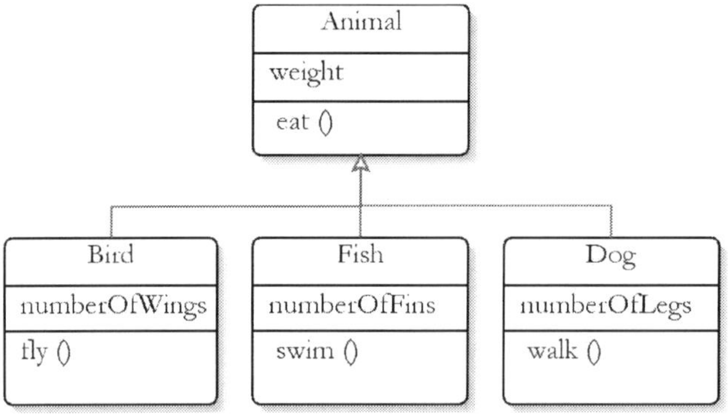

Figure 6.2: An example of inheritance

The is-a relationship between the subclasses and the superclass **Animal** is very apparent. A bird "is an" animal, a dog is an animal and a fish is an animal. A subclass is a special type of its superclass. For example, a bird is a special type of animal. The is-a relationship does not go the other way, however. An animal is not necessarily a bird or a dog.

Listing 6.3 presents the **Animal** class and its subclasses.

Listing 6.3: Animal and its subclasses

```
package app06;
class Animal {
    public float weight;
    public void eat() {
    }
}

class Bird extends Animal {
    public int numberOfWings = 2;
    public void fly() {
    }
}

class Fish extends Animal {
    public int numberOfFins = 2;
    public void swim() {
    }
}

class Dog extends Animal {
    public int numberOfLegs = 4;
    public void walk() {
    }
}
```

In this example, the **Animal** class defines a **weight** field that applies to all animals. It also declares an **eat** method because animals eat.

The **Bird** class is a special type of **Animal**, it inherits the **eat** method and the **weight** field. **Bird** also adds a **numberOfWings** field and a **fly** method. This shows that the more specific **Bird** class extends the functionality and behavior of the more generic **Animal** class.

A subclass inherits all public methods and fields of its superclass. For example, you can create a **Dog** object and call its **eat** method:

```
Dog dog = new Dog();
dog.eat();
```

The **eat** method is declared in the **Animal** class; the **Dog** class simply inherits it.

A consequence of the is-a relationship is that it is legal to assign an instance of a subclass to a reference variable of the parent type. For example, the following code is valid because **Bird** is a subclass of **Animal** and a **Bird** is always an **Animal**.

```
Animal animal = new Bird();
```

However, the following is illegal because there is no guarantee that an **Animal** is a **Dog**.:

```
Dog dog = new Animal();
```

6.2 Accessibility

From within a subclass you can access its superclass's public and protected methods and fields, but not the superclass's private methods. If the subclass and the superclass are in the same package, you can also access the superclass's default methods and fields.

Consider the **P** and **C** classes in Listing 6.4.

Listing 6.4: Showing accessibility

```
package app06;
public class P {
    public void publicMethod() {
    }
    protected void protectedMethod() {
    }
    void defaultMethod() {
    }
}
class C extends P {
    public void testMethods() {
        publicMethod();
        protectedMethod();
        defaultMethod();
    }
}
```

P has three methods, one public, one protected and one with the default access level. **C** is a subclass of **P**. As you can see in the **C** class's **testMethods** method, **C** can access its parent's public and protected methods. In addition, because **C** and **P** belong to the same package, **C** can also access **P**'s default method.

However, it does not mean you can expose **P**'s non-public methods through its subclass. For example, the following code will not compile:

```
package test;
import app06.C;
public class AccessibilityTest {
    public static void main(String[] args) {
        C c = new C();
        c.protectedMethod();
    }
}
```

protectedMethod is a protected method of **P**. It is not accessible from outside **P**, except from a subclass. Since **AccessibilityTest** is not a subclass of **P**, you cannot access **P**'s protected method through its subclass **C**.

6.3 Method Overriding

When you extends a class, you can change the behavior of a method in the parent class. This is called method overriding, and this happens when you write in a subclass a method that has the same signature as a method in the parent class. If only the name is the same but the list of arguments is not, then it is method overloading. (See Chapter 3, "Objects and Classes")

You override a method to change its behavior. To override a method, you simply have to write the new method in the subclass, without having to change anything in the parent class. You can override the superclass's public and protected methods. If the subclass and superclass are in the same package, you can also override methods with the default access level.

An example of method overriding is demonstrated by the **Box** class in Listing 6.5.

Listing 6.5: The Box class

```
package app06;
public class Box {
    public int length;
    public int width;
    public int height;

    public Box(int length, int width, int height) {
        this.length = length;
        this.width = width;
        this.height = height;
    }

    @Override
    public String toString() {
        return "I am a Box.";
    }

    @Override
    public Object clone() {
        return new Box(1, 1, 1);
    }
}
```

The **Box** class extends the **java.lang.Object** class. It is an implicit extension since the **extends** keyword is not used. **Box** overrides the public **toString** method and the protected **clone** method. Note that the **clone** method in **Box** is public whereas in **Object** it is protected. Increasing the visibility of a method defined in a superclass from protected to public is allowed. However, reducing visibility is illegal.

An overridden method is normally annotated with **@Override**. It is not required but it is good practice to do so.

What if you create a method that has the same signature as a private method in the superclass? It is not method overriding, since private methods are not visible from outside the class. It is just a method that happens to have the same signature as the private method.

Note
You cannot override a final method. To make a method final, use the **final** keyword in the method declaration. For example:

```
public final java.lang.String toUpperCase(java.lang.String s)
```

6.4 Calling the Constructors of the Superclass

A subclass is just like an ordinary class, you use the **new** keyword to create an instance of it. If you do not explicitly write a constructor in your subclass, the compiler will implicitly add a no-argument (no-arg) constructor.

When you instantiate a child class by invoking one of its constructors, the first thing the constructor does is call the no-argument constructor of the direct parent class. In the parent class, the constructor also calls the constructor of its direct parent class. This process repeats itself until it reaches the constructor of the **java.lang.Object** class. In other words, when you create a child object, all its parent classes are also instantiated.

This process is illustrated in the **Base** and **Sub** classes in Listing 6.6.

Listing 6.6: Calling a superclass's no-arg constructor

```
package app06;
class Base {
    public Base() {
        System.out.println("Base");
    }
    public Base(String s) {
        System.out.println("Base." + s);
    }
}
public class Sub extends Base {
    public Sub(String s) {
        System.out.println(s);
    }
    public static void main(String[] args) {
        Sub sub = new Sub("Start");
    }
}
```

If you run the **Sub** class, you'll see this on the console:

```
Base
Start
```

This proves that the first thing that the **Sub** class's constructor does is invoke the **Base** class's no-arg constructor. The Java compiler has quietly changed **Sub**'s constructor to the following without saving the modification to the source file.

```
public Sub(String s) {
    super();
    System.out.println(s);
}
```

The keyword **super** represents an instance of the direct superclass of the current object. Since **super** is called from an instance of **Sub**, **super** represents an instance of **Base**, its direct superclass.

You can explicitly call a parent's constructor from a subclass's constructor by using the **super** keyword, but **super** must be the first statement in the constructor. Using the **super** keyword is handy if you want another constructor in the superclass to be invoked. For example, you can modify the constructor in **Sub** to the following.

```
public Sub(String s) {
    super(s);
    System.out.println(s);
}
```

This constructor calls the single argument constructor of the parent class, by using **super(s)**. As a result, if you run the class you will see the following on the console.

```
Base.Start
Start
```

Now, what if the superclass does not have a no-arg constructor and you do not make an explicit call to another constructor from a subclass? This is illustrated in the **Parent** and **Child** classes in Listing 6.7.

Listing 6.7: Implicit calling to the parent's constructor that does not exist

```
package app06;
class Parent {
    public Parent(String s) {
        System.out.println("Parent(String)");
    }
}

public class Child extends Parent {
    public Child() {
    }
}
```

This will generate a compile error because the compiler adds an implicit call to the no-argument constructor in **Parent**, while the **Parent** class has only one constructor, the one that accepts a **String**. You can remedy this situation by explicitly calling the parent's constructor from the **Child** class's constructor:

```
public Child() {
    super(null);
}
```

Note

It actually makes sense for a child class to call its parent's constructor from its own constructor because an instance of a subclass must always be accompanied by an instance of each of its parents. This way, calls to a method that is not overridden in a child class can be passed to its parent until the first in the hierarchy is found.

6.5 Calling the Hidden Members of the Superclass

The **super** keyword has another purpose in life. It can be used to call a hidden member or an overridden method in a superclass. Since **super** represents an instance of the direct parent, super.*memberName* returns the specified member in the parent class. You can access any member in the superclass that is visible from the subclass. For example, Listing 6.8 shows two classes that have a parent-child relationship: **Tool** and **Pencil**.

Listing 6.8: Using super to access a hidden member

```
package app06;
class Tool {
    @Override
    public String toString() {
        return "Generic tool";
    }
}

public class Pencil extends Tool {
    @Override
    public String toString() {
        return "I am a Pencil";
    }

    public void write() {
        System.out.println(super.toString());
        System.out.println(toString());
    }

    public static void main(String[] args) {
        Pencil pencil = new Pencil();
        pencil.write();
    }
}
```

The **Pencil** class overrides the **toString** method in **Tool**. If you run the **Pencil** class, you will see the following on the console.

```
Generic tool
I am a Pencil
```

Unlike calling a parent's constructor, invoking a parent's method does not have to be the first statement in the caller method.

6.6 Type Casting

You can cast an object to another type. The rule is, you can only cast an instance of a subclass to its parent class. Casting an object to a parent class is called upcasting. Here is an example, assuming that **Child** is a subclass of **Parent**.

```
Child child = new Child();
```

```
Parent parent = child;
```

To upcast a **Child** object, all you need to do is assign the object to a reference variable of type **Parent**. Note that the **parent** reference variable cannot access members that are only available in **Child**.

Because **parent** in the snippet above references an object of type **Child**, you can cast it back to **Child**. This time, it is called downcasting because you are casting an object to a class down the inheritance hierarchy. Downcasting requires that you write the child type in brackets. For example:

```
Child child = new Child();
Parent parent = child;// parent pointing to an instance of Child
Child child2 = (Child) parent; // downcasting
```

Downcasting to a subclass is only allowed if the parent class reference is already pointing to an instance of the subclass. The following will generate a compile error.

```
Object parent = new Object();
Child child = (Child) parent; // illegal downcasting, compile error
```

6.7 Final Classes

You can prevent others from extending your class by making it final using the keyword **final** in the class declaration. **final** may appear after or before the access modifier. For example:

```
public final class Pencil
final public class Pen
```

The first form is more common.

Even though making a class final makes your code slightly faster, the difference is too insignificant to notice. Design consideration, and not speed, should be the reason you make a class final. For example, the **java.lang.String** class is final because the designer of the class did not want you to change the behavior of **String**.

6.8 The instanceof Operator

The **instanceof** operator can be used to test if an object is of a specified type. It is normally used in an **if** statement and its syntax is this.

```
if (objectReference instanceof type)
```

where *objectReference* references an object being investigated. For example, the following **if** statement returns **true**.

```
String s = "Hello";
if (s instanceof java.lang.String)
```

However, applying **instanceof** on a **null** reference variable returns **false**. For example, the following **if** statement returns **false**.

```
String s = null;
if (s instanceof java.lang.String)
```

Also, since a subclass "is a" type of its superclass, the following **if** statement, where **Child** is a subclass of **Parent**, returns **true**.

```
Child child = new Child();
if (child instanceof Parent)    // evaluates to true
```

Self Test

Question 1

Which of the following statements are true with regard to inheritance?

A. In Java a class can extend multiple classes
B. You create a subclass by using the **extends** keyword
C. In Java a class may only extend one parent class
D. You create a subclass by using the **import** keyword

Question 2

Which class is the root of all Java classes?

A. java.lang.Object
B. java.lang.Class
C. java.lang.System
D. java.lang.Runnable

Question 3

What do you call a class that extends another class?

A. A subclass
B. A final class
C. A child class
D. A base class

Question 4

What do you call a class that cannot be extended?

A. A subclass
B. A final class
C. A child class
D. An abstract class

Question 5

What do you call a class from which another class is derived?

A. A superclass
B. A final class
C. A parent class
D. A base class

Question 6

Which of the following statements are true?

A. A child class has an is-a relationship with its parent class
B. A parent class has a has-a relationship with all its children
C. A child class has an has-a relationship with its parent class
D. A child class has a has-a relationship only with its direct parent

Question 7

Consider the following two classes:

```
package com.example.inheritance;
class Parent {
    public void print() { ... }
    String describe() { ... }
    protected String[] copyElements(String[] sources) { ... }
    private float getNumber() { ... }
}

class Child extends Parent {
    public void doIt() {
        ...
    }
}
```

Which methods can be used in the **Child** class?

A. print, describe, getNumber
B. print, describe, copyElements, getNumber
C. print, describe, copyElements
D. print, describe, copyElements, toString

Question 8

Given

```
package biology;
class Insect {
}

class Butterfly extends Insect {
```

```
}

public class Insectarium {
    public static void main(String[] args) {
        Butterfly butterfly = new Butterfly();
        Insect insect = new Insect();
        boolean b1 = butterfly instanceof Insect;
        boolean b2 = butterfly instanceof Butterfly;
        boolean b3 = insect instanceof Butterfly;
        boolean b4 = insect instanceof Insect;

        System.out.println(b1);
        System.out.println(b2);
        System.out.println(b3);
        System.out.println(b4);
    }
}
```

After the last line of code is executed, what are the values of b1, b2, b3 and b4?

A. b1, b2, b3 and b4 are all true
B. b1, b2, b3 and b4 are all false
C. b1, b2 and b3 are true, b4 is false
D. b1, b2 and b4 are true, b3 is false

Question 9

Consider the following two classes:

```
package test;
class Device {
    public void printDescription() {
        System.out.println("I am a smart device");
    }
    private void printPrice() {}
}

class Computer extends Device {
    protected void printDescription() {
        System.out.println("I am a smart device");
    }
    protected void printPrice() {}
}
```

Which of the following statements is true?

A. The classes will compile with no error
B. There is a compile error caused by the **printDescription** method in **Computer**
C. There is a compile error caused by the **getPrice** method in **Computer**
D. There are compile errors caused by the **getPrice** and **printDescription** methods in **Computer**

Question 10

Given

```
package toolbox;
class Tool {
    public void printDescription() {
        System.out.println("I am a tool");
    }
}

class Hammer extends Tool {
    @Override
    public void printDescription() {
        System.out.println("I am a hammer");
        super.printDescription();
    }
}
```

What can be said of the two classes?

A. The @Override annotation in **Hammer** will cause a compile error
B. The two classes will compile and a call to **printDescription** in Hammer will print "I am a hammer" and "I am a tool"
C. There will be a compile error because a call to super must be the first line of code in a method
D. The two classes will compile and calling **printDescription** in Tool will print "I am a tool"

Answers to Self Test

Question 1

Which of the following statements are true with regard to inheritance?

A. In Java a class can extend multiple classes
B. You create a subclass by using the **extends** keyword
C. In Java a class may only extend one parent class
D. You create a subclass by using the **import** keyword

Answer: B, C.

You extend a class by using the extends keyword and a class can only be derived from a parent class.

Question 2

Which class is the root of all Java classes?

A. java.lang.Object
B. java.lang.Class
C. java.lang.System
D. java.lang.Runnable

Answer: A.

All classes are direct or indirect children of java.lang.Object.

Question 3

What do you call a class that extends another class?

A. A subclass
B. A final class
C. A child class
D. A base class

Answer: A, C.

A class that extends another class is called a subclass or child class.

Question 4

What do you call a class that cannot be extended?

A. A subclass
B. A final class
C. A child class
D. An abstract class

Answer: B.

A class that cannot be extended is called a final class.

Question 5

What do you call a class from which another class is derived?

A. A superclass
B. A final class
C. A parent class
D. A base class

Answer: A, C, D.

A class from which another class is derived is called a parent class or a superclass or a base class.

Question 6

Which of the following statements are true?

A. A child class has an is-a relationship with its parent class

B. A parent class has a has-a relationship with all its children
C. A child class has a has-a relationship with its parent class
D. A child class has a has-a relationship only with its direct parent

Answer: A.

A child class has an is-a relationship with its parent. For example, if class **Elephant** is derived from **Animal**, an **Elephant** is an **Animal**.

Question 7

Consider the following two classes:

```
package com.example.inheritance;
class Parent {
    public void print() { ... }
    String describe() { ... }
    protected String[] copyElements(String[] sources) { ... }
    private float getNumber() { ... }
}

class Child extends Parent {
    public void doIt() {
        ...
    }
}
```

Which methods can be used in the **Child** class?

A. print, describe, getNumber
B. print, describe, copyElements, getNumber
C. print, describe, copyElements
D. print, describe, copyElements, toString

Answer: C, D.

A child class has access to the public, protected and default methods of its parents. The **Child** class can use the **print**, **describe** and **copyElements** methods defined in **Parent**, so C is a correct answer. Since **Parent** automatically extends **java.lang.Object**, **Parent** also inherits methods from **java.lang.Object** including its **toString** method. All methods that **Parent** inherit from its parent are also inherited to **Child**, so D is also correct.

Question 8

Given

```
package biology;
class Insect {
}

class Butterfly extends Insect {
}
```

```
public class Insectarium {
    public static void main(String[] args) {
        Butterfly butterfly = new Butterfly();
        Insect insect = new Insect();
        boolean b1 = butterfly instanceof Insect;
        boolean b2 = butterfly instanceof Butterfly;
        boolean b3 = insect instanceof Butterfly;
        boolean b4 = insect instanceof Insect;

        System.out.println(b1);
        System.out.println(b2);
        System.out.println(b3);
        System.out.println(b4);
    }
}
```

After the last line of code is executed, what are the values of b1, b2, b3 and b4?

A. b1, b2, b3 and b4 are all true
B. b1, b2, b3 and b4 are all false
C. b1, b2 and b3 are true, b4 is false
D. b1, b2 and b4 are true, b3 is false

Answer: D.

The **instanceof** operator examines whether or not an object is of a certain type. An object of a class is of course an instance of that class. In addition, an object of a child class is also an instance of its parent class, even though it does not work the other way around. Therefore b1, b2 and b4 are true, but not b3.

Question 9

Consider the following two classes:

```
package test;
class Device {
    public void printDescription() {
        System.out.println("I am a smart device");
    }
    private void printPrice() {}
}

class Computer extends Device {
    protected void printDescription() {
        System.out.println("I am a smart device");
    }
    protected void printPrice() {}
}
```

Which of the following statements is true?

A. The classes will compile with no error
B. There is a compile error caused by the **printDescription** method in **Computer**
C. There is a compile error caused by the **getPrice** method in **Computer**

D. There are compile errors caused by the **getPrice** and **printDescription** methods in **Computer**

Answer: B.

The **printDescription** method in **Computer** reduces the visibility of the overriden method in the parent class from public to protected. This is not allowed in Java. The **getPrice** method in **Device** is not visible in **Computer**. Therefore, adding a method with the same signature has no effect.

Question 10

Given

```
package toolbox;
class Tool {
    public void printDescription() {
        System.out.println("I am a tool");
    }
}

class Hammer extends Tool {
    @Override
    public void printDescription() {
        System.out.println("I am a hammer");
        super.printDescription();
    }
}
```

What can be said of the two classes?

A. The @Override annotation in **Hammer** will cause a compile error
B. The two classes will compile and a call to **printDescription** in Hammer will print "I am a hammer" and "I am a tool"
C. There will be a compile error because a call to super must be the first line of code in a method
D. The two classes will compile and calling **printDescription** in Tool will print "I am a tool"

Answer: B, D.

The @Override annotation type can be used to annotate a method that overrides a method in a parent class. As long as the annotated method truly overrides a method in a parent class, it will not cause a compile error. The use of super to run a method in a parent class does not have to be the first line in a method, unlike the call to super in a constructor.

Chapter 7
Interfaces, Abstract Classes and Polymorphism

Java beginners often get the impression that an interface is simply a class without implementation. While this is not technically incorrect, it obscures the real purpose of having the interface in the first place. The interface is more than that. The interface should be regarded as a contract between a service provider and its clients. This chapter therefore focuses on the concepts before explaining how to write an interface.

The second topic in this chapter is the abstract class. Technically speaking, an abstract class is a class that cannot be instantiated and must be implemented by a subclass. However, the abstract class is important because in some situations it can take the role of the interface. You will learn how to use the abstract class too in this chapter.

Finally, this chapter discusses polymorphism, one of the main pillars in object-oriented programming.

7.1 The Concept of Interface

When learning about the interface for the first time, novices often focus on how to write one, rather than understanding the concept behind it. They would think an interface is something like a Java class declared with the **interface** keyword and whose methods have no body.

While the description is not inaccurate, treating an interface as an implementation-less class misses the big picture. A better definition of an interface is a contract. It is a contract between a service provider (server) and the user of such a service (client). Sometimes the server defines the contract, sometimes the client does.

Consider this real-world example. Microsoft Windows is the most popular operating system today, but Microsoft does not make printers. For printing, you still rely on those people at HP, Canon, Samsung, and the like. Each of these printer makers uses a proprietary technology. However, their products can all be used to print documents from any Windows application. How come?

This is because Microsoft said something to this effect to the printer manufacturers, "If you want your products useable on Windows (and we know you do), you must implement this **Printable** interface."

The interface is as simple as this:

```
interface Printable {
```

```
    void print(Document document);
}
```

where *document* is the document to be printed.

Implementing this interface, the printer makers then write printer drivers. Every printer has a different driver, but they all implement **Printable**. A printer driver is an implementation of **Printable**. In this case, these printer drivers are the service provider.

The client of the printing service is all Windows applications. It is easy to print on Windows because an application just needs to call the **print** method and pass a **Document** object. Because the interface is freely available, client applications can be compiled without waiting for an implementation to be available.

The point is, printing to different printers from different applications is possible thanks to the **Printable** interface. This interface is a contract between printing service providers and printing clients.

An interface can define both fields and methods. Prior to JDK 1.8 all methods in an interface were abstract, but starting from JDK 1.8 you can also write default and static methods in an interface. Unless specified otherwise, an interface method refers to an abstract method.

To be useful, an interface has to have an implementing class that actually performs the action.

Figure 7.1 illustrates the **Printable** interface and its implementation in an UML class diagram.

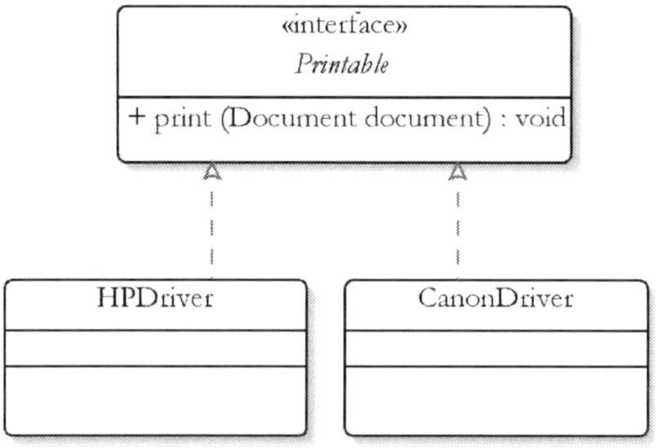

Figure 7.1: An interface and two implementation classes in a class diagram

In the class diagram, an interface has the same shape as a class, however the name is printed in italic and prefixed with <<interface>>. The **HPDriver** and **CanonDriver** classes are classes that implement the **Printable** interface. The implementations are of course different. In the **HPDriver** class, the **print** method contains code that enables printing to a HP printer. In **CanonDriver**, the code enables printing to a Canon driver. In a UML class diagram, a class and an interface are joined by a dash-line with an arrow. This type of relationship is often called realization because the class provides real implementation (code that actually works) of the abstraction provided by the interface.

Note

This case study is contrived but the problem and the solution are real. I hope this provides you with more understanding of what the interface really is. It is a contract.

7.2 The Interface, Technically Speaking

Now that you understand what the interface is, let's examine how you can create one. In Java, like the class, the interface is a type. Follow this format to write an interface:

```
accessModifier interface interfaceName {

}
```

Like a class, an interface has either the public or default access level. An interface can have fields and methods. All members of an interface are implicitly public. Listing 7.1 shows an interface named **Printable**.

Listing 7.1: The Printable interface

```
package app07;
public interface Printable {
    void print(Object o);
}
```

The **Printable** interface has a method, **print**. Note that **print** is public even though there is no **public** keyword in front of the method declaration. You are free to use the keyword **public** before the method signature, but it would be redundant.

Just like a class, an interface is a template for creating objects. Unlike an ordinary class, however, an interface cannot be instantiated. It simply defines a set of methods that Java classes can implement.

You compile an interface just you would a class. The compiler creates a .class file for each interface compiled successfully.

To implement an interface, you use the **implements** keyword after the class declaration. A class can implement multiple interfaces. For example, Listing 7.2 shows the **CanonDriver** class that implements **Printable**.

Listing 7.2: An implementation of the Printable interface

```
package app07;
public class CanonDriver implements Printable {
    @Override
    public void print(Object obj) {
        // code that does the printing
    }
}
```

Note that a method implementation should also be annotated with **@Override**.

Unless specified otherwise, all interface methods are abstract. An implementing class has to override all abstract methods in an interface. The relationship between an interface and its implementing class can be likened to a parent class and a subclass. An instance of the class is also an instance of the interface. For example, the following **if** statement evaluates to **true**.

```
CanonDriver driver = new CanonDriver();
if (driver instanceof Printable)     // evaluates to true
```

Some interfaces have neither fields nor methods, and are known as marker interfaces. Classes implement them as a marker. For example, the **java.io.Serializable** interface, has no fields nor methods. Classes implement it so that their instances can be serialized, i.e. saved to a file or to memory.

Fields in an Interface

Fields in an interface must be initialized and are implicitly public, static and final. However, you may redundantly use the modifiers **public**, **static**, and **final**. These lines of code have the same effect.

```
public int STATUS = 1;
int STATUS = 1;
public static final STATUS = 1;
```

Note that by convention field names in an interface are written in upper case.

It is a compile error to have two fields with the same name in an interface. However, an interface might inherit more than one field with the same name from its superinterfaces.

Abstract Methods

You declare abstract methods in an interface just as you would declare a method in a class. However, abstract methods in an interface do not have a body, they are immediately terminated by a semicolon. All abstract methods are implicitly public and abstract, even though it is legal to have the **public** and **abstract** modifiers in front of a method declaration.

The syntax of an abstract method in an interface is

```
[methodModifiers] ReturnType MethodName(listOfArgument)
        [ThrowClause];
```

where *methodModifiers* is **abstract** and **public**.

Extending An Interface

The interface supports inheritance. An interface can extend another interface. If interface **A** extends interface **B**, **A** is said to be a subinterface of **B**. **B** is the superinterface of **A**. Because **A** directly extends **B**, **B** is the direct superinterface of **A**. Any interfaces that extend **B** are indirect subinterfaces of **A**. Figure 7.2 shows an interface that extends another interface. Note that the type of the line connecting both interfaces is the same as the one used for extending a class.

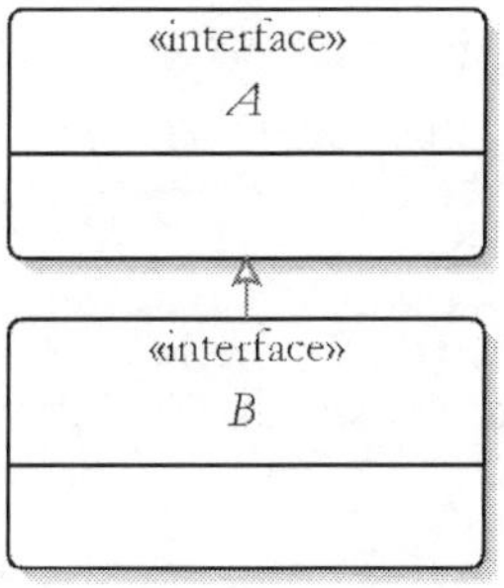

Figure 7.2: Extending an interface

What is the purpose of extending an interface? To safely add functionality to an interface without breaking existing code. This is so because you cannot add a new method to an interface once the interface has been published. Suppose an imaginary interface **XYZ** in JDK 1.7 was a popular interface with millions of implementation classes. Now, the designers of Java wanted to add a new method in **XYZ** in JDK 1.8. What would happen if a class that implemented the old **XYZ** and was compiled with a pre-JDK 1.8 compiler was deployed on JDK 1.8 (which would have shipped with the new version of **XYZ)**? It would break because the class had not provided the implementation for the new method.

The safe way would be to provide a new interface that extends **XYZ** so old software would still work and new applications can choose to implement the extension interface instead of **XYZ**.

Default Methods

Extending an interface is a safe way of adding functionality to the interface. However, you end up with two interfaces with similar functionality. This is acceptable if you only need to extend one or two interfaces. If you need to add features to hundred of interfaces, this has certainly become a serious issue.

This is exactly what the Java language designers faced when they were trying to add lambda expressions to Java 8 and add support for lambda in dozens of interfaces in the Collection Framework. Extending all the interfaces would double the number of interfaces and some would probably end up with ugly names such as **List2** or **ExtendedSet**.

Instead, they chose to add default methods. In other words, from JDK 1.8 onward, an interface can have default methods.

A default method in an interface is a method with implementation. A class implementing the interface does not have to implement the default method, which means you can add new methods to an interface without breaking backward compatibility.

To make a method in an interface a default method, add the keyword **default** in front of the method signature. Additionally, instead of terminating the signature with a semicolon, add a pair of brackets and write code in the brackets. Here is an example.

```
default java.lang.String getDescription() {
    return "This is a default method";
}
```

As you will learn later, a lot of Java interfaces in JDK 1.8 now have default methods.

When extending an interface with default methods, you have these options.

- Ignore the default methods, in effect inheriting them,
- Re-declare the default methods, which makes them abstract,
- Override the default methods.

Remember that the main reason Java now support default methods is for backward compatibility. By no means should you start writing programs without classes.

Static Methods

A static method in a class is shared by all instances of the class. In Java 8 and later you can have static methods in an interface so that all static methods associated with an interface can be written in the interface, rather than in a helper class.

The signature of a static method is similar to that of a default method. Instead of the keyword **default**, however, you use the keyword **static**. Static methods in an interface are public by default.

Static methods in an interface are rare. Of the close to 30 interfaces in the **java.util** package, only two contain static methods.

7.3 Abstract Classes

With the interface, you have to write an implementation class that perform the actual action. If there are many abstract methods in the interface, you risk wasting time overriding methods that you don't use. An abstract class has a similar role to an interface, i.e. provide a contract between a service provider and its clients, but at the same time an abstract class can provide partial implementation. Methods that must be explicitly overridden can be declared abstract. You still need to create an implementation class because you cannot instantiate an abstract class, but you don't need to override methods you don't want to use or change.

You create an abstract class by using the **abstract** modifier in the class declaration. To make an abstract method, use the **abstract** modifier in front of the method declaration. Listing 7.3 shows an abstract **DefaultPrinter** class as an example.

Listing 7.3: The DefaultPrinter class

```
package app07;
public abstract class DefaultPrinter {
    @Override
    public String toString() {
        return "Use this to print documents.";
    }
    public abstract void print(Object document);
}
```

There are two methods in **DefaultPrinter**, **toString** and **print**. The **toString** method has an implementation, so you do not need to override this method in an implementation class, unless you want to change its return value. The **print** method is declared abstract and does not have a body. Listing 7.4 presents a **MyPrinterClass** class that is the implementation class of **DefaultPrinter**.

Listing 7.4: An implementation of DefaultPrinter

```
package app07;
public class MyPrinter extends DefaultPrinter {
    @Override
    public void print(Object document) {
        System.out.println("Printing document");
        // some code here
    }
}
```

A concrete implementation class such as **MyPrinter** must override all abstract methods. Otherwise, it itself must be declared abstract.

Declaring a class abstract is a way to tell the class user that you want them to extend the class. You can still declare a class abstract even if it does not have an abstract method.

In UML class diagrams, an abstract class looks similar to a concrete class, except that the name is italicized. Figure 7.3 shows an abstract class.

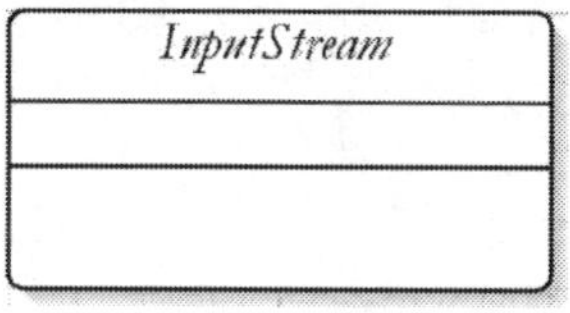

Figure 7.3: An abstract class

7.4 Polymorphism

In Java and other OOP languages, it is legal to assign to a reference variable an object whose type is different from the variable type, if certain conditions are met. In essence, if you have a reference variable **a** whose type is **A**, it is legal to assign an object of type **B**, like this

```
A a = new B();
```

provided one of the following conditions is met.

- **A** is a class and **B** is a subclass of **A**.
- **A** is an interface and **B** or one of its parents implements **A**.

As you have learned in Chapter 6, "Inheritance," this is called upcasting.

When you assign **a** an instance of **B** like in the code above, **a** is of type **A**. This means, you cannot call a method in **B** that is not defined in **A**. However, if you print the value of **a.getClass().getName()**, you'll get "B" and not "A." So, what does this mean? At compile time, the type of **a** is **A**, so the compiler will not allow you to call a method in **B** that is not defined in **A**. On the other hand, at runtime the type of **a** is **B**, as proven by the return value of **a.getClass().getName()**.

Now, here comes the essence of polymorphism. If **B** overrides a method (say, one named **play**) in **A**, calling **a.play()** will cause the implementation of **play** in **B** (and not in **A**) to be invoked. Polymorphism enables an object (in this example, the one referenced by

a) to determine which method implementation to choose (either the one in **A** or the one in **B**) when a method is called. Polymorphism dictates that the implementation in the runtime object be invoked. But, polymorphism does not stop here.

What if you call another method in **a** (say, a method called **stop**) and the method is not implemented in **B**? The JVM will be smart enough to know this and look into the inheritance hierarchy of **B**. **B**, as it happens, must be a subclass of **A** or, if **A** is an interface, a subclass of another class that implements **A**. Otherwise, the code would not have compiled. Having figured this out, the JVM will climb up the class hierarchy and find the implementation of **stop** and run it.

Now, there is more sense in the definition of polymorphism: Polymorphism is an OOP feature that enables an object to determine which method implementation to invoke upon receiving a method call.

Technically, though, how does Java achieve this? The Java compiler, as it turns out, upon encountering a method call such as **a.play()**, checks if the class/interface represented by **a** defines such a method (a **play** method) and if the correct set of parameters are passed to the method. But, that is the farthest the compiler goes. With the exception of static and final methods, it does not connect (or bind) a method call with a method body. The JVM determines how to bind a method call with the method body at runtime. In other words, except for static and final methods, method binding in Java happens at runtime and not at compile time. Runtime binding is also called late binding or dynamic binding. The opposite is early binding, in which binding occurs at compile time or link time. Early binding occurs in other languages, such as C.

Therefore, polymorphism is made possible by the late binding mechanism in Java. Because of this, polymorphism is rather inaccurately also called late binding, dynamic binding or runtime binding in other languages.

Consider the Java code in Listing 7.5.

Listing 7.5: An example of polymorphism

```
package app07;
class Employee {
    public void work() {
        System.out.println("I am an employee.");
    }
}

class Manager extends Employee {
    public void work() {
        System.out.println("I am a manager.");
    }

    public void manage() {
        System.out.println("Managing ...");
    }
}

public class PolymorphismDemo1 {
    public static void main(String[] args) {
        Employee employee;
        employee = new Manager();
        System.out.println(employee.getClass().getName());
```

```
        employee.work();
        Manager manager = (Manager) employee;
        manager.manage();
    }
}
```

Listing 7.5 defines two non-public classes: **Employee** and **Manager**. **Employee** has a method called **work**, and **Manager** extends **Employee** and adds a new method called **manage**.

The **main** method in the **PolymorphismDemo1** class defines an object variable called **employee** of type **Employee**:

```
Employee employee;
```

However, **employee** is assigned an instance of **Manager**, as in:

```
employee = new Manager();
```

This is legal because **Manager** is a subclass of **Employee**, so a **Manager** "is an" **Employee**. Because **employee** is assigned an instance of **Manager**, what is the outcome of **employee.getClass().getName()**? You're right. It's "Manager," not "Employee."

Then, the **work** method is called.

```
employee.work();
```

Guess what is written on the console?

```
I am a manager.
```

This means that it is the **work** method in the **Manager** class that got called, which was polymorphism in action.

Note

Polymorphism does not work with static methods because they are early-bound. For example, if the **work** method in both the **Employee** and **Manager** classes were static, a call to **employee.work()** would print "I am an employee." Also, since you cannot extend final methods, polymorphism will not work with final methods either.

Now, because the runtime type of **a** is **Manager**, you can downcast **a** to **Manager**, as the code shows:

```
Manager manager = (Manager) employee;
manager.manage();
```

After seeing the code, you might ask, why would you declare **employee** as **Employee** in the first place? Why didn't you declare **employee** as type **Manager**, such as this?

```
Manager employee;
employee = new Manager();
```

You do this to ensure flexibility in cases where you don't know whether the object reference (**employee**) will be assigned an instance of **Manager** or something else.

7.5 Polymorphism in Action

Suppose you have a **Greeting** interface that defines an abstract method named **greet**. This simple interface is given in Listing 7.6.

Listing 7.6: The Greeting interface

```
package app07;
public interface Greeting {
    public void greet();
}
```

The **Greeting** interface can be implemented to print a greeting in different languages. For example, the **EnglishGreeting** class in Listing 7.7 and the **FrenchGreeting** class in Listing 7.8 implement **Greeting** to greet the user in English and French, respectively.

Listing 7.7: The EnglishGreeting class

```
package app07;
public class EnglishGreeting implements Greeting {

    @Override
    public void greet() {
        System.out.println("Good Day!");
    }
}
```

Listing 7.8: The FrenchGreeting class

```
package app07;
public class FrenchGreeting implements Greeting {

    @Override
    public void greet() {
        System.out.println("Bonjour!");
    }
}
```

The **PolymorphismDemo2** class in Listing 7.9 shows polymorphism in action. It asks the user in what language they want to be greeted. If the user chooses English, then the **EnglishGreeting** class will be instantiated. If French is selected, **FrenchGreeting** will be instantiated. This is polymorphism because the class to be instantiated is only known at runtime, after the user types in a selection.

Listing 7.9: The PolymorphismDemo2 class

```
package app07;
import java.util.Scanner;

public class PolymorphismDemo2 {

    public static void main(String[] args) {
        String instruction = "What is your chosen language?" +
                "\nType 'English' or 'French'.";
        Greeting greeting = null;
```

```
        Scanner scanner = new Scanner(System.in);
        System.out.println(instruction);
        while (true) {
            String input = scanner.next();
            if (input.equalsIgnoreCase("english")) {
                greeting = new EnglishGreeting();
                break;
            } else if (input.equalsIgnoreCase("french")) {
                greeting = new FrenchGreeting();
                break;
            } else {
                System.out.println(instruction);
            }
        }

        scanner.close();
        greeting.greet();
    }
}
```

Self Test

Question 1

Which statements are true with regard to the interface?

A. All methods in an interface are abstract
B. All methods in an interface are public
C. You can use the public and protected modifier for a method in an interface
D. You can use the abstract modifier for a method in an interface

Question 2

Which statement is true with regard to the abstract class?

A. All fields and methods in an abstract class must be abstract
B. An abstract class may contain concrete methods and fields
C. You can create an instance of an abstract class
D. An abstract class can also be final

Question 3

The **java.util.ArrayList** is a class implementing the **java.util.List** interface. Which of these statements demonstrates polymorphism?

A. ArrayList<Integer> numbers = new ArrayList<>();
B. List<String> names = new ArrayList<>();
C. List list = new List();
D. ArrayList<Object> employees = new List<>();

Question 4

Given

```
package com.example.test;
interface Downloadable {
    Object download();
    void printDescription();
}
class Document implements Downloadable {
    @Override
    public Object download() {
        return null;
    }
}
```

The code fragment above will not compile. How do you fix it?

A. Remove the @Override annotation in class **Document**
B. Make the **Document** class abstract
C. Provide an implementation of printDescription in **Document**
D. None of the above

Question 5

Given the following class:

```
package test;
abstract class Paint {
    void changeColor(int colorCode) {}
    @Override
    public String toString() {
        return "Paint";
    }
}
```

Which is the correct statement?

A. The **Paint** class must not be abstract since it has no abstract methods/fields
B. The **Paint** class will not compile unless the **abstract** modifier is removed
C. The **Paint** class compiles and is an abstract class
D. The **Paint** class will not compile because an abstract class must not override a method from a parent class

Question 6

6. Consider the following code snippet:

```
package papermatter;
class PaperCollection {
    public static void print() {
        System.out.print("PaperCollection.print()");
    }
```

```
    @Override
    public String toString() {
        return "PaperCollection";
    }
}

class Book extends PaperCollection {
    public static void print() {
        System.out.print("Book.print()");
    }

    @Override
    public String toString() {
        return "Book";
    }
}

public class Printer {
    public static void main(String[] args) {
        PaperCollection paper = new Book();
        paper.print();
        System.out.println(" | " + paper.toString());
    }
}
```

What is printed in the standard out when the code is executed?

A. Book.print() | Book
B. PaperCollection.print() | Book
C. Book.print() | PaperCollection
D. PaperCollection.print() | PaperCollection

Question 7

Which access modifiers can be used for an interface?

A. public
B. protected
C. default
D. private

Question 8

Given

```
package demo.oop;
class Display {
    public void display() {
        System.out.print("Display.display()");
    }
}
class Monitor extends Display {
    public long pixelCount() {
```

```
        return 1024 * 768;
    }
}
public class Printer {
    public static void main(String[] args) {
        Display display = new Monitor();
        // some code
        long pixelCount = display.pixelCount();
    }
}
```

Which of the following statements are true?

A. The code will compile
B. The code will not compile because the **pixelCount** method is not part of **Display**.
C. The code will compile but will thrown a **NullPointerException**
D. The code is a perfect example of polymorphism

Question 9

Given two interfaces and a class:

```
interface Swimmable {
    void swim();
}

interface Walkable {
    void walk();
}

class Animal {
}
```

You need to create a class named **Dog** that extends Animal and implements **Swimmable** and **Walkable**. Which statements about the **Dog** class are correct?

A. Java does not support multiple inheritance, so the **Dog** class cannot be written because a class can only implement one interface
B. The **Dog** class would have the following declaration: class Dog extends Animal implements Walkable, Swimmable { }
C. The **Dog** class would have the following declaration: class Dog extends Animal, Walkable, Swimmable { }
D. The **Dog** class would have the following declaration: class Dog implements Walkable, Swimmable extends Animal { }
E. The **Dog** class would have the following declaration: class Dog extends Animal implements Swimmable, Walkable { }

Question 10

The **Readable** and **Writable** interfaces shown below happen to have methods with the same signature

```
interface Readable {
```

```
    void perform(int howManyTimes);
}

interface Writable {
    void perform(int howManyTimes);
}
```

You need to write a class that implements both interfaces. Which statements are true?

A. You cannot implement interfaces with the same name
B. You can implement both interfaces and you need to provide two implementations of perform()
C. You can implement both interfaces and you need to provide one implementation of perform()
D. It is not necessary to implement both Readable and Writable since they have exactly the same set of methods. You can just implement either one and have the same effect as implementing both interfaces

---

Answers to Self Test

Question 1

Which statements are true with regard to the interface?

A. All methods in an interface are abstract
B. All methods in an interface are public
C. You can use the public and protected modifier for a method in an interface
D. You can use the abstract modifier for a method in an interface

Answer: B, D.

A is incorrect because Java 8 interfaces can have default and static methods as well as abstract methods. It would have been correct if we were talking about Java 7 and previous versions.

B is correct because all methods in an interface are public even if defined without the public modifier.

C is incorrect because a method in an interface cannot be protected.

D is correct because you can use the keyword **abstract** for abstract methods in an interface. However, the use of the keyword is redundant as all methods that declare no method body are implicitly abstract.

Question 2

Which statement is true with regard to the abstract class?

A. All fields and methods in an abstract class must be abstract
B. An abstract class may contain concrete methods and fields
C. You can create an instance of an abstract class
D. An abstract class can also be final

Answer: B.

An abstract class may contain concrete fields and methods and it cannot be instantiated. An abstract class must be extended and therefore an abstract class cannot also be a final class.

Question 3

The **java.util.ArrayList** is a class implementing the **java.util.List** interface. Which of these statements demonstrates polymorphism?

A. ArrayList<Integer> numbers = new ArrayList<>();
B. List<String> names = new ArrayList<>();
C. List list = new List();
D. ArrayList<Object> employees = new List<>();

Answer: B.

Polymorphism allows an instance of class B to be assigned to a reference variable of type A if

- **A** is a class and **B** is a subclass of **A**
- **A** is an interface and **B** or one of its parents implements **A**

A will not cause a compile error but it is not polymorphism. B is polymorphism as **List** is an interface and **ArrayList** is a class implementing **List**. C is invalid because you cannot instantiate an interface. D is also incorrect and will generate a compile error because you cannot instantiate an interface and assigning an instance of a **List** to a reference variable of type **ArrayList** is not permitted.

Question 4

Given

```
package com.example.test;
interface Downloadable {
    Object download();
    void printDescription();
}
class Document implements Downloadable {
    @Override
    public Object download() {
        return null;
    }
}
```

The code fragment above will not compile. How do you fix it?

A. Remove the @Override annotation in class **Document**
B. Make the **Document** class abstract
C. Provide an implementation of printDescription in **Document**
D. None of the above

Answer: B, C.

A class that implements an interface must implement all its methods. The code will not compile because the **Document** class is missing an implementation of **printDescription**. You can fix it by either making **Document** abstract or provide an implementation of **printDesription** in **Document**.

Question 5

Given the following class:

```
package test;
abstract class Paint {
    void changeColor(int colorCode) {}
    @Override
    public String toString() {
        return "Paint";
    }
}
```

Which is the correct statement?

A. The **Paint** class must not be abstract since it has no abstract methods/fields
B. The **Paint** class will not compile unless the **abstract** modifier is removed
C. The **Paint** class compiles and is an abstract class
D. The **Paint** class will not compile because an abstract class must not override a method from a parent class

Answer: C.

An abstract class does not have to have an abstract member. Since **Paint** is abstract, it may not be instantiated.

Question 6

6. Consider the following code snippet:

```
package papermatter;
class PaperCollection {
    public static void print() {
        System.out.print("PaperCollection.print()");
    }
    @Override
    public String toString() {
        return "PaperCollection";
    }
}

class Book extends PaperCollection {
    public static void print() {
        System.out.print("Book.print()");
    }

    @Override
    public String toString() {
```

```
        return "Book";
    }
}

public class Printer {
    public static void main(String[] args) {
        PaperCollection paper = new Book();
        paper.print();
        System.out.println(" | " + paper.toString());
    }
}
```

What is printed in the standard out when the code is executed?

A. Book.print() | Book
B. PaperCollection.print() | Book
C. Book.print() | PaperCollection
D. PaperCollection.print() | PaperCollection

Answer: B.

Polymorphism does not work on static methods or static fields because they are early-bound. The **paper** variable references an instance of **Book**, however calling a static method on **paper** will invoke the method on **PaperCollection**, not **Book**.

Question 7

Which access modifiers can be used for an interface?

A. public
B. protected
C. default
D. private

Answer: A, C.

An interface, like a class, can have the public or default access modifier.

Question 8

Given

```
package demo.oop;
class Display {
    public void display() {
        System.out.print("Display.display()");
    }
}
class Monitor extends Display {
    public long pixelCount() {
        return 1024 * 768;
    }
}
public class Printer {
```

```
    public static void main(String[] args) {
        Display display = new Monitor();
        // some code
        long pixelCount = display.pixelCount();
    }
}
```

Which of the following statements are true?

A. The code will compile
B. The code will not compile because the **pixelCount** method is not part of **Display**.
C. The code will compile but will thrown a **NullPointerException**
D. The code is a perfect example of polymorphism

Answer: B.

Since **display** is of type **Display**, you cannot call the **pixelCount** method on it. You can upcast **display** to **Monitor** like so to fix the compiler error:

```
long pixelCount = ((Monitor) display).pixelCount();
```

Question 9

Given two interfaces and a class:

```
interface Swimmable {
    void swim();
}

interface Walkable {
    void walk();
}

class Animal {
}
```

You need to create a class named **Dog** that extends Animal and implements **Swimmable** and **Walkable**. Which statements about the **Dog** class are correct?

A. Java does not support multiple inheritance, so the **Dog** class cannot be written because a class can only implement one interface
B. The **Dog** class would have the following declaration: class Dog extends Animal implements Walkable, Swimmable { }
C. The **Dog** class would have the following declaration: class Dog extends Animal, Walkable, Swimmable { }
D. The **Dog** class would have the following declaration: class Dog implements Walkable, Swimmable extends Animal { }
E. The **Dog** class would have the following declaration: class Dog extends Animal implements Swimmable, Walkable { }

Answer: B, E.

Java does not support multiple inheritance so you can only extend one class. However, you can implement multiple interfaces. The syntax of a class that extends another class and implements interfaces is as follows.

```
[public] class className extends parentClass implements interface1,
        interface2, ...
```

The implemented interfaces can be in any order, so B and E are both correct.

Question 10

The **Readable** and **Writable** interfaces shown below happen to have methods with the same signature

```
interface Readable {
    void perform(int howManyTimes);
}

interface Writable {
    void perform(int howManyTimes);
}
```

You need to write a class that implements both interfaces. Which statements are true?

A. You cannot implement interfaces with the same name
B. You can implement both interfaces and you need to provide two implementations of perform()
C. You can implement both interfaces and you need to provide one implementation of perform()
D. It is not necessary to implement both Readable and Writable since they have exactly the same set of methods. You can just implement either one and have the same effect as implementing both interfaces

Answer: C.

You need to implement both interfaces so you can instantiate your class and assign it to a variable of type **Readable** or **Writable**. Since the perform methods have the same signature, you just need one implementation. In fact, it would generate a compile error if you tried to provide two implementations since both methods would have the same signature.

Chapter 8
Error Handling

Error handling is an important feature in any programming language. A good error handling mechanism makes it easier for programmers to write robust applications and to prevent bugs from creeping in. In some languages, programmers are forced to use multiple **if** statements to detect all possible conditions that might lead to an error. This could make code excessively complex. In a larger program, this could easily lead to spaghetti like code.

Java offers the **try** statement as a nice approach to error handling. With this strategy, part of the code that could potentially lead to an error is isolated in a block. Should an error occur, this error is caught and resolved locally. This chapter teaches you this.

8.1 Catching Exceptions

There are two types of errors, compile error and runtime error. Compile errors or compilation errors are due to errors in the source code. For example, if you forgot to terminate a statement with a semicolon, the compiler will tell you that and refuse to compile your code. Compile errors are caught by the compiler at compile time. Runtime errors, on the other hand, can only be caught when the program is running, i.e. at runtime, because the compiler could not have caught them. For example, running out of memory is a runtime error and a compiler could not have predicted this. Or, if a program tries to parse a user input to an integer, the input is only available when the program is running. If the user enters non-digits, then the parsing process will fail and a runtime error thrown. A runtime error, if not handled, will cause the program to quit abruptly.

In your program you can isolate code that may cause a runtime error using a **try** statement, which normally is accompanied by the **catch** and **finally** statements. Such isolation typically occurs in a method body. If an error is encountered, Java stops the processing of the **try** block and jump to the **catch** block. Here you can gracefully handle the error or notify the user by 'throwing' a **java.lang.Exception** object. Another scenario is to re-throw the exception or a new **Exception** object back to the code that called the method. It is then up to the client how he or she would handle the error. If a thrown exception is not caught, the application will crash.

This is the syntax of the **try** statement.

```
try {
    [code that may throw an exception]
} [catch (ExceptionType-1 e) {
    [code that is executed when ExceptionType-1 is thrown]
}] [catch (ExceptionType-2 e) {
    [code that is executed when ExceptionType-2 is thrown]
```

```
}]
   ...
} [catch (ExceptionType-n e) {
    [code that is executed when ExceptionType-n is thrown]
}]
[finally {
    [code that runs regardless of whether an exception was thrown]]
}]
```

The steps for error handling can be summarized as follows:

1. Isolate code that could lead to an error in the **try** block.
2. For each individual **catch** block, write code that is to be executed if an exception of that particular type occurs in the **try** block.
3. In the **finally** block, write code that will be run whether or not an error has occurred.

Note that the **catch** and **finally** blocks are optional, but one or both of them must exist. Therefore, you can have **try** with one or more **catch** blocks, **try** with **finally** or **try** with **catch** and **finally**.

The previous syntax shows that you can have more than one **catch** block. This is because some code may throw different types of exceptions. When an exception is thrown from a **try** block, control is passed to the first **catch** block. If the type of exception thrown matches the exception or is a subclass of the exception in the first **catch** block, the code in the **catch** block is executed and then control goes to the **finally** block, if one exists.

If the type of the exception thrown does not match the exception type in the first **catch** block, the JVM goes to the next **catch** block and does the same thing until it finds a match. If no match is found, the exception object will be thrown to the method caller. If the caller does not put the offending code that calls the method in a **try** block, the program will crash.

To illustrate the use of this error handling, consider the **NumberDoubler** class in Listing 8.1. When the class is run, it will prompt you for input. You can type anything, including non-digits. If your input is successfully converted to a number, it will double it and print the result. If your input is invalid, the program will print an "Invalid input" message.

Listing 8.1: The NumberDoubler class

```
package app08;
import java.util.Scanner;

public class NumberDoubler {
    public static void main(String[] args) {
        Scanner scanner = new Scanner(System.in);
        String input = scanner.next();
        try {
            double number = Double.parseDouble(input);
            System.out.printf("Result: %s", number);
        } catch (NumberFormatException e) {
            System.out.println("Invalid input.");
        }
        scanner.close();
    }
```

```
}
```

The **NumberDoubler** class uses the **java.util.Scanner** class to take user input.

```
Scanner scanner = new Scanner(System.in);
String input = scanner.next();
```

It then uses the static **parseDouble** method of the **java.lang.Double** class to convert the string input to a **double**. Note that the code that calls **parseDouble** resides in a **try** block. This is necessary because **parseDouble** may throw a **java.lang.NumberFormatException**, as indicated by the signature of the **parseDouble** method:

```
public static double parseDouble(String s)
        throws NumberFormatExcpetion
```

The **throws** statement in the method signature tells you that it may throw a **NumberFormatException** and it is the responsibility of the method caller to catch it.

Without the **try** block, invalid input will give you this embarrassing error message before the system crashes:

```
Exception in thread "main" java.lang.NumberFormatException:
```

8.2 try without catch

A try statement can be used with **finally** without a catch block. You normally use this syntax to ensure that some code always gets executed whether or not an unexpected exception has been thrown in the **try** block. For example, after opening a database connection, you want to make sure the connection's **close** method is called after you're done with it. To illustrate this scenario, consider the following pseudocode that opens a database connection.

```
Connection connection = null;
try {

    // open connection
    // do something with the connection and perform other tasks

} finally {
    if (connection != null) {
        // close connection
    }
}
```

If something unexpected occurs in the **try** block, the **close** method will always be called to release the resource.

8.3 Catching Multiple Exceptions

Java 7 and later allow you to catch multiple exceptions in a single **catch** block if the caught exceptions are to be handled by the same code. The syntax of the **catch** block is as follows, two exceptions being separated by the pipe character |.

```
catch(exception-1 | exception-2 ... e) {

    // handle exceptions

}
```

For example, the **java.net.ServerSocket** class's **accept** method can throw four exceptions: **java.nio.channels.IllegalBlockingModeException**, **java.net.SocketTimeoutException**, **java.lang.SecurityException**, and **java.io.Exception**. If, say, the first three exceptions are to be handled by the same code, you can write your **try** block like this:

```
try {
    serverSocket.accept();
} catch (SocketTimeoutException | SecurityException |
        IllegalBlockingModeException e) {

    // handle exceptions

} catch (IOException e) {

    // handle IOException

}
```

8.4 The try-with-resources Statement

Many Java operations involve some kind of resource that has to be closed after use. Before JDK 7, you used **finally** to make sure a **close** method is guaranteed to be called:

```
try {

    // open resource

} catch (Exception e) {

} finally {
    // close resource
}
```

This syntax can be tedious especially if the **close** method can throw an exception and can be null. For example, here's a typical code fragment to open a database connection.

```
Connection connection = null;
try {

    // create connection and do something with it

} catch (SQLException e) {

} finally {
    if (connection != null) {
        try {
            connection.close();
        } catch (SQLException e) {
        }
    }
}
```

You see, you need quite a bit of code in the **finally** block just for one resource, and it's not uncommon to have to open multiple resources in a single **try** block. JDK 7 added a new feature, the try-with-resource statement, to make resource closing automatic. Its syntax is as follows.

```
try ( resources ) {

    // do something with the resources

} catch (Exception e) {
    // do something with e
}
```

For example, here is opening a database connection would look like in Java 7 and later.

```
Connection connection = null;
try (Connection connection = openConnection();
        // open other resources, if any) {

    // do something with connection

} catch (SQLException e) {

}
```

Not all resources can be automatically closed. Only resource classes that implement **java.lang.AutoCloseable** can be automatically closed. Fortunately, in JDK 7 many input/output and database resources have been modified to support this feature.

8.5 The java.lang.Exception Class

Erroneous code can throw any type of exception. For example, an invalid argument may throw a **java.lang.NumberFormatException**, and calling a method on a null reference variable throws a **java.lang.NullPointerException**. All Java exception classes derive from the **java.lang.Exception** class. It is therefore worthwhile to spend some time examining this class.

Among others, the **Exception** class overrides the **toString** method and adds a **printStackTrace** method. The **toString** method returns the description of the exception. The **printStackTrace** method has the following signature.

```
public void printStackTrace()
```

This method prints the description of the exception followed by a stack trace for the **Exception** object. By analyzing the stack trace, you can find out which line is causing the problem. Here is an example of what **printStackTrace** may print on the console.

```
java.lang.NullPointerException
    at MathUtil.doubleNumber(MathUtil.java:45)
    at MyClass.performMath(MyClass.java: 18)
    at MyClass.main(MyClass.java: 90)
```

This tells you that a **NullPointerException** has been thrown. The line that throws the exception is Line 45 of the **MathUtil.java** class, inside the **doubleNumber** method. The **doubleNumber** method was called by **MyClass.performMath**, which in turns was called by **MyClass.main**.

Most of the time a **try** block is accompanied by a **catch** block that catches the **java.lang.Exception** in addition to other **catch** blocks. The **catch** block that catches **Exception** must appear last. If other **catch** blocks fail to catch the exception, the last **catch** will do that. Here is an example.

```
try {
    // code
} catch (NumberFormatException e) {
    // handle NumberFormatException
} catch (Exception e) {
    // handle other exceptions
}
```

You may want to use multiple **catch** blocks in the code above because the statements in the **try** block may throw a **java.lang.NumberFormatException** or other type of exception. If the latter is thrown, it will be caught by the last **catch** block.

Be warned, though: The order of the **catch** blocks is important. You cannot, for example, put a **catch** block for handling **java.lang.Exception** before any other **catch** block. This is because the JVM tries to match the thrown exception with the argument of the **catch** blocks in the order of appearance. **java.lang.Exception** catches everything; therefore, the **catch** blocks after it would never be executed.

If you have several **catch** blocks and the exception type of one of the **catch** blocks is derived from the type of another **catch** block, make sure the more specific exception type appears first. For example, when trying to open a file, you need to catch the **java.io.FileNotFoundException** just in case the file cannot be found. However, you may want to make sure that you also catch **java.io.IOException** so that other I/O-related exceptions are caught. Since **FileNotFoundException** is a child class of **IOException**, the **catch** block that handles **FileNotFoundException** must appear before the **catch** block that handles **IOException**.

8.6 Throwing an Exception from a Method

When catching an exception in a method, you have two options to handle the error that occurs inside the method. You can either handle the error in the method, thus quietly catching the exception without notifying the caller (this has been demonstrated in the previous examples), or you can throw the exception back to the caller and let the caller handle it. If you choose the second option, the calling code must catch the exception that is thrown back by the method.

Listing 8.2 presents a **capitalize** method that changes the first letter of a **String** to upper case.

Listing 8.2: The capitalize method

```
public String capitalize(String s) throws NullPointerException {
    if (s == null) {
        throw new NullPointerException(
                "You passed a null argument");
    }
    Character firstChar = s.charAt(0);
    String theRest = s.substring(1);
    return firstChar.toString().toUpperCase() + theRest;
}
```

If you pass a null to **capitalize**, it will throw a new **NullPointerException**. Pay attention to the code that instantiates the **NullPointerException** class and throws the instance:

```
        throw new NullPointerException(
                "Your passed a null argument");
```

The **throw** keyword is used to throw an exception. Don't confuse it with the **throws** statement which is used at the end of a method signature to indicate that the method may throw an exception of the given type.

The following example shows code that calls **capitalize**.

```
String input = null;
try {
    String capitalized = util.capitalize(input);
    System.out.println(capitalized);
} catch (NullPointerException e) {
    System.out.println(e.toString());
}
```

Note

A constructor can also throw an exception.

8.7 User-Defined Exceptions

You can create a user-defined exception by subclassing **java.lang.Exception**. There are several reasons for having a user-defined exception. One of them is to create a customized error message.

For example, Listing 8.3 shows the **AlreadyCapitalizedException** class that derives from **java.lang.Exception**.

Listing 8.3: The AlreadyCapitalizedException class

```
package app08;
public class AlreadyCapitalizedException extends Exception {
    @Override
    public String toString() {
        return "Input has already been capitalized";
    }
}
```

You can throw an **AlreadyCapitalizedException** from the **capitalize** method in Listing 8.2. The modified **capitalize** method is given in Listing 8.4.

Listing 8.4: The modified capitalize method

```
public String capitalize(String s)
        throws NullPointerException, AlreadyCapitalizedException {
    if (s == null) {
        throw new NullPointerException(
                "Your passed a null argument");
    }
    Character firstChar = s.charAt(0);
    if (Character.isUpperCase(firstChar)) {
        throw new AlreadyCapitalizedException();
    }
    String theRest = s.substring(1);
    return firstChar.toString().toUpperCase() + theRest;
}
```

Now, **capitalize** may throw one of two exceptions. You comma-delimit multiple exceptions in a method signature.

Clients that call **capitalize** must now catch both exceptions. This code shows a call to **capitalize**.

```
StringUtil util = new StringUtil();
String input = "Capitalize";
try {
    String capitalized = util.capitalize(input);
    System.out.println(capitalized);
} catch (NullPointerException e) {
    System.out.println(e.toString());
} catch (AlreadyCapitalizedException e) {
    e.printStackTrace();
}
```

Since **NullPointerException** and **AlreadyCapitalizedException** do not have a parent-child relationship, the order of the **catch** blocks above is not important.

When a method throws multiple exceptions, rather than catch all the exceptions, you can simply write a **catch** block that handles **java.lang.Exception**. Rewriting the code above:

```
StringUtil util = new StringUtil();
```

```
String input = "Capitalize";
try {
    String capitalized = util.capitalize(input);
    System.out.println(capitalized);
} catch (Exception e) {
    System.out.println(e.toString());
}
```

While it's more concise, the latter lacks specifics and does not allow you to handle each exception separately.

8.8 Note on Exception Handling

The **try** statement imposes some performance penalty. Therefore, do not use it over-generously. If it is not hard to test for a condition, then you should do the testing rather than depending on the **try** statement. For example, calling a method on a null object throws a **NullPointerException**. Therefore, you could always surround a method call with a **try** block:

```
try {
    ref.method();
...
```

However, it is not hard at all to check if **ref** is null prior to calling **methodA**. Therefore, the following code is better because it eliminates the **try** block.

```
if (ref != null) {
    ref.methodA();
}
```

The **NullPointerException** is one of the most common exceptions a developer has to handle. Java 8 adds the **java.util.Optional** class that can reduce the amount of code for handling the **NullPointerException**.

Self Test

Question 1

Consider the following code snippet:

```
int[] wheels = { 1, 2, 4, 5 };
try {
    int i = wheels[10];
} catch (Exception e) {
    e.printStackTrace();
} catch (ArrayIndexOutOfBoundsException e) {
    e.printStackTrace();
}
```

What will happen if you try to compile and run the code?

A. The code will compile and run without problems
B. The code will compile and throw an **ArrayIndexOutOfBoundsException** when run
C. The code will compile and throw a runtime exception other than an **ArrayIndexOutOfBoundsException**
D. The code will not compile

Question 2

Consider the following code fragment:

```
Car[] cars = ...;
try {
    Car car = cars[8];
} catch (NullPointerException e) {
    e.printStackTrace();
} catch (ArrayIndexOutOfBoundsException e) {
    e.printStackTrace();
}
```

What will happen if you try to compile and run the code?

A. The code will compile and run without problems
B. The code will compile and may throw an ArrayIndexOutOfBoundsException when run
C. The code will compile and may throw a NullPointerException when run
D. The code will not compile

Question 3

Which of the following statements are correct?

A. A try statement must be accompanied by at least one catch clause
B. A try statement must have a finally clause or at least a catch clause
C. A try statement can stand alone with a finally clause or a catch clause
D. A try statement can have multiple catch clauses

Question 4

How do you write a method that may throw an exception?

A. By using the throws keyword
B. By using the throw keyword
C. By throwing an instance of Exception
D. None of the above

Question 5

Given

```
package test;
```

```
public class Printer {
    public void print() {
        print();
    }

    public static void main(String[] args) {
        Printer printer = new Printer();
        printer.print();
    }
}
```

What runtime exception or error will be thrown when the class is executed?

A. java.lang.NullPointerException
B. java.lang.OutOfMemoryError
C. java.lang.ArrayIndexOutOfBoundsException
D. java.lang.StackOverflowError

Question 6

Which statements about errors and exceptions are correct?

A. All Java exceptions are derived from **java.lang.Exception**
B. An error is a serious problem that the Java program should not try to catch
C. All errors are derived from **java.lang.Error**
D. Both **java.lang.Error** and **java.lang.Exception** are direct children of **java.lang.Throwable**

Question 7

Given

```
class ArrayMismatchedException {
}

public class ArrayUtil {
    public static void main(String[] args) {
        try {
            // some code
        } catch (ArrayMismatchedException e) {
        }
    }
}
```

What happens if you try to compile and run the ArrayUtil class?

A. The code will compile and run without problems
B. The code will not compile because there is no code in the try block
C. The code will not compile because **ArrayMismatchedException** is not derived from **java.lang.Exception**
D. The code will not compile because **ArrayMistmatchedException** is not derived from **java.lang.Throwable**

Question 8

Consider the following code.

```
package test;
import java.util.ArrayList;
import java.util.List;
public class ArtistManagement {
    public static void main(String[] args) {
        List<String> artists = new ArrayList<>();
        try {
            artists.add(1, "Will Biteman");
            artists.add(2, "Hermann Longlegs");
        } catch (Exception e) {
            e.printStackTrace();
        }
        for (String artist : artists) {
            System.out.println(artist);
        }
    }
}
```

What happens if you try to compile and run the ArrayUtil class?

A. The code will compile and run without problems
B. The code will not compile
C. The program will print the two elements in **artists**
D. The code will compile but will throw a runtime exception

Question 9

Given

```
package demo1;
public class ExceptionDemo {
    public static void main(String[] args) {
        try {
            int count = Integer.parseInt(args[0]);
        } catch (NumberFormatException e) {
            System.err.println("Error: Not a number");
        } catch (Exception e) {
            e.printStackTrace();
        }
    }
}
```

What exception will be thrown if the program is invoked without arguments?

A. NumberFormatException
B. NullPointerException
C. RuntimeException
D. ArrayIndexOutOfBoundsException

Question 10

What can be said of try-with-resource?

A. It is a new feature in JDK 1.7
B. The resource must implement **java.lang.AutoCloseable**
C. It can be used without a catch or a finally block
D. It can be used with any resource

Answers to Self Test

Question 1

Consider the following code snippet:

```
int[] wheels = { 1, 2, 4, 5 };
try {
    int i = wheels[10];
} catch (Exception e) {
    e.printStackTrace();
} catch (ArrayIndexOutOfBoundsException e) {
    e.printStackTrace();
}
```

What will happen if you try to compile and run the code?

A. The code will compile and run without problems
B. The code will compile and throw an **ArrayIndexOutOfBoundsException** when run
C. The code will compile and throw a runtime exception other than an **ArrayIndexOutOfBoundsException**
D. The code will not compile

Answer: D.

Because **ArrayIndexOutOfBoundsException** is a subclass of **Exception**, a catch block that catches an **ArrayIndexOutOfBoundsException** must appear before a catch block that catches an **Exception**. In this case, here is the compile error message: Unreachable catch block for **ArrayIndexOutOfBoundsException**.

Question 2

Consider the following code fragment:

```
Car[] cars = ...;
try {
    Car car = cars[8];
} catch (NullPointerException e) {
    e.printStackTrace();
} catch (ArrayIndexOutOfBoundsException e) {
    e.printStackTrace();
```

```
}
```

What will happen if you try to compile and run the code?

A. The code will compile and run without problems
B. The code will compile and may throw an ArrayIndexOutOfBoundsException when run
C. The code will compile and may throw a NullPointerException when run
D. The code will not compile

Answer: B, C.

Because **ArrayIndexOutOfBoundsException** and **NullPointerException** do not have a parent-child relationship, the position of the two catch blocks may be interchangeable. Since it is unknown what is assigned to cars, the code may throw a runtime exception and there is no guarantee the code will run without problems.

Question 3

Which of the following statements are correct?

A. A try statement must be accompanied by at least one catch clause
B. A try statement must have a finally clause or at least a catch clause
C. A try statement can stand alone with a finally clause or a catch clause
D. A try statement can have multiple catch clauses

Answer: B, D.

A try statement must have a finally clause or at least a catch clause. In addition, a try statement may be accompanied by multiple catch clauses.

Question 4

How do you write a method that may throw an exception?

A. By using the **throws** keyword
B. By using the **throw** keyword
C. By throwing an instance of **Exception**
D. None of the above

Answer: A.

You use **throws** to indicate that a method may throw an exception.

Question 5

Given

```
package test;
public class Printer {
    public void print() {
        print();
    }
```

```
    public static void main(String[] args) {
        Printer printer = new Printer();
        printer.print();
    }
}
```

What runtime exception or error will be thrown when the class is executed?

A. java.lang.NullPointerException
B. java.lang.OutOfMemoryError
C. java.lang.ArrayIndexOutOfBoundsException
D. java.lang.StackOverflowError

Answer: D.

A **StackOverflowError** is thrown if a program recurses too deeply, as clearly is the case here when a method calls itself.

Question 6

Which statements about errors and exceptions are correct?

A. All Java exceptions are derived from **java.lang.Exception**
B. An error is a serious problem that the Java program should not try to catch
C. All errors are derived from **java.lang.Error**
D. Both **java.lang.Error** and **java.lang.Exception** are direct children of **java.lang.Throwable**

Answer: A, B, C, D.

All statements are correct. A problem that may occur when an application is running is either an exception or an error. An error is a serious problem that should not be caught. An exception, on the other hand, may be caught to make sure the program does not crash and cause embarrassment.

Question 7

Given

```
class ArrayMismatchedException {
}

public class ArrayUtil {
    public static void main(String[] args) {
        try {
            // some code
        } catch (ArrayMismatchedException e) {
        }
    }
}
```

What happens if you try to compile and run the ArrayUtil class?

A. The code will compile and run without problems

B. The code will not compile because there is no code in the try block
C. The code will not compile because **ArrayMismatchedException** is not derived from **java.lang.Exception**
D. The code will not compile because **ArrayMistmatchedException** is not derived from **java.lang.Throwable**

Answer: D.

All exceptions must be derived from **java.lang.Throwable**.

Question 8

Consider the following code.

```
package test;
import java.util.ArrayList;
import java.util.List;
public class ArtistManagement {
    public static void main(String[] args) {
        List<String> artists = new ArrayList<>();
        try {
            artists.add(1, "Will Biteman");
            artists.add(2, "Hermann Longlegs");
        } catch (Exception e) {
            e.printStackTrace();
        }
        for (String artist : artists) {
            System.out.println(artist);
        }
    }
}
```

What happens if you try to compile and run the ArrayUtil class?

A. The code will compile and run without problems
B. The code will not compile
C. The program will print the two elements in **artists**
D. The code will compile but will throw a runtime exception

Answer: D.

The program will throw an ArrayIndexOutOfBoundsException because it attempts to insert an element at position 2 when the ArrayList is empty.

Question 9

Given

```
package demo1;
public class ExceptionDemo {
    public static void main(String[] args) {
        try {
            int count = Integer.parseInt(args[0]);
        } catch (NumberFormatException e) {
```

```
            System.err.println("Error: Not a number");
        } catch (Exception e) {
            e.printStackTrace();
        }
    }
}
```

What exception will be thrown if the program is invoked without arguments?

A. NumberFormatException
B. NullPointerException
C. RuntimeException
D. ArrayIndexOutOfBoundsException

Answer: D.

If a program is invoked without arguments, the JVM will still create an array that is passed to the **main** method. Therefore, it will not throw a **NullPointerException**. Rather, it will throw an **ArrayIndexOutOfBoundsException** because it tries to access the first element of an empty array.

Question 10

What can be said of try-with-resource?

A. It is a new feature in JDK 1.7
B. The resource must implement **java.lang.AutoCloseable**
C. It can be used without a catch or a finally block
D. It can be used with any resource

Answer: A, B.

try-with-resource is a new feature in JDK 1.7 that can close a resource automatically. The resource must implement the **java.lang.AutoCloseable** interface.

Chapter 9
Dates and Times

Support for dates and times has been available since Java version 1.0, mainly through the **java.util.Date** class. However, **Date** was poorly designed. For examples, months in **Date** start at 1 but days start at 0. A lot of its methods were deprecated in JDK 1.1 at the same time the **java.util.Calendar** was brought in to take over some of the functionality in **Date**. The duo were the main classes for dealing with dates and times, right up to JDK 1.7, even though they had been considered inadequate and not easy to work with, causing many to resort to third party alternatives such as Joda Time (http://joda.org). The new Date and Time API in JDK 1.8 resolves many of the issues in the old API and is similar to the Joda Time API.

9.1 Date and Time API Overview

The new Date and Time API makes it extremely easy to work with dates and times. The **java.time** package contains the core classes in the API. In addition, there are four other packages whose members are used less often: **java.time.chrono**, **java.time.format**, **java.time.temporal** and **java.time.zone**.

Within the **java.time** package, the **Instant** class represents a point on the time-line and is often used to time an operation. The **LocalDate** class models a date without the time component and time zone, suitable, for example, to represent a birthday.

If you need a date as well as a time, then **LocalDateTime** is for you. For instance, an order shipping date probably requires a time in addition to a date to make the order easier to track. If you need a time but do not care about the date, then you can use **LocalTime**.

On top of that, if a time zone is important, the Date and Time API provides the **ZonedDateTime** class. As the name implies, this class models a date-time with a time zone. For instance, you can use this class to calculate the flight time between two airports located in different time zones.

Then there are two classes for measuring an amount of time, **Duration** and **Period**. These two are similar except that **Duration** is time-based and **Period** is date-based. **Duration** provides a quantity of time to nanosecond precision. This class is good, for example, to model a flight time as it is often given in the number of hours and minutes. On the other hand, **Period** is suitable when you are only concerned with the number of days, months or years, such as when calculating your father's age.

The **java.time** package also comes with two enums, **DayOfWeek** and **Month**. **DayOfWeek** represents the day of the week, from **MONDAY** to **SUNDAY**. The **Month** enum represents the twelve months of the year, from **JANUARY** to **DECEMBER**.

Working with dates and times frequently involves parsing and formatting. The Date and Time API addresses these two issues by providing **parse** and **format** methods in all its major classes. In addition, the **java.time.format** contains a **DateTimeFormatter** class for formatting dates and times.

9.2 The Instant Class

An **Instant** object represents a point on the time-line. The reference point is the standard Java epoch, which is 1970-01-01T00:00:00Z (January 1, 1970 00:00 GMT). The **EPOCH** field of the **Instant** class returns an **Instant** representing the Java epoch. Instants after the epoch have positive values and instants prior to that have negative values.

The static method **now** of **Instant** returns an **Instant** object that represents the current time:

```
Instant now = Instant.now();
```

The **getEpochSecond** method returns the number of seconds that have elapsed since the epoch. The **getNano** method returns the number of nanoseconds since the beginning of the last second.

A popular use of the **Instant** class is to time an operation, as demonstrated in Listing 9.1.

Listing 9.1: Using Instant to time an operation

```
package app09;
import java.time.Duration;
import java.time.Instant;

public class InstantDemo1 {
    public static void main(String[] args) {
        Instant start = Instant.now();
        // do something here
        Instant end = Instant.now();
        System.out.println(Duration.between(start, end).toMillis());
    }
}
```

As shown in Listing 9.1, the **Duration** class is used to return the difference between two **Instants**. You will learn more about **Duration** later in this chapter.

9.3 LocalDate

The **LocalDate** class models a date without a time component. It also has no time zone. Table 9.1 shows some of the more important methods in **LocalDate**.

Method	Description
now	A static method that returns today's date.
of	A static method that creates a **LocalDate** from the specified year, month and date.
getDayOfMonth, getMonthValue, getYear	Returns the day, month or year part of this **LocalDate** as an **int**.
getMonth	Returns the month of this **LocalDate** as a **Month** enum constant.
plusDays, minusDays	Adds or subtracts the given number of days to or from this **LocalDate**.
plusWeeks, minusWeeks	Adds or subtracts the given number of weeks to or from this **LocalDate**.
plusMonths, minusMonths	Adds or subtracts the given number of months to or from this **LocalDate**.
plusYears, minusYears	Adds or subtracts the given number of years to or from this **LocalDate**.
isLeapYear	Checks if the year specified by this **LocalDate** is a leap year.
isAfter, isBefore	Checks if this **LocalDate** is after or before the given date.
lengthOfMonth	Returns the number of days in the month in this **LocalDate**.
withDayOfMonth	Returns a copy of this **LocalDate** with the day of month set to the given value.
withMonth	Returns a copy of this **LocalDate** with the month set to the given value.
withYear	Returns a copy of this **LocalDate** with the year set to the given value.

Table 9.1: More important methods of LocalDate

LocalDate offers various methods to create a date. For example, to create a **LocalDate** that represents today's date, use the static method **now**.

```
LocalDate today = LocalDate.now();
```

To create a **LocalDate** that represents a specific year, month and day, use its **of** method, which is also static. For instance, the following snippet creates a **LocalDate** that represents December 31, 2015.

```
LocalDate endOfYear = LocalDate.of(2015, 12, 31);
```

The method **of** has another override that accepts a constant of the **java.time.Month** enum as the second argument. For example, here is the code to construct the same date using the second method override.

```
LocalDate endOfYear = LocalDate.of(2015, Month.DECEMBER, 31);
```

There are also methods for obtaining the day, month or year of a **LocalDate**, such as **getDayOfMonth**, **getMonth**, **getMonthValue** and **getYear**. They all do not take any argument and either return an **int** or a **Month** enum constant. In addition, there is a **get** method that takes a **TemporalField** and returns a part of this **LocalDate**. For example, passing **ChronoField.YEAR** to **get** returns the year component of a **LocalDate**.

```
int year = localDate.get(ChronoField.YEAR));
```

ChronoField is an enum that implements the **TemporalField** interface, therefore you can pass a **ChronoField** constant to **get**. Both **TemporalField** and **ChronoField** are part of the **java.time.temporal** package. However, not all constants in **ChronoField** can be passed to **get** as not all of them are supported. For example, passing **ChronoField.SECOND_OF_DAY** to **get** throws an exception. As such, instead of **get**, it is better to use **getMonth**, **getYear** or a similar method to obtain a component of a **LocalDate**.

In addition, there are methods for copying a **LocalDate**, such as **plusDays**, **plusYears**, **minusMonths**, and so on. For example, to get a **LocalDate** that represents tomorrow, you can create a **LocalDate** that represents today and then calls its **plusDays** method.

```
LocalDate tomorrow = LocalDate.now().plusDays(1);
```

To get a **LocalDate** that represents yesterday, you can use the **minusDays** method.

```
LocalDate yesterday = LocalDate.now().minusDays(1);
```

In addition, there are **plus** and **minus** methods to get a copy of a **LocalDate** in a more generic way. Both accept an **int** and a **TemporalUnit**. The signatures of these methods are as follows.

```
public LocalDate plus(long amountToAdd,
        java.time.temporal.TemporalUnit unit)

public LocalDate minus(long amountToSubtract,
        java.time.temporal.TemporalUnit unit)
```

As an example, to get a **LocalDate** that represents a past date exactly two decades ago from today, you can use this code.

```
LocalDate pastDate = LocalDate.now().minus(2, ChronoUnit.DECADES);
```

ChronoUnit is an enum that implements **TemporalUnit**, so you can pass a **ChronoUnit** constant to the **plus** or **minus** method.

A **LocalDate** is immutable and therefore cannot be changed. Any method that returns a **LocalDate** returns a new instance of **LocalDate**.

Listing 9.2 shows an example of **LocalDate**.

Listing 9.2: LocalDate example

```
package app09;
import java.time.LocalDate;
import java.time.temporal.ChronoField;
import java.time.temporal.ChronoUnit;

public class LocalDateDemo1 {
    public static void main(String[] args) {
        LocalDate today = LocalDate.now();
        LocalDate tomorrow = today.plusDays(1);
        LocalDate oneDecadeAgo = today.minus(1,
                ChronoUnit.DECADES);
        System.out.println("Day of month: "
                + today.getDayOfMonth());
        System.out.println("Today is " + today);
        System.out.println("Tomorrow is " + tomorrow);
        System.out.println("A decade ago was " + oneDecadeAgo);
        System.out.println("Year : "
```

```
                + today.get(ChronoField.YEAR));
        System.out.println("Day of year:" + today.getDayOfYear());
    }
}
```

9.4 Period

The **Period** class models a date-based amount of time, such as five days, a week or three years. Some of its more important methods are presented in Table 9.2.

Method	Description
between	Creates a **Period** between two **LocalDates**.
ofDays, ofWeeks, ofMonths, ofYears	Creates a **Period** representing the given number of days/weeks/months/years.
of	Creates a **Period** from the given numbers of years, months and days.
getDays, getMonths, getYears	Returns the number of days/months/years of this period as an **int**.
isNegative	Returns **true** if any of the three components of this **Period** is negative. Returns **false** otherwise.
isZero	Returns **true** if all of the three components of this **Period** are zero. Otherwise, returns **false**.
plusDays, minusDays	Adds or subtracts the given number of days to or from this **Period**.
plusMonths, minusMonths	Adds or subtracts the given number of months to or from this **Period**.
plusYears, minusYears	Adds or subtracts the given number of years to or from this **Period**.
withDays	Returns a copy of this **Period** with the specified number of days.
withMonths	Returns a copy of this **Period** with the specified number of months.
withYears	Returns a copy of this **Period** with the specified number of years.

Table 9.2 More important methods of Period

Creating a **Period** is easy, thanks to the static factory methods **between**, **of**, and **ofDays/ofWeeks/ofMonths/ofYears**. For example, here is how you create a **Period** representing two weeks.

```
Period twoWeeks = Period.ofWeeks(2);
```

To create a **Period** representing one year, two months and three days, use the **of** method.

```
Period p = Period.of(1, 2, 3);
```

To obtain the year/month/day component of a **Period**, call its **getYears/getMonths/getDays** method. For instance, the **howManyDays** variable in the following code snippet will have a value of 14.

```
Period twoWeeks = Period.ofWeeks(2);
int howManyDays = twoWeeks.getDays();
```

Finally, you can create a copy of a **Period** using the **plus*XXX*** or **minus*XXX*** methods as well as one of the **with*XXX*** methods. A **Period** is immutable so these methods return new **Period** instances.

As an example, the code in Listing 9.3 shows an age calculator that calculates a person's age. It creates a **Period** from two **LocalDate**s and calls its **getDays**, **getMonths**, and **getYears** methods.

Listing 9.3: Using Period

```
package app09;
import java.time.LocalDate;
import java.time.Period;

public class PeriodDemo1 {
    public static void main(String[] args) {
        LocalDate dateA = LocalDate.of(1978, 8, 26);
        LocalDate dateB = LocalDate.of(1988, 9, 28);
        Period period = Period.between(dateA, dateB);
        System.out.printf("Between %s and %s"
                + " there are %d years, %d months"
                + " and %d days%n", dateA, dateB,
                period.getYears(),
                period.getMonths(),
                period.getDays());
    }
}
```

When run, the **PeriodDemo1** class in Listing 9.3 will print this string.

```
Between 1978-08-26 and 1988-09-28 there are 10 years, 1 months and 2
days
```

9.5 LocalDateTime

The **LocalDateTime** class models a date-time without a time zone. Table 9.3 shows some of the more important methods in **LocalDateTime**. The methods are similar to those of **LocalDate** plus some other methods for modifying the time component, such as **plusHours**, **plusMinutes** and **plusSeconds**, that are not available in **LocalDate**.

Method	Description
now	A static method that returns the current date and time.
of	A static method that creates a **LocalDateTime** from the specified year, month, date, hour, minute, second and millisecond.
getYear, getMonthValue, getDayOfMonth, getHour, getMinute, getSecond	Returns the year, month, day, hour, minute or second part of this **LocalDateTime** as an **int**.
plusDays, minusDays	Adds or subtracts the given number of days to or from the current **LocalDateTime**.
plusWeeks, minusWeeks	Adds or subtracts the given number of weeks to or from the current **LocalDateTime**.
plusMonths, minusMonths	Adds or subtracts the given number of months to or from the current **LocalDateTime**.
plusYears, minusYears	Adds or subtracts the given number of years to or from the current **LocalDateTime**.
plusHours, minusHours	Adds or subtracts the given number of hours to or from the current **LocalDateTime**.
plusMinutes, minusMinutes	Adds or subtracts the given number of minutes to or from the current **LocalDateTime**.
plusSeconds, minusSeconds	Add or subtracts the given number of seconds to or from the current **LocalDateTime**.
IsAfter, isBefore	Checks if this **LocalDateTime** is after or before the given date-time.
withDayOfMonth	Returns a copy of this **LocalDateTime** with the day of month set to the given value.
withMonth, withYear	Returns a copy of this **LocalDateTime** with the month or year set to the given value.
withHour, withMinute, withSecond	Returns a copy of this **LocalDateTime** with the hour/minute/second set to the given value.

Table 9.3: More important methods of LocalDateTime

LocalDateTime offers various static methods to create a date-time. The method **now** comes with three overrides and return the current date-time. The no-argument override is the easiest to use:

```
LocalDateTime now = LocalDateTime.now();
```

To create a **LocalDateTime** with a specific date and time, use the **of** method. This method has a number of overrides and allows you to pass the individual component of a date-time or a **LocalDate** and a **LocalTime**. Here are the signatures of some of the **of** methods.

```
public static LocalDateTime of(int year, int month, int dayOfMonth,
        int hour, int minute)

public static LocalDateTime of(int year, int month, int dayOfMonth,
        int hour, int minute)

public static LocalDateTime of(int year, Month month,
        int dayOfMonth, int hour, int minute)

public static LocalDateTime of(int year, Month month,
```

```
        int dayOfMonth, int hour, int minute)
public static LocalDateTime of(LocalDate date, LocalTime time)
```

For instance, the following snippet creates a **LocalDateTime** that represents December 31, 2015 at eight o'clock in the morning.

```
LocalDateTime endOfYear = LocalDateTime.of(2015, 12, 31, 8, 0);
```

You can create a copy of a **LocalDateTime** using the **plus*XXX*** or **minus*XXX*** method. For example, this code creates a **LocalDateTime** that represents the same time tomorrow.

```
LocalDateTime now = LocalDateTime.now();
LocalDateTime sameTimeTomorrow = now.plusHours(24);
```

9.6 Time Zones

The Internet Assigned Numbers Authority (IANA) maintains a database of time zones that you can download from this web page:

```
http://www.iana.org/time-zones
```

For easy viewing, however, you can just visit this Wikipedia page:

```
http://en.wikipedia.org/wiki/List_of_tz_database_time_zones
```

The Java Date and Time API caters for time zones too. The abstract class **ZoneId** (in the **java.time** package) represents a zone identifier. It has a static method called **getAvailableZoneIds** that returns all zone identifiers. Listing 9.4 shows how you can print a sorted list of all time zones using this method.

Listing 9.4: Listing all zone identifiers

```
package app09;
import java.time.ZoneId;
import java.util.ArrayList;
import java.util.Collections;
import java.util.List;
import java.util.Set;

public class TimeZoneDemo1 {
    public static void main(String[] args) {
        Set<String> allZoneIds = ZoneId.getAvailableZoneIds();
        List<String> zoneList = new ArrayList<>(allZoneIds);

        Collections.sort(zoneList);
        for (String zoneId : zoneList) {
            System.out.println(zoneId);
        }
        // alternatively, you can use this line of code to
        // print a sorted list of zone ids
        // ZoneId.getAvailableZoneIds().stream().sorted().
        //        forEach(System.out::println);
    }
```

```
}
```

getAvailableZoneIds returns a **Set** of **String**s. You can sort the **Set** using **Collections.sort()** or more elegantly by calling its **stream** method. You could have written this code to sort the zone identifiers.

```
ZoneId.getAvailableZoneIds().stream().sorted()
        .forEach(System.out::println);
```

Chapter 20, "Working with Streams" explains what streams are.

getAvailableZoneIds returns a **Set** of 586 zone identifiers. Here are some of the zone identifiers from the code above.

```
Africa/Cairo
Africa/Johannesburg
America/Chicago
America/Los_Angeles
America/Mexico_City
America/New_York
America/Toronto
Antarctica/South_Pole
Asia/Hong_Kong
Asia/Shanghai
Asia/Tokyo
Australia/Melbourne
Australia/Sydney
Canada/Atlantic
Europe/Amsterdam
Europe/London
Europe/Paris
US/Central
US/Eastern
US/Pacific
```

9.7 ZonedDateTime

The **ZonedDateTime** class models a date-time with a time zone. For example, the following is a zoned date-time:

```
2015-12-31T10:59:59+01:00 Europe/Paris
```

A **ZonedDateTime** is always immutable and the time component is stored to nanosecond precision.

Table 9.4 shows the more important methods in **ZonedDateTIme**.

Method	Description
now	A static method that returns the current date and time of the system's default zone.
of	A static method that creates a **ZonedDateTime** from the specified date-time and zone identifier.
getYear, getMonthValue, getDayOfMonth, getHour, getMinute, getSecond, getNano	Returns the year, month, day, hour, minute, second or nanosecond part of this **ZoneDateTime** as an **int**.
plusDays, minusDays	Adds or subtracts the given number of days to or from the current **ZonedDateTime**.
plusWeeks, minusWeeks	Adds or subtracts the given number of weeks to or from the current **ZonedDateTime**.
plusMonths, minusMonths	Adds or subtracts the given number of months to or from the current **ZonedDateTime**.
plusYears, minusYears	Adds or subtracts the given number of years to or from the current **ZonedDateTime**.
plusHours, minusHours	Adds or subtracts the given number of hours to or from the current **ZonedDateTime**.
plusMinutes, minusMinutes	Adds or subtracts the given number of minutes to or from the current **ZonedDateTime**.
plusSeconds, minusSeconds	Add or subtracts the given number of seconds to or from the current **ZonedDateTime**.
IsAfter, isBefore	Checks if this **ZonedDateTime** is after or before the given zoned date-time.
getZone	Returns the zone ID of this **ZonedDateTime**.
withYear, withMonth, withDayOfMonth	Returns a copy of this **ZonedDateTime** with the year/month/day of month set to the given value.
withHour, withMinute, withSecond	Returns a copy of this **ZonedDateTime** with the hour/minute/second set to the given value.
withNano	Returns a copy of this **ZonedDateTime** with the nanosecond set to the given value.

Table 9.4: More important methods of ZonedDateTime

Like **LocalDateTime**, the **ZonedDateTime** class offers the static methods **now** and **of** to construct a **ZonedDateTime**. **now** creates a **ZonedDateTime** representing the date and time of execution. The no-argument override of **now** creates a **ZonedDateTime** with the computer's default time zone.

```
ZonedDateTime now = ZonedDateTime.now();
```

Another override of **now** lets you pass a zone identifier:

```
ZonedDateTime parisTime =
        ZonedDateTime.now(ZoneId.of("Europe/Paris"));
```

The method **of** also comes with several overrides. In all cases, you need to pass a zone identifier. The first override allows you to pass each component of a zoned date-time, from the year to the nanosecond.

```
public static ZonedDateTime of(int year, int month, int dayOfMonth,
        int hour, int minute, int second, int nanosecond,
        ZoneId zone)
```

The second override of **of** takes a **LocalDate**, a **LocalTime** and a **ZoneId**:

```
public static ZonedDateTime of(LocalDate date, LocalTime time,
        ZoneId zone)
```

The last override of of takes a **LocalDateTime** and a **ZoneId**.

```
public static ZonedDateTime of(LocalDateTime datetime, ZoneId zone)
```

Like **LocalDate** and **LocalDateTime**, **ZonedDateTime** offers methods to create a copy of an instance using the **plus***XXX*, **minus***XXX* and **with***XXX* methods.

For instance, these lines of code creates a **ZonedDateTime** with the default time zone and calls its **minusDays** method to create the same **ZonedDateTime** three days earlier.

```
ZonedDateTime now = ZonedDateTime.now();
ZonedDateTime threeDaysEarlier = now.minusDays(3);
```

9.8 Duration

The **Duration** class models a time-based duration. It is similar to **Period** except that a **Duration** has a time component to nanosecond precision and takes into account the time zones between **ZonedDateTime**s. Table 9.5 shows the more important methods in **Duration**.

Method	Description
between	Creates a **Duration** between two temporal objects, such as between two **LocalDateTime**s or two **LocalZonedDateTime**s.
ofYears, ofMonths, ofWeeks, ofDays, ofHours, ofMinutes, ofSeconds, ofNano	Creates a **Duration** representing the given number of years/months/weeks/days/hours/minutes/seconds/nanoseconds.
of	Creates a **Duration** from the given number of temporal units.
toDays, toHours, toMinutes	Returns the number of days/hours/minutes of this **Duration** as an int.
isNegative	Returns **true** if this **Duration** is negative. Returns **false** otherwise.
isZero	Returns **true** if this **Duration** is zero length. Otherwise, returns **false**.
plusDays, minusDays	Adds or subtracts the given number of days to or from this **Duration**.
plusMonths, minusMonths	Adds or subtracts the given number of months to or from this **Duration**.
plusYears, minusYears	Adds or subtracts the given number of years to or from this **Duration**.
withSeconds	Returns a copy of this **Duration** with the specified number of seconds.

Table 9.5: More important methods in Duration

You can create a **Duration** by calling its **between** or **of** static method. The code in Listing 9.5 creates a **Duration** between two **LocalDateTimes**, between January 26, 2015 11:10 and January 26, 2015 12:40.

Listing 9.5: Creating a Duration between two LocalDateTimes

```
package app09;
import java.time.Duration;
import java.time.LocalDateTime;

public class DurationDemo1 {

    public static void main(String[] args) {
        LocalDateTime dateTimeA = LocalDateTime
                .of(2015, 1, 26, 8, 10, 0, 0);
        LocalDateTime dateTimeB = LocalDateTime
                .of(2015, 1, 26, 11, 40, 0, 0);
        Duration duration = Duration.between(
                dateTimeA, dateTimeB);
        System.out.printf("There are %d hours and %d minutes.%n",
                duration.toHours(),
                duration.toMinutes() % 60);
    }
}
```

The result of running the **DurationDemo1** class is this.

```
There are 3 hours and 30 minutes.
```

The code in Listing 9.6 creates a **Duration** between two **ZoneDateTimes**, with the same date-time but different timezones.

Listing 9.6: Creating a Duration between two ZonedDateTimes

```
package app09;
import java.time.Duration;
import java.time.LocalDateTime;
import java.time.Month;
import java.time.ZoneId;
import java.time.ZonedDateTime;

public class DurationDemo2 {

    public static void main(String[] args) {
        ZonedDateTime zdt1 = ZonedDateTime.of(
                LocalDateTime.of(2015, Month.JANUARY, 1,
                        8, 0),
                ZoneId.of("America/Denver"));
        ZonedDateTime zdt2 = ZonedDateTime.of(
                LocalDateTime.of(2015, Month.JANUARY, 1,
                        8, 0),
                ZoneId.of("America/Toronto"));
        Duration duration = Duration.between(zdt1, zdt2);
        System.out.printf("There are %d hours and %d minutes.%n",
                duration.toHours(),
                duration.toMinutes() % 60);
```

```
    }
}
```

Running the **DurationDemo2** class prints this on the console.

```
There are -2 hours and 0 minutes.
```

This is expected, because there are two hours difference between the time zones America/Denver and America/Toronto.

As a more complex example, the code in Listing 9.7 shows a bus travel time calculator. It has one method, **calculateTravelTime**, which takes a departure **ZonedDateTime** and an arrival **ZonedDateTime**. The code calls the **calculateTravelTime** method twice. Both times the bus departs from Denver, Colorado at 8 in the morning Denver time and arrives in Toronto at 8 in the next morning Toronto time. The first time the bus leaves on March 8, 2014 and the second time it leaves on March 18, 2014.

What are the travel time in both occasions?

Listing 9.7: Travel time calculator

```
package app09;
import java.time.Duration;
import java.time.LocalDateTime;
import java.time.Month;
import java.time.ZoneId;
import java.time.ZonedDateTime;

public class TravelTimeCalculator {

    public Duration calculateTravelTime(
            ZonedDateTime departure, ZonedDateTime arrival) {
        return Duration.between(departure, arrival);
    }

    public static void main(String[] args) {
        TravelTimeCalculator calculator =
                new TravelTimeCalculator();
        ZonedDateTime departure1 = ZonedDateTime.of(
                LocalDateTime.of(2014, Month.MARCH, 8,
                        8, 0),
                ZoneId.of("America/Denver"));
        ZonedDateTime arrival1 = ZonedDateTime.of(
                LocalDateTime.of(2014, Month.MARCH, 9,
                        8, 0),
                ZoneId.of("America/Toronto"));
        Duration travelTime1 = calculator
                .calculateTravelTime(departure1, arrival1);
        System.out.println("Travel time 1: "
                + travelTime1.toHours() + " hours");

        ZonedDateTime departure2 = ZonedDateTime.of(
                LocalDateTime.of(2014, Month.MARCH, 18,
                        8, 0),
```

```
                ZoneId.of("America/Denver"));
        ZonedDateTime arrival2 = ZonedDateTime.of(
                LocalDateTime.of(2014, Month.MARCH, 19,
                        8, 0),
                ZoneId.of("America/Toronto"));
        Duration travelTime2 = calculator
                .calculateTravelTime(departure2, arrival2);
        System.out.println("Travel time 2: "
                + travelTime2.toHours() + " hours");
    }
}
```

The result is this.

```
Travel time 1: 21 hours
Travel time 2: 22 hours
```

Why the difference? Because in 2014 daylight saving time began on Sunday, March 9 at 2AM. As such, you 'lost' one hour between March 8, 2014 and March 9, 2014.

9.9 Formatting A Date-Time

You use a **java.time.format.DateTimeFormatter** to format a local or zoned date-time. The **LocalDate**, **LocalDateTime**, **LocalTime** and **ZoneDateTime** classes offer a **format** method that has the following signature.

```
public java.lang.String format(java.time.format.DateTimeFormatter
        formatter)
```

It is clear that to format a date or time, you must first create an instance of **DateTimeFormatter**.

The code in Listing 9.8 formats the current date using two formatters.

Listing 9.8: Formatting dates

```
package app09;
import java.time.LocalDateTime;
import java.time.format.DateTimeFormatter;
import java.time.format.FormatStyle;

public class DateTimeFormatterDemo1 {
    public static void main(String[] args) {
        DateTimeFormatter formatter1 = DateTimeFormatter
                .ofLocalizedDateTime(FormatStyle.MEDIUM);
        LocalDateTime example = LocalDateTime.of(
                2000, 3, 19, 10, 56, 59);
        System.out.println("Format 1: " + example
                .format(formatter1));
        DateTimeFormatter formatter2 = DateTimeFormatter
                .ofPattern("MMMM dd, yyyy HH:mm:ss");
        System.out.println("Format 2: " +
                example.format(formatter2));
```

```
    }
}
```

The results are as follows (the first result depends on your locale).

```
Format 1: 19-Mar-2000 10:56:59 AM
Format 2: March 19, 2000 10:56:59
```

9.10 Parsing A Date-Time

There are two **parse** methods in many of the classes in the Java Date and Time API. The first requires a formatter, the second does not. The one that does not will parse the date-time based on the default pattern. To use your own pattern, use a **DateTimeFormatter**. The **parse** methods will throw a **DateTimeParseException** if the string passed cannot be parsed.

Listing 9.9 contains an age calculator to demonstrate date parsing.

Listing 9.9: An age calculator

```
package app09;
import java.time.LocalDate;
import java.time.Period;
import java.time.format.DateTimeFormatter;
import java.time.format.DateTimeParseException;
import java.util.Scanner;

public class AgeCalculator {
    DateTimeFormatter formatter = DateTimeFormatter
            .ofPattern("yyyy-M-d");
    public Period calculateAge(LocalDate birthday) {
        LocalDate today = LocalDate.now();
        return Period.between(birthday, today);
    }

    public LocalDate getBirthday() {
        Scanner scanner = new Scanner(System.in);
        LocalDate birthday;
        while (true) {
            System.out.println("Please enter your birthday "
                    + "in yyyy-MM-dd format (e.g. 1980-9-28): ");
            String input = scanner.nextLine();
            try {
                birthday = LocalDate.parse(input, formatter);
                return birthday;
            } catch(DateTimeParseException e) {
                System.out.println("Error! Please try again");
            }
        }
    }

    public static void main(String[] args) {
```

```
        AgeCalculator ageCalculator = new AgeCalculator();
        LocalDate birthday = ageCalculator.getBirthday();
        Period age = ageCalculator.calculateAge(birthday);
        System.out.printf("Today you are %d years, %d months"
                + " and %d days old%n",
                age.getYears(), age.getMonths(), age.getDays());
    }
}
```

The **AgeCalculator** class has two methods, **getBirthday** and **calculateAge**. The **getBirthday** method employs a **Scanner** to read user input and parses the input into a **LocalDate** using the class level **DateTimeFormatter**. The **getBirthday** method keeps begging for a date until the user types in a date in the correct format, in which case the method returns. The **calculateAge** method takes a birthday and creates a **Period** between the birthday and today.

If you run this example, you will see this on your console.

```
Please enter your birthday in yyyy-MM-dd format (e.g. 1980-9-28):
```

If you enter a date in the correct format, the program will print the calculated age, such as the following.

```
Today you are 79 years, 0 months and 15 days old
```

Self Test

Question 1

Which of the following is part of the new Date and Time API added in Java 8?

A. java.util.Date
B. java.util.Time
C. java.time.LocalDate
D. java.time.LocalDateTime
E. java.time.Period

Answer: C, D, E.

A is incorrect because **java.util.Date** has been around since Java 1.

B is incorrect because **java.util.Time** does not exist.

C, D and E are correct because **LocalDate**, **LocalDateTime** and **Period** are some of the classes in the new Date and Time API.

Question 2

If today was January 1, 2015, what would the code below print?

```
LocalDate localDate = LocalDate.now();
localDate = localDate.withMonth(6).withDayOfMonth(30);
localDate = localDate.plusMonths(-1);
```

```
System.out.println(localDate.getMonth());
```

A. JANUARY
B. DECEMBER
C. JUNE
D. MAY

Answer: D.

The code will always print **MAY** no matter when it is run. This is because **withMonth(6)** sets the date to June and **plusMonths(-1)** changes it to May.

Question 3

What is the output of this code?

```
LocalDate localDate = LocalDate.of(2008, 3, 30);
localDate = localDate.minusMonths(1);
System.out.println(localDate);
```

A. 2008-02-31
B. 2008-02-30
C. 2008-02-29
D. 2008-02-28
E. 2008-02-27

Answer: C.

Since 2008 was a leap year, moving March 30, 2008 back by one month returns February 29, 2008.

Question 4

Which of the following expressions return 10 o'clock? (Choose all that apply)

A. LocalTime.NOON.minus(2, ChronoUnit.HOURS)
B. LocalTime.of(10, 00)
C. LocalTime.of(22, 00)
D. LocalTime.of(10, 0, 0)

Answer: A, B, C, D.

A, B, D return a time representing 10 am. C returns a time representing 10pm.

Question 5

What can be inserted into line 2 so that the code always prints true?

```
1. LocalDateTime dt1 = LocalDateTime.now();
2. ...
3. System.out.println(dt2.equals(dt1));
```

A. LocalDateTime dt2 = LocalDateTime.of(LocalDate.now(), dt1.toLocalTime());
B. LocalDateTime dt2 = LocalDateTime.of(LocalDate.now(), LocalTime.now());
C. LocalDateTime dt2 = LocalDateTime.of(dt1.toLocalDate, dt1.toLocalTime());

D. LocalDateTime dt2 = LocalDateTime.now();

Answer: C.

A LocalDateTime can be created from a LocalDate and a LocalTime.

Option A would be correct most of the time because calling LocalDate.now() to create dt1 and calling LocalDate.now() to create dt2 would almost always return the same date, except when the code is run close to midnight, in which case there is a slim chance the second LocalDate.now() might return a different date. Therefore, there is no guarantee dt2.equals(dt1) returns true.

B is incorrect because calling LocalTime.now() twice will return different times.

C. is correct because dt2 is constructed from components of dt1.

D is incorrect because calling LocalDateTime.now() twice returns different local date times.

Question 6

What is the output of the following code?

```
Period period = Period.of(0,  0,  1);
LocalDate today = LocalDate.now();
for (int i = 0; i < 30; i++) {
    System.out.println(today.plus(period));
}
```

A. It prints 30 dates from the first of this month to the 30th
B. It prints 30 dates starting from today's date
C. It prints today's date 30 times
D. It prints 30 dates from the last day of this month

Answer: C.

This is a trick question. Calling LocalDate.plus(period) does not change the LocalDate. To have a different date, the expression must be assigned to itself:

```
today = today.plus(period)
```

Question 7

What is the output of the following code?

```
DateTimeFormatter formatter1 = DateTimeFormatter
        .ofLocalizedDateTime(FormatStyle.SHORT);
LocalDateTime date1 = LocalDateTime.of(
        2000, 1, 1, 0, 0, 0);
System.out.println(date1.format(formatter1));
```

A. 2000-1-1 00:00 AM
B. 2000/1/1 00:00 AM
C. 2000/01/01 00:00
D. The output cannot be determined

Answer: D.

The **ofLocalizedDateTime** method return a **DateTimeFormatter** that depends on the computer settings. Therefore, the output cannot be determined.

Question 8

How do you parse a local date using the new Date and Time API?

A. By using DateTimeFormatter.parse()
B. By using DateTimeFormatter.format()
C. By using DateTimeParser.parse()
D. By using LocalDate.parse()

Answer: D.

A is incorrect because **DateTimeFormatter** does not have a parse method.

B is incorrect because **DateTimeFormatter.format()** formats a date.

C is incorrect because **DateTimeParser** is not part of the Date and Time API.

D is correct.

Question 9

Which pattern can be used to parse the string “2015 4 4” as April 4, 2015?

A. yyyy MM dd
B. yyyy M dd
C. yyyy MM d
D. yyyy M d

Answer: D.

A is incorrect because with this pattern the date would have to presented as 2015 04 04.

B is incorrect because with this pattern the date would have to be presented as 2015 4 04

C is incorrect because with this pattern the date would have to be presented as 2014 04 4.

D is the correct answer.

Question 10

What is the output of the following code?

```
LocalDate date1 = LocalDate.of(2016, 12, 20);
LocalDate date2 = LocalDate.of(2016, 11, 21);
Period period = Period.between(date1, date2);
System.out.println(period.getDays());
```

A. 0

B. 1
C. 30
D. -29

Answer: D.

The **between** method calculates the period between the first argument and the second argument. Since **date2** is earlier than **date2**, the result must be negative.

Chapter 10
Lambda Expressions

The lambda expression is the most important new feature in Java SE 8. Long considered a missing feature in Java, it has made the Java language complete. At least for now. In this chapter you will learn what lambda expressions are and why they are a nice addition to the language. You will also be introduced to new technical terms such as single abstract method (SAM) and functional interface.

Before you get acquainted with lambda expressions, however, you should first learn about anonymous inner classes. This is because a lambda expression is basically a shorter way of doing the same thing with an anonymous inner class. Knowing what anonymous inner classes are helps you understand lambda expressions better. The first section of this chapter is therefore a brief discussion of anonymous inner classes.

10.1 Anonymous Inner Classes

An anonymous inner class is a nested class, which is a class that is defined within another class. An anonymous inner class does not have a name and is mainly used for writing an interface implementation that will only be used locally within a method. An anonymous inner class is used when there is no point in defining a separate class for the implementation because the implementation will only be used once.

For example, the **AnonymousInnerClassDemo1** class in Listing 10.1 creates an anonymous inner class that is an implementation of **Printable**.

Listing 10.1: Using an anonymous inner class

```
package app10;
interface Printable {
    void print(String message);
}

public class AnonymousInnerClassDemo1 {
    public static void main(String[] args) {

        Printable printer = new Printable() {
            public void print(String message) {
                System.out.println(message);
            }
        }; // this is a semicolon

        printer.print("Beach Music");
    }
```

```
}
```

The interesting thing here is that you create an anonymous inner class by using the **new** keyword followed by what looks like a class's constructor (in this case **Printable()**). However, note that **Printable** is an interface and does not have a constructor. **Printable()** is followed by the implementation of the **print** method. Also, note that after the closing brace, you use a semicolon to terminate the statement that instantiates the anonymous inner class.

In addition, you can also create an anonymous inner class by extending an abstract or concrete class, as demonstrated in the code in Listing 10.2.

Listing 10.2: Using an anonymous inner class with an abstract class

```
package app10;
abstract class Printable2 {
    void print(String message) {
    }
}

public class AnonymousInnerClassDemo2 {
    public static void main(String[] args) {
        Printable2 printer = new Printable2() {
            public void print(String message) {
                System.out.println(message);
            }
        }; // this is a semicolon

        printer.print("Beach Music");
    }
}
```

Now that you know what the anonymous inner class is, you are ready to learn about lambda expressions.

10.2 Why Lambda Expressions?

Also known as closures, lambda expressions can make certain constructs shorter and more readable, especially when you are dealing with inner classes.

Consider the following code snippet that defines an anonymous inner class out of the **java.lang.Runnable** interface and instantiates the class.

```
Runnable runnable = new Runnable() {
    @Override
    public void run() {
        System.out.println("Running...");
    }
}
```

The code can be replaced with a lambda expression as short as this:

```
Runnable runnable = () -> System.out.println("Running...")
```

In other words, if you need to pass a **Runnable** to a **java.util.concurrent.Executor** like so

```
executor.execute(new Runnable() {
    @Override
    public void run() {
        System.out.println("Running...");
    }
});
```

you can use a lambda expression to produce code with the same effect:

```
executor.execute(() -> System.out.println("Running..."));
```

Short and sweet. And clearer and more expressive too.

10.3 Functional Interfaces

Before I explain the lambda expression further, I will introduce the functional interface. A functional interface is an interface that has exactly one abstract method that does not override a method in **java.lang.Object**. A functional interface is also called a single abstract method (SAM) interface. For example, **java.lang.Runnable** is a functional interface because it has only one abstract method, **run**. A functional interface may have any number of default and static methods and methods that override public methods in **java.lang.Object** and still qualifies as a functional interface. For example, the **Calculator** interface in Listing 10.3 is a functional interface with a single abstract method called **calculate**. It is a functional interface even though it has two default methods and another abstract method overriding the **toString** method from **java.lang.Object**.

Listing 10.3: A functional interface

```
package app10;
public interface Calculator {

    double calculate(int a, int b);

    public default int subtract(int a, int b) {
        return a - b;
    }

    public default int add(int a, int b) {
        return a * b;
    }

    @Override
    public String toString();
}
```

Examples of functional interfaces in the core Java library include **java.lang.Runnable**, **java.lang.AutoCloseable**, **java.lang.Comparable** and **java.util.Comparator**. In addition, the new package **java.util.function** contains dozens of functional interfaces and is discussed in the section "Predefined Functional Interfaces" later in this chapter.

Optionally, a functional interface can be annotated with **@FunctionalInterface**.

Why is the functional interface important? Because you can use a lambda expression to create the equivalent of an anonymous inner class from a functional interface. You cannot use an interface that is not a functional interface for this purpose.

So, let the fun begin.

10.4 Lambda Expression Syntax

The **Calculator** interface in Listing 10.3 has a **calculate** method that can be the basis of a lambda expression. The method allows you to define any mathematical operation that takes two integers and return a double. For instance, here are two lambda expressions based on **Calculator**.

```
Calculator addition = (int a, int b) -> (a + b);
System.out.println(addition.calculate(5, 20)); // prints 25.0

Calculator division  = (int a, int b) -> (double) a / b;
System.out.println(division.calculate(5, 2)); // prints 2.5
```

The lambda expression is such an elegant design. How many more lines of code would you need to implement the same program without lambda expressions?

Now that you have acquainted yourself with the lambda expression, I will show you its formal syntax.

```
(parameter list) -> expression
```

or

```
(parameter list) -> {
    statements
}
```

The parameter list is the same as the list of parameters of the abstract method in the underlying functional interface. However, the type for each parameter is optional. In other words, both of these expressions are valid.

```
Calculator addition = (int a, int b) -> (a + b);

Calculator addition = (a, b) -> (a + b);
```

To summarize, a lambda expression is a shortcut to defining an implementation of a functional interface. A lambda expression is equivalent to an instance of a functional interface implementation. Since it is possible to pass objects as parameters to a method, it is too possible to pass lambda expressions as parameters to a method.

10.5 Predefined Functional Interfaces

The **java.util.function** package is a new package in JDK 8. It contains more than forty predefined functional interfaces that can make it easier for you to write lambda expressions. Some of the predefined functional interfaces are shown in Table 10.1.

Functional Interface	Description
Function	Models a function that can take one parameter and return a result. The result can be of a different type than the parameter.
BiFunction	Models a function that can take two parameters and return a result. The result can be of a different type than any of the parameters.
UnaryOperator	Represents an operation on a single operand that returns a result whose type is the same as the type of the operand. A **UnaryOperator** can be thought of as a **Function** whose return value is of the same type as the parameter. In fact, **UnaryOperator** is a subinterface of **Function.**
BiOperator	Represents an operation on two operands. The result and the operands must be of the same type.
Predicate	A Function that takes a parameter and returns **true** or **false** based on the value of the parameter.
Supplier	Represents a supplier of results.
Consumer	An operation that takes a parameter and returns no result.

Table 10.1: Core functional interfaces

Function, BiFunction and Other Variants

The **Function** interface is used to create a one-argument function that returns a result. It is a parameterized type and here is its definition.

```
public interface Function<T, R>
```

Here, T represents the type of the argument and R the type of the result.

Function has one abstract method, **apply**, whose signature is as follows.

```
R apply(T argument)
```

This is the method you need to override when using **Function**. For example, the class in Listing 10.4 defines a **Function** for converting miles to kilometers. The **Function** takes an Integer as an argument and returns a **Double**.

Listing 10.4: The FunctionDemo1 class

```
package app10.function;
import java.util.function.Function;

public class FunctionDemo1 {
    public static void main(String[] args) {
        Function<Integer, Double> milesToKms =
                (input) -> 1.6 * input;
        int miles = 3;
```

```
        double kms = milesToKms.apply(miles);
        System.out.printf("%d miles = %3.2f kilometers\n",
                miles, kms);
    }
}
```

If you run the **FunctionDemo1** class, you will see this on your console.

```
3 miles = 4.80 kilometers
```

A variant of **Function**, **BiFunction** takes two arguments and returns a result. Listing 10.5 shows an example of **BiFunction**. It uses **BiFunction** to create a function that calculates an area given a width and a length. Invoking the function is done by calling its **apply** method.

Listing 10.5: The BiFunctionDemo1 class

```
package app10.function;
import java.util.function.BiFunction;

public class BiFunctionDemo1 {
    public static void main(String[] args) {
        BiFunction<Float, Float, Float> area =
                (width, length) -> width * length;
        float width = 7.0F;
        float length = 10.0F;
        float result = area.apply(width, length);
        System.out.println(result);
    }
}
```

Running the **BiFunctionDemo1** class prints the following on the console.

```
70.0
```

In addition to **BiFunction**, there are also variants that are specializations of **Function**. For example, the **IntFunction** interface always takes an **Integer** and requires only one parameterized type for the result type. Its **apply** method returns an **int**.

```
R apply(int input)
```

The **LongFunction** and **DoubleFunction** interfaces are similar to **IntFunction**, except they take a long and a double as an argument, respectively.

Then, there are variants that do not require parameterized arguments at all, because they have been designed for a specific argument type and a specific return type. For instance, the **IntToDoubleFunction** interface can be used to create a function that accepts an int and returns a double. Instead of **apply**, the interface offers an **applyAsDouble** method. An example of **IntToDoubleFunction** interface is given in Listing 10.6. It is a function that converts a temperature on the Celcius scale to Fahrenheit.

Listing 10.6: The IntToDoubleFunctionDemo1 class

```
package app10.function;
import java.util.function.IntToDoubleFunction;

public class IntToDoubleFunctionDemo1 {
```

```
    public static void main(String[] args) {
        IntToDoubleFunction celciusToFahrenheit =
                (input) -> 1.8 * input + 32;
        int celcius = 100;
        double fahrenheit =
                celciusToFahrenheit.applyAsDouble(celcius);
        System.out.println(celcius + "\u2103" + " = "
                + fahrenheit + "\u2109\n");
    }
}
```

This is the output of **IntToDoubleFunctionDemo1**.

```
100℃ = 212.0℉
```

Similar to **IntToDoubleFunction** are **LongToDoubleFunction** and **LongToIntFunction**. I am sure you can guess what they do from their names.

The **UnaryOperator** interface is another specialization of **Function** whose operand type is the same the return type. Its declaration is as follows.

public interfaceUnaryOperator<T> extends Function<T,T>**BinaryOperator** is a specialization of **BiFunction**. **BinaryOperator** represents an operation with two operands of the same type and returns a result that has the same type as the operands.

Predicate

A **Predicate** is a function that takes a parameter and returns **true** or **false** based on the value of the parameter. It has a single abstract method called **test**.

For example, the **PredicateDemo1** class in Listing 10.7 defines a **Predicate** that evaluates a string input and returns true if every character in the string is a number.

Listing 10.7: The PredicateDemo1 class

```
package app10.function;
import java.util.function.Predicate;

public class PredicateDemo1 {
    public static void main(String[] args) {
        Predicate<String> numbersOnly = (input) -> {
            for (int i = 0; i < input.length(); i++) {
                char c = input.charAt(i);
                if ("0123456789".indexOf(c) == -1) {
                    return false;
                }
            }
            return true;
        };

        System.out.println(numbersOnly.test("12345"));// true
        System.out.println(numbersOnly.test("100a")); // false
    }
}
```

Supplier

A **Supplier** takes no parameter and returns a value. Implementations must override its **get** abstract method and returns an instance of the interface's type parameter.

Listing 10.8 shows an example of **Supplier**. It defines a **Supplier** that returns a one-digit random number and uses a **for** loop to print five random numbers.

Listing 10.8: The SupplierDemo1 class

```
package app10.function;
import java.util.Random;
import java.util.function.Supplier;

public class SupplierDemo1 {
    public static void main(String[] args) {
        Supplier<Integer> oneDigitRandom = () -> {
            Random random = new Random();
            return random.nextInt(10);
        };
        for (int i = 0; i < 5; i++) {
            System.out.println(
                    oneDigitRandom.get());
        }
    }
}
```

There are also specialized variants of **Supplier**, such as **DoubleSupplier** (returns a **Double**), **IntSupplier** and **LongSupplier**.

Consumer

A **Consumer** is an operation that returns no result. It has one abstract method called **accept**.

Listing 10.9 shows an example of **Consumer** that takes a string and print it center-justified.

Listing 10.9: Consumer example

```
package app10.function;
import java.util.function.Consumer;
import java.util.function.Function;

public class ConsumerDemo1 {
    public static void main(String[] args) {
        Function<Integer, String> spacer = (count) -> {
            StringBuilder sb = new StringBuilder(count);
            for (int i = 0; i < count; i++) {
                sb.append(" ");
            }
            return sb.toString();
        };

        int lineLength = 60; // characters
```

```
        Consumer<String> printCentered =
                (input) -> {
                    int length = input.length();
                    String spaces = spacer.apply(
                            (lineLength - length) / 2);
                    System.out.println(spaces + input);
                };

        printCentered.accept("A lambda expression a day");
        printCentered.accept("makes you");
        printCentered.accept("look smarter");
    }
}
```

The example in Listing 10.9 features a **Consumer** that takes a **String** and prints it after prefixing it with a certain number of spaces. The maximum number of characters in each line is 60 and the spaces are obtained by calling a **Function** named spacer. The implementation of the Consumer's **accept** method is given by this Lambda expression.

```
(input) -> {
    int length = input.length();
    String spaces = spacer.apply(
            (lineLength - length) / 2);
    System.out.println(spaces + input);
}
```

The function **spacer** returns the specified number of spaces and is defined as

```
Function<Integer, String> spacer = (count) -> {
    StringBuilder sb = new StringBuilder(count);
    for (int i = 0; i < count; i++) {
        sb.append(" ");
    }
    return sb.toString();
};
```

The function employs a **for** loop that appends a space to a **StringBuilder** *count* number of times, where *count* is the parameter to the function. When the loop exits, it returns the **String** representation of the **StringBuilder**.

If you run the **ConsumerDemo1** class, you will see this on your console.

```
A lambda expression a day
        makes you
       look smarter
```

Self Test

Question 1

Consider this interface:

```
interface Computable {
    double compute(double a, double b);
}
```

Which of the following lambda expressions can be created out of the **Computable** interface?

A. Computable multiply = (x, y) -> x * y;
B. Computable div = (double x, double y) -> x / y;
C. Computable add = (int x, int y) -> x / y;
D. Computable add = (a, b) => x / y;

Answer: A, B.

A and B are correct. C is incorrect because the method **compute** expects two **double** arguments, not **ints**. D is incorrect because -> is the operator for lambda expressions, not =>.

Question 2

Consider this interface:

```
interface Formatter {
    String format(double a, double b);
    String format(int a, int b);
}
```

Which of the following lambda expressions can be created out of the **Formatter** interface?

A. Formatter f1 = (x, y) -> { return x + "," + y };
B. Formatter f2 = (double x, double y) -> x + "" + y;
C. Formatter f3 = (int x, int y) -> x + y;
D. Formatter cannot be used to construct a lambda expression.

Answer: D.

Formatter is not a functional interface because it has more than one abstract method. As such, it cannot be used as the assignment target for a lambda expression.

Question 3

Which of the following statements are true? (Choose all that apply)

A. A functional interface may only have one method
B. A functional interface may have more than one method
C. A functional interface may not have default methods
D. A functional interface can be used as the assignment target for a lambda expression

Answer: B, D.

A is incorrect because a functional interface may have multiple methods as long as only one of them is abstract.

B is correct because a functional interface may have more than one method as long as one of them is abstract.

C is incorrect because a functional interface may have default methods.

D is correct because a function interface can be used as the assignment target for a lambda expression.

Question 4

Which of the following are predefined functional interfaces? (Choose all that apply)

A. Function
B. BiFunction
C. TriFunction
D. UnaryFunction

Answer: A, B.

Function and **BiFunction** are predefined functional interfaces. **TriFunction** and **UnaryFunction** are not.

Question 5

Which of the following statements are true? (Choose all that apply)

A. A **Predicate** is a function that takes a parameter and returns true or false
B. **Predicate** is a predefined functional interface
C. The **Predicate** interface has a single abstract method called **predicate**
D. The **Predicate** interface has a single abstract method called **test**

Answer: A, B, D.

The **Predicate** interface is one of the predefined functional interfaces. It has an abstract method named **test** that returns true or false depending on the given argument.

Question 6

Consider this lambda expression that uses **Predicate**:

```
Predicate<String> cap = s -> s.charAt(0) == s.toUpperCase().charAt(0);
```

Which of the following expressions return true? (Choose all that apply)

A. cap.test("Abc")
B. cap.test("abc")
C. cap.test("ABC")
D. cap.test("aBC")

Answer: A, C.

The lambda expression tests if the first character of a **String** is capitalized. Therefore, A and C return true.

Question 7

Which of the following statements are true with regard to **Supplier**?

A. Supplier is a predefined functional interface

B. Supplier has an abstract method called supply
C. Supplier has an abstract method called test
D. Supplier takes two arguments

Answer: A.

Supplier is a predefined functional interface with an abstract method called **get**. The method takes no argument.

Question 8

Consider the following lambda expression:

```
Supplier<String> supplier = () -> "ABC";
```

Which of the following statements are correct? (Choose all that apply)

A. System.out.print(supplier.get()) prints "ABC"
B. System.out.print(supplier) also prints "ABC"
C. System.out.print(supplier.getClass().getName()) prints "java.lang.String"
D. System.out.print(supplier.getClass().getName()) prints "java.util.function.Supplier"

Answer: A.

A is correct because **Supplier.get()** returns the object being supplied.

B is incorrect and it will print the **Supplier** and not what is being supplied.

C and D are incorrect because **supplier** is a lambda expression and not an instance of **Supplier**. In fact, the statement prints a String having this format:

nameOfContainingClass$$Lambda$*someId*

Question 9

Consider the following code:

```
package test;
import java.util.ArrayList;
import java.util.List;
import java.util.function.Consumer;

public class Tester {
    public static void main(String[] args) {
        List<String> list = new ArrayList<String>();
        Consumer<String> consumer = (s) -> {
            if (s.length() % 2 == 0)
                list.add(s.toUpperCase());
```

```
        };
        consumer.accept("hello");
        consumer.accept("world!");
        for (String s : list) {
            System.out.print(s);
        }
    }
}
```

What is printed on the console?

A. WORLD!
B. helloworld!
C. HELLOWORLD!
D. an empty string

Answer: A.

The Consumer accepts a String and adds it the uppercase of it to the List if the number of characters in the String is even.

Question 10

Consider the following lambda expression that uses a **BiPredicate**:

```
BiPredicate<Double, Integer> pr = (x, y) -> x > y;
```

Which of the following statements is/are true?

A. pr must be called with two arguments.
B. Passing 0 and 0 to pr.test returns false
C. Passing 10 and 0 to pr.test returns true
D. Passing 10 and 0 to pr.test returns false

Answer: A.

A is correct because a **BiPredicate** takes two arguments.

B, C and D cause compile errors as passing two ints to a method that takes a **Double** and an **Integer** is illegal.

Appendix A
Mock Exam 1

The following are questions for the first mock exam. Each question may have more than one correct answer. Each of the questions also shows which exam topic it relates to.

Question 1 (7.1. Describe inheritance and its benefits)

The keyword **extends** can be used

A. to create a subclass from another class
B. to create a subinterface from another interface
C. to make a class implement an interface
D. to make an interface implement another interface

Question 2 (6.3. Create and overload constructors; including impact on default constructors)

Given the following class

```
class RocketScience {
    public String description;
    public String getDescription() {
       return description;
    }
}
```

Which of the following statements are correct?

A. The class will not compile because it has no constructor.
B. The class will compile.
C. All Java classes, including abstract classes, need at least one constructor.
D. The class will compile but will throw an exception when instantiated.

Question 3 (6.3. Create and overload constructors; including impact on default constructors)

Given

```
abstract class Abstract {
      public Abstract() {
      }
}
```

Which of these statements is true?

A. The class will not compile because an abstract class must not have a constructor.
B. The class will compile but cannot be instantiated.
C. The class will compile and can be instantiated.
D. The class will not compile because **Abstract** is a keyword and cannot be used as a class name.

Question 4 (1.4. Import other Java packages to make them accessible in your code)

Which of the following statements about the default package is true.

A. You cannot import a class in the default package.
B. A class in the default package can only be used in other classes in the default package.
C. A class in the default package can be imported into classes in non-default packages.
D. A class in the default package can import classes in non-default packages.

Question 5 (2.1. Declare and initialize variables (including casting of primitive data types))

Which ones are valid variable declarations?

A. long row_count;
B. long $;
C. long table$;
D. long _g5;
E. int $final_;
F. int static;

Question 6 (1.2. Define the structure of a Java class)

Here is the content of the **Computer.java** file.

```
1.    package test;
2.
3.    class A {
4.
5.    }
6.
7.    final class b {
8.
9.    }
```

Which of the following statements is (are) true?

A. The code will not compile because the file does not contain a **Computer** class.
B. A compile error at line 7 because a class name must start with a capital.
C. Compile errors at lines 3 and 7 because **Computer.java** may only contain a class with the same name as the file.

D. The code will compile.

Question 7 (9.1. Manipulate data using the StringBuilder class and its methods)

What is the output of this code snippet:

```
StringBuilder sb = new StringBuilder("Best phone cameras!");
System.out.println(sb.replace(1,  5,  "Worst"));
```

A. Worst phone cameras!
B. WorstBest phone cameras!
C. BWorstphone cameras!
D. Worstphone cameras!

Question 8 (3.3. Create if and if/else and ternary constructs)

Consider the following code snippet:

```
1. for (int i=10; i<20; i=i+2) {
2.     ...
3.          System.out.println(i);
4.     }
5. }
```

What can be inserted in line 2 to make the code print 10? (Choose all that apply)

A. if (i == 10) {
B. if (i % 5 == 0) {
C. if (i = 10) {
D. if (i % 2 == 5)

Question 9 (1.3. Create executable Java applications with a main method; run a Java program from the command line; including console output)

Given

```
package com.example;
public class Printer {
    public static void main(String[] args) {
        System.out.print(args[1]);
        System.out.print(args[2]);
    }
}
```

The program is invoked using this command.

```
java com.example.Printer Sonic "Drill" 'Toxic'
```

What is printed on the console?

A. SonicDrill

B. Sonic"Drill"
C. "Drill"'Toxic'
D. DrillToxic

Question 10 (3.2. Use Java operators; including parenthesis to override operator precedence)

Consider the following code:

```
int a = 2 + 3 * 6;
int b = (2 + 3) * 6;
System.out.println(a + b);
```

What is printed on the standard out upon the execution of the code?

A. 60
B. 50
C. 40
D. 30

Question 11 (1.1. Define the scope of variables)

Consider the following code snippet that contains named regions R, S, T, U, V and X.

```
int m = 0;
// ------- R --------
while (m < 5) {
  // ------- S --------
    for (int n = 0; n < 3; n++) {
      // ------- T --------
        System.out.println(m);
        System.out.println(n);
      // ------- U --------
    }
  // ------- V --------
  m++;
}
// ------- X --------
```

Which of the following statements are true?

A. *n* cannot be used in region R.
B. *m* and *n* can be used in region T.
C. *m* and *n* can be used in region U.
D. *m* and *n* can be used in region V.
E. *m* can be used in regions S, T, U and V.
F. *m* and *n* are out of scope in Region X.

Question 12 (1.3. Create executable Java applications with a main method; run a Java program from the command line; including console output)

Given

```
package test;
public class Hello {
    protected static void main(String[] args) {
        System.out.println("Hello, World!");
    }
}
```

Which of the following statements is (are) true?

A. The program does not compile.
B. The program compiles.
C. The program can be executed.
D. The program cannot be executed.

Question 13 (2.1. Declare and initialize variables (including casting of primitive data types))

Consider this code snippet:

```
int i = 015;
if (i == 13L)
    System.out.println("Equal");
else
    System.out.println("Not equal");
```

What will be printed on the console when the code is executed?

A. Nothing will be printed.
B. Equal
C. Not equal
D. Equal Not equal

Question 14 (6.4. Apply access modifiers)

Given the following class declaration

```
modifier class Pointer {}
```

Which modifiers can be used for class **Pointer**?

A. public
B. private
C. protected
D. final
E. static
F. abstract

Question 15 (6.4. Apply access modifiers)

Given the following method declaration

```
modifier int calculate(int a, int b)
```

Which modifiers can be used for class **Nested**?

A. public
B. private
C. protected
D. final
E. static
F. abstract
G. strictfp

Question 16 (6.4. Apply access modifiers)

Given the following interface declaration

```
modifier interface Device {}
```

Which modifiers can be used for interface **Device**?

A. public
B. private
C. protected
D. final
E. static
F. abstract

Question 17 (7.4. Use super and this to access objects and constructors)

Given

```
package test;
public class Parent {
    public Parent() {
        System.out.print("Parent...");
    }
    public static void main(String[] args) {
        Child1 c1 = new Child1();
        Child2 c2 = new Child2();
    }
}

class Child1 extends Parent {
    public Child1() {
        super();
        System.out.print("Child1...");
    }
}

class Child2 extends Parent {
    public Child2() {
        System.out.print("Child2...");
    }
```

```
}
```

What will be printed on the console when the **Parent** class is executed?

A. Child1...Child2...
B. Parent...Child1...Child2...
C. Child1...Parent...Child2...
D. Parent...Child1...Parent...Child2...

Question 18 (7.4. Use super and this to access objects and constructors)

Consider the following code

```
package test;
public class Parent {
    public Parent() {
        System.out.print("Parent...");
    }
    public static void main(String[] args) {
        Child1 c1 = new Child1("Joe");
        Child2 c2 = new Child2("Jane");
    }
}

class Child1 extends Parent {
    public Child1(String name) {
        super();
        System.out.print("Child1...");
    }
}

class Child2 extends Parent {
    public Child2(String name) {
        System.out.print("Child2...");
    }
}
```

Which of the following statements is (are) true?

A. The program will not compile because the **Parent** class does not have a constructor that takes a **String**.
B. The program will not compile because **Child1** and **Child2** do not have a constructor that matches the signature of the only constructor in **Parent**.
C. The program will compile and when executed it will print **Child1...Parent...Child2...**
D. The program will compile and when executed it will print **Parent...Child1...Parent...Child2...**

Question 19 (7.4. Use super and this to access objects and constructors)

Given

```
package test;
```

```
public class Parent {
    public Parent(String name) {
        System.out.print("Parent...");
    }
       public static void main(String[] args) {
           Child1 c1 = new Child1("Joe");
           Child2 c2 = new Child2("Jane");
       }
}

class Child1 extends Parent {
    public Child1(String name) {
        super(name);
        System.out.print("Child1...");
    }
}

class Child2 extends Parent {
    public Child2(String name) {
        System.out.print("Child2...");
    }
}
```

Which of the following statements is (are) true?

A. The program will not compile because the **Parent** class does not have a no-argument constructor.
B. The program will not compile because the constructor in **Child2** will try to call the default constructor in **Parent** and such a constructor does not exist.
C. The program will compile and when executed it will print **Child1...Parent...Child2...**
D. The program will compile and when executed it will print **Parent...Child1...Parent...Child2...**

Question 20 (1.4. Import other Java packages to make them accessible in your code)

Given

```
1.  package test;
2.  ...
3.  public class MathUtil {
4.      double twoPis = PI * 2;
5.  }
```

To prevent line 4 from causing a compile error, which line must be inserted into line 2?

A. import static Math.PI;.
B. import static java.lang.Math;
C. import static java.lang.Math.PI;
D. import java.lang.Math.PI;

Question 21 (1.4. Import other Java packages to make them accessible in your code)

Consider the following code snippet:

```
1.  import static java.lang.Integer.MAX_VALUE;
2.  public class Storage {
3.      public static void main(String[] args) {
4.          int i = MAX_VALUE;
5.      }
6.  }
```

What do you have to insert into line 1 so you can use the static field **MAX_VALUE** in the **Integer** class?

A. import static java.lang.Integer.MAX_VALUE;.
B. import static java.lang.Integer;
C. import java.lang.Integer.MAX_VALUE;
D. import java.lang.Integer;

Question 22 (4.1. Declare, instantiate, initialize and user a one-dimensional array)

Which of the following are valid array declarations? (Choose all that apply)

A. int stats[] = {Integer.MIN_VALUE, Integer.MAX_VALUE };
B. double[] remainders[] = {1, 2, 3};
C. short[] smallNumbers = new short[5];
D. String keys[] = new ArrayList<String>();

Question 23 (9.2. Creating and manipulating Strings)

Assuming **s** is a **String**, which of the following expressions returns the number of characters in **s**?

A. s.size
B. s.size()
C. s.length
D. s.length()
E. s.chars
F. s.chars()

Question 24 (6.2. Apply the static keyword to methods and fields)

Given the following class:

```
package demo;
public class Demo100 {
    private void doSomething() {
        System.out.println("Hello, World!");
    }
```

```
    public static void main(String[] args) {
        doSomething();
    }
}
```

What is the output of the program?

A. The program will print "Hello, World!"
B. The program will print an empty string
C. The program will fail to compile because the doSomething method is private
D. The program will fail to compile because you cannot access a non-static method from a static method

Question 25 (2.1. Declare and initialize variables (including casting of primitive data types))

Consider the following code snippet:

```
package util;
public class NumberUtil {
    public int getTodaysNumber() {
        private int i = 9;
        return i;
    }
}
```

Which statement is true with regard to the class above?

A. The program will compile
B. The getTodaysNumber method returns 9
C. The getTodaysNumber method can be accessed from static methods
D. The program will not compile

Question 26 (3.1. Use Java operators; including parentheses to override operator precedence)

Examine the following code:

```
package com.example.test;
public class Test101 {
    public static void main(String[] args) {
        int i = 10;
        System.out.println(i < 11);
    }
}
```

What is the output of this class?

A. 10<11
B. 1011
C. true
D. false

Question 27 (6.1. Create methods with arguments and return values; including overloaded methods)

Consider this code snippet:

```
 1. public class MathUtil {
 2.     public static int add(int a, int b) {
 3.         a++;
 4.         b++;
 5.         return a + b;
 6.     }
 7.     public static void main(String[] args) {
 8.         int m = 10;
 9.         int n = 20;
10.         int o = add(m, n);
11.         //
12.     }
13. }
```

Which of the following statement(s) is/are true?

A. At line 11 the value of m is 11
B. At line 11 the value of n is 21
C. At line 11 the value of m is 10
D. At line 11 the value of n is 20

Question 28 (6.3. Create and overload constructors; including impact on default constructors)

What can be said about this class?

```
public class Printer {
    private String name;
    public Printer() {
        this("Default");
    }
    public Printer(String name) {
        this.name = name;
    }
    public static void main(String[] args) {
        Printer printer = new Printer();
    }
}
```

A. The code creates two instances of **Printer**
B. The code creates one instance of **Printer**
C. The code calls the no-argument constructor and then the one-argument constructor
D. The name field will be assigned the value "Default"

Question 29 (5.1. Create and use while loops)

What is the output of the following class?

```
public class Loop1 {
    public static void main(String[] args) {
        int x = 0;
        while (x < 5)
            while (x < 3)
                System.out.print(x++);
    }
}
```

A. 012 then stops
B. 123 then stops
C. 012 then loops indefinitely
D. 123 then loops indefinitely

Question 30 (3.4. Use a switch statement)

Given the following code

```
public class Printer {
    public static void main(String[] args) {
       int x1 = 1;
       int x2 = 2;
       int y = 4;
       switch (y) {
       case x1:
           System.out.println("one");
           break;
       case x2:
           System.out.println("two");
           break;
       default:
           System.out.println("unknown");
       }
    }
}
```

Which of the statement(s) is/are true?

A. The program prints "one"
B. The program prints "two"
C. The program prints "unknown"
D. Compile error

Question 31 (7.2. Develop code that demonstrates the use of polymorphism; including overriding and object type versus reference type)

Given the following code:

```
interface Printable {}
class Document{}
class EBook extends Document implements Printable {}
```

Which of the following statements will not cause a compile error?

A. Printable printable1 = new Printable();
B. Printable printable2 = new Document();
C. Printable printable3 = new EBook();
D. Document document1 = new Document();
E. Document document2 = new EBook();
F. EBook ebook1 = new EBook();
G. EBook ebook2 = new Document();

Question 32 (1.3. Create executable Java applications with a main method; run a Java program from the command line; including console output)

Consider the following code:

```
package test;
public class TasteOfMain {
    public static void main(String[] args) {
        System.out.println(args.length);
    }
}
```

The class is invoked with this command line command

```
java test.TasteOfMain \ \\\ \\
```

What is the value of **args.length**?

A. 1
B. 2
C. 3
D. 4

Question 33 (2.4. Explain an object's lifecycle (creation, "dereference by assignment" and garbage collection))

Given

```
1.  class Resident {
```

```
 2.       public void live() {
 3.       }
 4.   }
 5.
 6.   public class Printer {
 7.       public static void main(String[] args) {
 8.           Resident r1 = new Resident();
 9.           Resident r2 = new Resident();
10.           r1 = null;
11.           System.out.println(r1);
12.           r2 = r1;
13.           System.out.println(r2);
14.       }
15.   }
```

Which of the following statements are true?

A. Two objects will be garbage collected at line 14.
B. One object will be garbage collected at line 12.
C. The object referenced by **r1** is eligible for garbage collection at line 11.
D. The object referenced by **r2** is eligible for garbage collection at line 13.

Question 34 (9.1. Manipulate data using the StringBuilder class and its methods)

Given

```
package test;
public class StatementComposer {

    public String getStatement(int id, String name) {
        StringBuilder s = new StringBuilder();
        s.append("SELECT * FROM employees WHERE ");
        s.append("id = " + id);
        s.append(" OR ");
        if (name == null) {
            s.delete(s.length() - 4, s.length());
        } else {
            s.append("name = '" + name + "'");
        }
        return s.toString();
    }
    public static void main(String[] args) {
        StatementComposer sc = new StatementComposer();
        System.out.println(sc.getStatement(3, null));
    }
}
```

What is the output of the class?

A. SELECT * FROM employees WHERE id = 3
B. SELECT * FROM employees WHERE id =
C. SELECT * FROM employees WHERE id = 3 OR name = 'null'

D. SELECT * FROM employees WHERE id = 3 OR name = null

Question 35 (3.2. Test equality between Strings and other objects using == and equals())

What is the output of this program?

```
package test;
public class StringTest {
    public static void main(String[] args) {
        String s1 = "Java";
        String s2 = "Rocks";
        String s3 = "JavaRocks";
        System.out.print(s3 == s1 + s2);
        System.out.print(".");
        System.out.print(s3.equals(s1 + s2));
    }
}
```

A. false.false
B. false.true
C. true.true
D. true.false

Question 36 (2.7. Creating and manipulating Strings)

Consider the following method:

```
public String getSubstring(String s) {
    int index1 = s.indexOf(".");
    int index2 = -1;
    if (index1 != -1) {
        index2 = s.indexOf(".", index1 + 1);
    }
    if (index2 == -1) {
        return s.substring(index1);
    } else {
        return s.substring(index1, index2);
    }
}
```

What is the method's return value if the string "Hello.World" is passed to it?

A. Hello
B. World
C. .World
D. HelloWorld

Question 37 (3.3. Create if and if/else and ternary constructs)

What is the value of **y** after this code is executed?

```
int i = 10;
int y = 50;
if (i + y < 70) {
    if (i + y < 60) {
        y = 500;
    } else {
        y = 5000;
    }
}
```

A. 50
B. 500
C. 5000
D. 10

Question 38 (9.4. Declare and use an ArrayList of a given type)

Which statement(s) creates an **ArrayList** of **String**s with an initial capacity of 20? (Choose all that apply)

A. ArrayList<String> names = new ArrayList<>();
B. ArrayList<String> names = new ArrayList<>(20);
C. ArrayList<String> names = new ArrayList<String>();
D. ArrayList<String> names = new ArrayList<String>(20);

Question 39 (4.2. Declare, instantiate, initialize and use multi-dimensional array)

Here is a multidimensional array:

```
int[][] tableCells = {{1, 2, 3, 4}, {5, 6, 7, 8}, {9, 10, 11}};
```

What is the value of **tableCells[1][3]**?

A. 3
B. 9
C. 8
D. 11

Question 40 (4.2. Declare, instantiate, initialize and use multidimensional array)

Which of the following are valid declarations of multidimensional arrays? (Choose all that apply)

A. int[][] tableCells = new int[0][0];
B. String names[][] = {};
C. String[] employees[] = {{"Henry Wong", "Hendrick Takada"}};
D. long diameters[] = null;
E. long wheels[][] = null;
F. Object[][] cars = new cars[][];

Question 41 (4.2. Declare, instantiate, initialize and use multidimensional array)

Consider the following class:

```
 1. package test;
 2. public class MultiDimArray {
 3.
 4.     public static void main(String[] args) {
 5.         int[][] stickers = new int[4][];
 6.         for (int i = 0; i < stickers.length; i++) {
 7.             stickers[i] = new int[4];
 8.         }
 9.         System.out.println(stickers[0][0]);
10.     }
11.}
```

What happens if you try to compile and run this class?

A. Compile error at line 5
B. Compile error at line 7
C. It compiles and prints 0
D. It compiles and throws a runtime exception

Question 42 (5.3. Create and use do/while loops)

Consider the following code.

```
package test;
public class Repeater {
    public static void main(String[] args) {
        if (args.length == 0) return;
        int input = 0;
        try {
            input = Integer.parseInt(args[0]);
            do {
                System.out.print(input + " ");
                input += 5;
            } while(input < 5);
        } catch (NumberFormatException e) {
            System.out.println("Not an integer");
        }
    }
}
```

What does the class print if it is invoked using this command line command?

```
java test.Repeater 50 20
```

A. Nothing
B. 50 55 60 65 70
C. 5
D. 50

Question 43 (5.4. Compare loop constructs)

Consider the following while loop:

```
1. int x = 0;
2. while (true) {
3.     x++;
4.     if (x > 5) break;
5.     System.out.println(x);
6. }
```

Which of the following **for** statement can be used to replace line 2 without changing what the code does?

A. for (int x = 0; x < 5; x++) {
B. for (; x < 5;) {
C. for (; ;) {
D. for (int y = 0; y < 5; y++) {

Question 44 (5.5. Use break and continue)

Consider this **for** loop:

```
for (int i = 0; i < 10; i++) {
    if (i % 2 == 0) continue;
    if (i % 5 == 0) break;
    System.out.print(i + " ");
}
```

What is printed on the console if the code snippet is executed?

A. 1 2 3 4 5 6 7 8 9
B. 1 3 5 7 9
C. 1 3 5
D. 1 3

Question 45 (6.5. Apply encapsulation principles to a class)

Which of the following statements are true about encapsulation?

A. Instance variables are made private
B. For each instance variable, there is a get method that returns the instance variable. This method is public
C. For each instance variable that is writable, there is a set method that is public.
D. Class fields are made protected.

Question 46 (6.6. Determine the effect upon object references and primitive values when they are passed into methods that change the values)

Consider the following code:

```
package test;
public class MathGenius {
    public void printDouble(int a, int b) {
        a *= 2;
        b *= 2;
        System.out.print(a + "__");
        System.out.print(b);
    }
    public static void main(String[] args) {
        int x = 10;
        int y = 20;
        new MathGenius().printDouble(x, y);
        System.out.print("__" + x + "__" + y);
    }
}
```

What is the output of the program?

A. 20__40__20__40
B. 20__40__10__20
C. 10__20__10__20
D. 10__20__20__40

Question 47 (6.6. Determine the effect upon object references and primitive values when they are passed into methods that change the values)

Consider the following code:

```
package test;
class Point {
    int x, y;
    Point(int x, int y) {
        this.x = x;
        this.y = y;
    }
    public void setX(int x) {
        this.x = x;
    }
    public void setY(int y) {
        this.y = y;
    }
    public int getX() {
        return x;
    }
    public int getY() {
        return y;
    }
    public String toString() {
        return x + "__" + y;
    }
}
```

```
public class PointDemo {
    public void enlargeAndPrintPoint(Point point) {
        point.setX(point.getX() * 2);
        point.setY(point.getY() * 2);
        System.out.print(point);
    }
    public static void main(String[] args) {
        Point point = new Point(100, 200);
        new PointDemo().enlargeAndPrintPoint(point);;
        System.out.print("__" + point);
    }
}
```

What is the output of the program?

A. 200__400__200__400
B. 200__400__100__200
C. 100__200__100__200
D. 100__200__200__400

Question 48 (7.2. Develop code that demonstrates the use of polymorphism; including overriding and object type versus reference type)

Given

```
package temporary;
class Animal {
    public void walk() {
        System.out.print("Animal.walk()");
    }
}
class Giraffe extends Animal {
    public int getLegCount() {
        return 4;
    }
}
public class Main {
    public static void main(String[] args) {
        Animal animal = new Giraffe();
        // some code
        int legCount = animal.getLegCount();
    }
}
```

Which of the following statements are true?

A. This is polymorphism in action.
B. The code will compile
C. The code will not compile because the **getLegCount** method is not part of **Animal**.
D. The code will compile but will thrown a **NullPointerException**

Question 49 (7.3. Determine when casting is necessary)

Consider the following code:

```
 1. package test;
 2. class Request {
 3.     public void parse(String request) {
 4.         System.out.print("Request.parse()");
 5.     }
 6. }
 7. class HttpRequest extends Request {
 8.     public String getHttpMethod() {
 9.         return "post";
10.     }
11. }
12. public class Server {
13.     public static void main(String[] args) {
14.         Request request1 = new Request();
15.         HttpRequest httpRequest1 = (HttpRequest) request1;
16.         HttpRequest httpRequest2 = new HttpRequest();
17.         httpRequest2.parse("");
18.     }
19. }
```

Which of the following methods are untrue?

A. Compile error at line 15
B. Compile error at line 17
C. No compile error, but there will be a runtime error if the class is executed
D. No compile error and no runtime error if the class is execute

Question 50 (8.1. Differentiate among checked exceptions, unchecked exceptions, and Errors)

Which of the following statements are true?

A. A checked exception is internal to the program
B. Errors should not be caught
C. A runtime exception is an unchecked exception
D. A runtime exception is a checked exception
E. Applications can recover from checked exceptions

Question 51 (8.2. Create a try-catch block and determine how exceptions alter normal program flow)

Consider the following code:

```
package test;
public class VideoGame {
    public static void main(String[] args) {
        int playerCount = 1;
        try {
```

```
            playerCount = Integer.parseInt(args[0]);
            if (playerCount > 1) {
                System.out.println("Multiple players found.");
            } else {
                System.out.println("One player");
            }
        } catch (ArrayIndexOutOfBoundsException e) {
            System.out.println("Please determine the number of players");
        } catch (NumberFormatException e) {
            System.out.println("Unrecognized number of players");
        }
    }
}
```

What is the output of the program if invoked using "**java test.VideoGame 1.0**"?

A. A runtime exception occurs
B. The program prints "Multiple players found"
C. The program prints "One player"
D. The program prints "Unrecognized number of players"

Question 52 (8.5. Recognize common exception classes (such as NullPointerException. ArithmeticException, ArrayIndexOutOfBoundsException, ClassCastException))

Which of the following are not runtime exceptions?

A. ClassCastException
B. NullPointerException
C. ArrayIndexOutOfBoundsException
D. NumberFormatException
E. OutOfMemoryError

Question 53 (8.5. Recognize common exception classes (such as NullPointerException. ArithmeticException, ArrayIndexOutOfBoundsException, ClassCastException))

Which of the following are caused by external errors?

A. ClassCastException
B. OutOfMemoryError
C. RuntimeException
D. StackOverflowError
E. Throwable

Question 54 (7.2. Develop code that demonstrates the use of polymorphism; including overriding and object type versus reference type)

Let class **Circle** extend class **Shape**. Given the following code

```
Circle circle = new Circle();
Shape shape = new Shape();
```

Which of the following expressions evaluate to true?

A. circle instanceof Shape
B. circle instanceof Object
C. shape instanceof Circle
D. (Shape) circle instanceof Circle

Question 55 (7.1. Describe inheritance and its benefits)

Consider the following two classes:

```
package inheritance;
class Parent {
    public void print() { ... }
    String describe() { ... }
    protected String[] copyNames(String[] sources) { ... }
    private boolean isResident() { ... }
}

class Sub extends Parent {
    public void doIt() {
        ...
    }
}
```

Which methods can be used in the **Sub** class?

A. print, describe, doIt
B. print, describe, copyNames, isResident
C. print, describe, copyNames
D. print, describe, copyNames, toString

Question 56 (2.3. Know how to read or write to object fields)

Consider the following code:

```
package test;
public class Holder {
    float length = 100F;
    static {
        width = 23.00F;
    }
    static {
        width = 25.00F;
    }
    static float width = 12.30F;
    public static void main(String[] args) {
        Holder h1 = new Holder();
        h1.length++;
```

```
        h1.width++;
        Holder h2 = new Holder();
        System.out.print(h2.width + ", ");
        System.out.print(h2.length);
    }
}
```

What is the output of the program?

A. 25.0, 100.0
B. 12.3, 100.0
C. 26.0, 100.0
D. 26.0, 110.0
E. 13.3, 100.0
F. 13.3, 110.0

Question 57 (3.1. Use Java operators; including parentheses to override operator precedence)

What is the value of **b**?

```
byte b = 2 ^ 6;
```

A. 64
B. 8
C. 4
D. 2

Question 58 (9.4. Declare and use an ArrayList of a given type)

Given the following code:

```
package test;
import java.util.ArrayList;
public class Roller {
    public static void main(String[] args) {
        ArrayList<String> collector = new ArrayList<String>();
        collector.add("Study");
        collector.add(Integer.toOctalString(Integer.MAX_VALUE));

        ArrayList<String> names = new ArrayList<>();
        names.addAll(collector);
        names.add("Study");
        names.add(null);
        System.out.println(names.size());
    }
}
```

What is printed on the console?

A. 0
B. 2
C. 3

D. 4

Question 59 (7.5. Use abstract classes and interfaces)

Consider the following code:

```
 1. package test;
 2. abstract class Base {
 3.     public Base() {}
 4.     public Base(String s) {}
 5. }
 6. final class Impl extends Base {
 7. }
 8. public class Tester {
 9.     public static void main(String[] args) {
10.         Base base1 = new Base();
11.         Base base2 = new Impl();
12.         new Impl().toString();
13.         ((Base) new Impl()).toString();
14.     }
15. }
```

Does the code compile?

A. It compiles
B. No, compile error at line 10
C. No, compile error at line 12
D. No, compile error at line 13

Question 60 (6.1. Create methods with arguments and return values; including overloaded method)

Consider the following class:

```
class Engineer {
    public double calculate(double a, double b) { return 0; }
    private double calculate(double[] numbers) { return 0; }
    private void demandPayRise() {}
    public static void demandPayRise(BigDecimal byHowMuch) {}
    public long thinkInNumbers(int... numbers) { return 0; }
    public long thinkInNumbers(int a, int b) {return 1; }
}
```

Which of the following statements are true?

A. calculate are method overloads
B. demandPayRise are method overloads
C. thinkInNumbers are method overloads
D. calculate are not method overloads because they don't have the same access modifiers.
E. demandPayRise are not method overloads because one is static and the other is not.
F. thinkInNumbers are not method overloads because it is ambiguous which method

will be called when two **int**s are passed in.

Question 61 (4.1. Declare, instantiate, initialize and use a one-dimensional array)

Given

```
1. public class ArrayUtil2 {
2.     public static void main(String[] args) {
3.         char[] characters = { '1', '2', '3', '4'};
4.         int[] numbers = characters;
5.         for (char c : characters) {
6.             System.out.print(c);
7.         }
8.     }
9. }
```

A. The code prints 1234
B. Compile error at line 4
C. Compile error at line 5
D. Compile error at lines 4 and 5

Question 62 (5.2. Create and use for loops including the enhanced for loop)

Given

```
1. public class ArrayUtil2 {
2.     public static void main(String[] args) {
3.         Character[] characters = { '1', '2', '3', '4'};
4.         Object[] numbers = characters;
5.         for (char c : characters) {
6.             System.out.print(c);
7.         }
8.     }
9. }
```

Which of the following statement(s) is/are true?

A. The code prints 1234
B. Compile error at line 4
C. Compile error at line 5
D. Compile error at lines 4 and 5

Question 63 (2.2. Differentiate between object reference variables and primitive variables)

Which of the following are primitive wrappers?

A. Boolean
B. Char
C. Character

D. Int
E. Integer
F. Double
G. String
H. float

Question 64 (8.3. Describe the advantages of Exceptions handling)

Which of the following statements are true?

A. The **try** statement can be used to handle errors in your program
B. The **try-with-resources** statement closes all resources that implements **AutoCloseable**
C. You should catch all errors in your program
D. All exception classes are subclasses of **java.lang.Throwable**

Question 65 (8.4. Create and invoke a method that throws an exception)

Consider the following code:

```
public class VideoGame {
    public static void execute() {}
    public static void exit() {}
    public static void main(String[] args) {
        switch (args[0]) {
        default:
            exit();
            break;
        case "1":
        case "2":
        case "3":
            execute();
            break;
        }
    }
}
```

Which of the following statements are true?

A. The program may throw an exception
B. The **execute** method will be called if the value of the first argument to the program is “1”, “2” or “3”.
C. There is a compile error because the default case must be the last case in a switch statement
D. Nothing will be invoked if the value of the first argument to the program is “1” or “2”

Question 66 (6.1. Create methods with arguments and return values; including overloaded method)

Given the following code:

```
 1. package science;
 2. public class MathGenius {
 3.     public int add(int... numbers) {
 4.         int result = 0;
 5.         for (int n : numbers) {
 6.             result += n;
 7.         }
 8.         return result;
 9.     }
10.     public static void main(String[] args) {
11.         MathGenius mathGenius = new MathGenius();
12.         // some code
13.         System.out.println(result);
14.     }
15. }
```

Which of the following statements may replace the code in line 12 so the program will print **10**. (Choose all that apply).

A. int result = mathGenius.add({1, 2, 3, 4});
B. int result = mathGenius.add(new int[] {1, 2, 3, 4});
C. int result = mathGenius.add(1, 2, 3, 4);
D. int result = mathGenius.add(4, 3, 2, 1);

Question 67 (2.3. Know how to read or write to object fields)

Consider the following code:

```
public class Employee {
    protected String firstName;
    public int age;
    private String lastName;
    boolean member;
}
-----------------------------------
import test.sense.Employee;
public class Manager extends Employee {
    public void configure() {
        this.age = 12;
        this.firstName = "Aurora";
        this.lastName = "Valentino";
        this.member = false;
    }
}
```

Assuming **Employee** and **Manager** are not in the same package, which of the following statements in the **Manager** class will generate a compile error?

A. this.age = 12;
B. this.firstName = "Aurora";
C. this.lastName = "Valentino";
D. this.member = false;

Question 68 (2.3. Know how to read or write to object fields)

Examine the following code.

```
class Person {
    protected String firstName;
    public int age;
    private String lastName;
    boolean member;
}

class HR {
    public static void main(String[] args) {
        Person person = new Person();
        person.age = 30;
        person.firstName = "Brad";
        person.lastName = "Sumitomo";
        person.member = false;
    }
}
```

Assuming **Person** and **HR** are classes in the same package, which statements will not generate a compile error?

A. person.age = 30;
B. person.firstName = "Brad";
C. person.lastName = "Sumitomo";
D. person.member = false;

Question 69 (6.1. Create methods with arguments and return values; including overloaded method)

Consider the signature of the following method:

```
public int handle(int a, int b)
```

Which of these method signatures are the overloads of the method above?

A. public static int handle(int a, int b)
B. public void handle(int[] args)
C. private String handle(int x, int y)
D. public Object handle(long a, long b)

Question 70 (7.5. Use abstract classes and interfaces)

Consider these two interfaces:

```
interface Printable {
    float getCost();
}

interface Uploadable {
    double getCost();
```

}

Is it possible for a class to implement both interfaces?

A. Yes, a class can always implement any set of interfaces
B. Yes, and you must provide two implementations of getCost()
C. Yes, and you must only provide one implementation of getCost()
D. No, it is not possible. The class will not compile

Question 71 (1.5. Compare and contrast the features and components of Java such as: platform independence, object orientation, encapsulation, etc.)

Which of the following options are part of what makes Java platform-independent? (Choose all that apply)

A. Java programs are compiled into bytecode
B. Small programs are compiled into native code
C. The JVM is available in many platforms
D. The JVM can run Java bytecode

Question 72 (2.5. Develop code that uses wrapper classes such as Boolean, Double, and Integer)

Which of the following statements are valid? (Choose all that apply)

A. double w = Double.MAX_VALUE;
B. Integer s = new Integer(123);
C. Long t = new Integer(9);
D. long u = new Integer(99);

Question 73 (2.5. Develop code that uses wrapper classes such as Boolean, Double, and Integer)

What is the value of **s** after the following line of code is executed?

```
int s = new Double(23.8).intValue();
```

A. 23.8
B. 23
C. 24
D. 0

Question 74 (9.3 Create and manipulate calendar data using classes from java.time.LocalDateTime, java.time.LocalDate, java.time.LocalTime, java.time.format.DateTimeFormatter, java.time.Period)

Consider the following code snippet:

```
String pattern = ...;
DateTimeFormatter formatter = DateTimeFormatter.ofPattern(pattern);
LocalDate date = LocalDate.parse("24 04 2019", formatter);
```

Which date pattern can be used to parse "24 04 2019" to April 24, 2019? (Choose all that apply)

A. dd mm yyyy
B. dd MM yyyy
C. d M yyy
D. dd MMM yyyy

Question 75 (9.3 Create and manipulate calendar data using classes from java.time.LocalDateTime, java.time.LocalDate, java.time.LocalTime, java.time.format.DateTimeFormatter, java.time.Period)

Which of the following lines of code can be used to create a date representing yesterday?

A. LocalDate yesterday = LocalDate.now().minusDays(1);
B. LocalDate yesterday2 = LocalDate.now().plusDays(-1);
C. LocalDate yesterday3 = LocalDate.now().plus(1, TemporalUnit.DAYS);
D. LocalDate yesterday4 = LocalDate.now().minus(1, ChronoUnit.DAYS);

Question 76 (9.5 Write a simple Lambda expression that consumes a Lambda Predicate expression)

Which statements are true with regard to **java.util.function.Predicate**?

A. **Predicate** is a predefined functional interface
B. **Predicate** can take primitive arguments
C. **Predicate** can take an array argument
D. **Predicate** can take one or two arguments

Question 77 (9.5 Write a simple Lambda expression that consumes a Lambda Predicate expression)

Which of the following are valid statements?

A. Predicate<Integer> abc = x -> x == 0;
B. Predicate<Void> s = (x) -> 2 == 1;
C. Predicate<> w = (x) -> 2 == 1;
D. Predicate<Long> t = x -> {return true};

Appendix B
Mock Exam 1 Answers

The following are answers to the questions in the first mock exam. Each question may have more than one correct answer. Each of the questions also shows which exam topic it relates to.

Question 1 (7.1. Describe inheritance and its benefits)

The keyword **extends** can be used

A. to create a subclass from another class
B. to create a subinterface from another interface
C. to make a class implement an interface
D. to make an interface implement another interface

Answer: A, B.

The keyword **extends** can be used to create a child class from another class or a subinterface from another interface. C is incorrect because **extends** cannot be used to make a class implement an interface. For this, you use the keyword **implements**. Also in Java an interface cannot implement another interface, so D is incorrect.

Question 2 (6.3. Create and overload constructors; including impact on default constructors)

Given the following class

```
class RocketScience {
    public String description;
    public String getDescription() {
        return description;
    }
}
```

Which of the following statements are correct?

A. The class will not compile because it has no constructor.
B. The class will compile.
C. All Java classes, including abstract classes, need at least one constructor.
D. The class will compile but will throw an exception when instantiated.

Answer: B, C.

All Java classes, even abstract ones, need at least one constructor. If no constructor is declared explicitly in a class, the compiler will create a default constructor, which means C is correct. Therefore, the class above will compile, which means B is correct.

Question 3 (6.3. Create and overload constructors; including impact on default constructors)

Given

```
abstract class Abstract {
        public Abstract() {
        }
}
```

Which of these statements is true?

A. The class will not compile because an abstract class must not have a constructor.
B. The class will compile but cannot be instantiated.
C. The class will compile and can be instantiated.
D. The class will not compile because **Abstract** is a keyword and cannot be used as a class name.

Answer: B.

All Java classes, even abstract ones, need at least one constructor, so A is incorrect. However, you cannot instantiate an abstract class. Therefore, the class will compile but cannot be instantiated, so B is correct and C is incorrect. In addition, **abstract** is a Java keyword, but **Abstract** is not, which means D is incorrect.

Question 4 (1.4. Import other Java packages to make them accessible in your code)

Which of the following statements about the default package is true.

A. You cannot import a class in the default package.
B. A class in the default package can only be used in other classes in the default package.
C. A class in the default package can be imported into classes in non-default packages.
D. A class in the default package can import classes in non-default packages.

Answer: A, B, D.

You cannot import a class in the default package. However, a class in the default package can use other classes in the default package without importing them, so statement B is also true. Finally, a class in the default package can import other classes in non-default packages.

Question 5 (2.1. Declare and initialize variables (including casting of primitive data types))

Which ones are valid variable declarations?

A. long row_count;
B. long $;
C. long table$;
D. long _g5;
E. int $final_;
F. int static;

Answer: A, B, C, D, E.

A and D are correct because the underscore character can be used in an identifier. B, C and E are also correct because $ can be used in a Java identifier, even though it is normally only used in machine-generated code. F is invalid because **static** is a reserved keyword and cannot be used as a variable name.

Question 6 (1.2. Define the structure of a Java class)

Here is the content of the **Computer.java** file.

```
1.   package test;
2.
3.   class A {
4.
5.   }
6.
7.   final class b {
8.
9.   }
```

Which of the following statements is (are) true?

A. The code will not compile because the file does not contain a **Computer** class.
B. A compile error at line 7 because a class name must start with a capital.
C. Compile errors at lines 3 and 7 because **Computer.java** may only contain a class with the same name as the file.
D. The code will compile.

Answer: D.

A is incorrect because the rule that says a Java class must reside in a file with the same name as the class only applies to public classes. The code above has no compile error and will compile, so D is correct and B and C are incorrect.

Question 7 (9.1. Manipulate data using the StringBuilder class and its methods)

What is the output of this code snippet:

```
StringBuilder sb = new StringBuilder("Best phone cameras!");
System.out.println(sb.replace(1,  5,  "Worst"));
```

A. Worst phone cameras!
B. WorstBest phone cameras!
C. BWorstphone cameras!
D. Worstphone cameras!

Answer: C.

Here is the signature of the **StringBuilder** class's **replace** method:

```
public StringBuilder replace(int start, int end, String substring)
```

It works by first removing the characters between the two **int** arguments, including the character at the start position but not including the character at the end position. Note that the positions specified are zero-based, which means position 0 refers to the first character. The method then inserts the specified substring at the start position.

sb.replace(1, 5, "Worst") removes the second, third, fourth and fifth characters (resulting "Bphone cameras!") and inserts the word "Worst" at position 1 (resulting "BWorstphone cameras!").

Question 8 (3.3. Create if and if/else and ternary constructs)

Consider the following code snippet:

```
1. for (int i=10; i<20; i=i+2) {
2.      ...
3.           System.out.println(i);
4.      }
5. }
```

What can be inserted in line 2 to make the code print 10? (Choose all that apply)

A. if (i == 10) {
B. if (i % 5 == 0) {
C. if (i = 10) {
D. if (i % 2 == 5)

Answer: A, B.

Note that the update statement in the **for** loop is **i=i+2**, which means the loop will have five iterations with i equal to 10, 12, 14, 16 and 18.

A is correct because the expression (i == 10) returns true only if i equals 10 and therefore the **println** method will only be called when i equals 10.

B is correct because the % operator is the remainder operator that calculates the remainder of a division operation. 10 % 5 = 0, whereas 12 % 5 = 2, 14 % 5 = 4, 16 % 2 = 1, 18 % 5 = 3.

C is incorrect because = is the assignment operator and this will cause a compile error.

D is incorrect because i % 2 will not return 5 for any integer.

Question 9 (1.3. Create executable Java applications with a main method; run a Java program from the command line; including console output)

Given

```
package com.example;
public class Printer {
```

```
    public static void main(String[] args) {
        System.out.print(args[1]);
        System.out.print(args[2]);
    }
}
```

The program is invoked using this command.

```
java com.example.Printer Sonic "Drill" 'Toxic'
```

What is printed on the console?

A. SonicDrill
B. Sonic"Drill"
C. "Drill"'Toxic'
D. DrillToxic

Answer: D.

The first element of **args** is args[0]. The program therefore prints the second and third arguments. Quotes are stripped before being passed to the program.

Question 10 (3.2. Use Java operators; including parenthesis to override operator precedence)

Consider the following code:

```
int a = 2 + 3 * 6;
int b = (2 + 3) * 6;
System.out.println(a + b);
```

What is printed on the standard out upon the execution of the code?

A. 60
B. 50
C. 40
D. 30

Answer: B.

The multiplication sign has precedence over addition, so 2 + 3 * 6 = 20 because the multiplication (3 * 6) is evaluated first and its result is added to 2. On the other hand, parentheses have precedence over multiplication, so (2 + 3) * 6 is 30. The result of a + b is therefore 20 + 30 = 50.

Question 11 (1.1. Define the scope of variables)

Consider the following code snippet that contains named regions R, S, T, U, V and X.

```
int m = 0;
// ------- R --------
while (m < 5) {
  // ------- S --------
    for (int n = 0; n < 3; n++) {
```

```
        // ------- T --------
          System.out.println(m);
          System.out.println(n);
        // ------- U --------
      }
    // ------- V --------
    m++;
  }
  // ------- X --------
```

Which of the following statements are true?

A. *n* cannot be used in region R.
B. *m* and *n* can be used in region T.
C. *m* and *n* can be used in region U.
D. *m* and *n* can be used in region V.
E. *m* can be used in regions S, T, U and V.
F. *m* and *n* are out of scope in Region X.

Answer: A, B, C, E.

A is correct because the scope of **n** is only in the for block. Therefore, n cannot be used in region R.

B is correct because **m** and **n** are visible in region T.

C is correct because **m** and **n** are visible in region U

D is incorrect because **n** is not visible in region V.

E is correct because **m** is in scope in regions S, T, U and V.

F is incorrect because only **n** is out of scope in region X. **m** is still visible in region X.

Question 12 (1.3. Create executable Java applications with a main method; run a Java program from the command line; including console output)

Given

```
package test;
public class Hello {
    protected static void main(String[] args) {
        System.out.println("Hello, World!");
    }
}
```

Which of the following statements is (are) true?

A. The program does not compile.
B. The program compiles.
C. The program can be executed.
D. The program cannot be executed.

Answer: B, D.

Nothing prevents you from naming a protected static void method **main**. However to make a class executable, the **main** method must be public and static, return no value, and accept one argument that is a String array.

Question 13 (2.1. Declare and initialize variables (including casting of primitive data types))

Consider this code snippet:

```
int i = 015;
if (i == 13L)
    System.out.println("Equal");
else
    System.out.println("Not equal");
```

What will be printed on the console when the code is executed?

A. Nothing will be printed.
B. Equal
C. Not equal
D. Equal Not equal

Answer: B.

Remember that 015 is an octal number that is equivalent to 13. Comparing an **int** with a **long** having the same value evaluates to true.

Question 14 (6.4. Apply access modifiers)

Given the following class declaration

```
modifier class Pointer {}
```

Which modifiers can be used for class **Pointer**?

A. public
B. private
C. protected
D. final
E. static
F. abstract

Answer: A, D, F.

Only **public**, **final** and **abstract** are valid modifiers for top level class declarations.

Question 15 (6.4. Apply access modifiers)

Given the following method declaration

```
modifier int calculate(int a, int b)
```

Which modifiers can be used for class **Nested**?

A. public
B. private
C. protected
D. final
E. static
F. abstract
G. strictfp

Answer: A, B, C, D, E, F, G.

All these modifiers can be used on methods. However, you cannot use **final** and **abstract** on the same method.

Question 16 (6.4. Apply access modifiers)

Given the following interface declaration

```
modifier interface Device {}
```

Which modifiers can be used for interface **Device**?

A. public
B. private
C. protected
D. final
E. static
F. abstract

Answer: A, F.

Only public and abstract are valid modifiers for top level interfaces. The use of abstract is valid but redundant as all interfaces are implicitly abstract.

Question 17 (7.4. Use super and this to access objects and constructors)

Given

```
package test;
public class Parent {
    public Parent() {
        System.out.print("Parent...");
    }
    public static void main(String[] args) {
        Child1 c1 = new Child1();
        Child2 c2 = new Child2();
    }
}

class Child1 extends Parent {
    public Child1() {
        super();
        System.out.print("Child1...");
    }
}
```

```
class Child2 extends Parent {
    public Child2() {
        System.out.print("Child2...");
    }
}
```

What will be printed on the console when the **Parent** class is executed?

A. Child1...Child2...
B. Parent...Child1...Child2...
C. Child1...Parent...Child2...
D. Parent...Child1...Parent...Child2...

Answer: D.

Instantiating a child class will also instantiate all its parents. **super()** is automatically called from a constructor if the first line of code in the constructor is not **super()**.

Question 18 (7.4. Use super and this to access objects and constructors)

Consider the following code

```
package test;
public class Parent {
    public Parent() {
        System.out.print("Parent...");
    }
    public static void main(String[] args) {
        Child1 c1 = new Child1("Joe");
        Child2 c2 = new Child2("Jane");
    }
}

class Child1 extends Parent {
    public Child1(String name) {
        super();
        System.out.print("Child1...");
    }
}

class Child2 extends Parent {
    public Child2(String name) {
        System.out.print("Child2...");
    }
}
```

Which of the following statements is (are) true?

A. The program will not compile because the **Parent** class does not have a constructor that takes a **String**.
B. The program will not compile because **Child1** and **Child2** do not have a constructor that matches the signature of the only constructor in **Parent**.
C. The program will compile and when executed it will print

Child1...Parent...Child2...

D. The program will compile and when executed it will print **Parent...Child1...Parent...Child2...**

Answer: D.

By default, a constructor (regardless of its signature) in a derived class will call the no-argument constructor of its parent, unless there is another **super** statement that calls a non-default constructor of its parent.

Question 19 (7.4. Use super and this to access objects and constructors)

Given

```
package test;
public class Parent {
    public Parent(String name) {
        System.out.print("Parent...");
    }
       public static void main(String[] args) {
           Child1 c1 = new Child1("Joe");
           Child2 c2 = new Child2("Jane");
       }
}

class Child1 extends Parent {
    public Child1(String name) {
        super(name);
        System.out.print("Child1...");
    }
}

class Child2 extends Parent {
    public Child2(String name) {
        System.out.print("Child2...");
    }
}
```

Which of the following statements is (are) true?

A. The program will not compile because the **Parent** class does not have a no-argument constructor.
B. The program will not compile because the constructor in **Child2** will try to call the default constructor in **Parent** and such a constructor does not exist.
C. The program will compile and when executed it will print **Child1...Parent...Child2...**
D. The program will compile and when executed it will print **Parent...Child1...Parent...Child2...**

Answer: B.

By default, a constructor (regardless of its signature) in a derived class will call the no-argument constructor of its parent, unless there is another **super** statement that calls a non-default constructor of its parent.

Question 20 (1.4. Import other Java packages to make them accessible in your code)

Given

```
1.  package test;
2.  ...
3.  public class MathUtil {
4.      double twoPis = PI * 2;
5.  }
```

To prevent line 4 from causing a compile error, which line must be inserted into line 2?

A. import static Math.PI;.
B. import static java.lang.Math;
C. import static java.lang.Math.PI;
D. import java.lang.Math.PI;

Answer: C.

To use a static member of a type in another type, import static that member prefixed by the fully-qualified name of the type containing the static member.

Question 21 (1.4. Import other Java packages to make them accessible in your code)

Consider the following code snippet:

```
1.  import static java.lang.Integer.MAX_VALUE;
2.  public class Storage {
3.      public static void main(String[] args) {
4.          int i = MAX_VALUE;
5.      }
6.  }
```

What do you have to insert into line 1 so you can use the static field **MAX_VALUE** in the **Integer** class?

A. import static java.lang.Integer.MAX_VALUE;.
B. import static java.lang.Integer;
C. import java.lang.Integer.MAX_VALUE;
D. import java.lang.Integer;

Answer: A.

To use a static member of a type in another type, import static that member prefixed by the fully-qualified name of the type containing the static member.

Question 22 (4.1. Declare, instantiate, initialize and user a one-dimensional array)

Which of the following are valid array declarations? (Choose all that apply)

A. int stats[] = {Integer.MIN_VALUE, Integer.MAX_VALUE };
B. double[] remainders[] = {1, 2, 3};
C. short[] smallNumbers = new short[5];
D. String keys[] = new ArrayList<String>();

Answer: A, C.

A and C are valid array declarations.

B is incorrect because **remainders** is a multidimensional array and expects a multidimensional array but is assigned a one-dimensional array.

D is incorrect because an **ArrayList** is not an array.

Question 23 (9.2. Creating and manipulating Strings)

Assuming **s** is a **String**, which of the following expressions returns the number of characters in **s**?

A. s.size
B. s.size()
C. s.length
D. s.length()
E. s.chars
F. s.chars()

Answer: D.

A and B are incorrect because there is no accessible member of the **String** class that is named **size**.

C is incorrect because **String** does not have a field named **length**.

D is correct. The **length** method returns the number of characters in the **String**.

E is incorrect because **String** does not have a field called **chars**.

F is incorrect because even though there is a **chars** method in **String**, it does not return the number of characters in a **String**.

Question 24 (6.2. Apply the static keyword to methods and fields)

Given the following class:

```
package demo;
public class Demo100 {
    private void doSomething() {
        System.out.println("Hello, World!");
    }

    public static void main(String[] args) {
        doSomething();
    }
}
```

What is the output of the program?

A. The program will print "Hello, World!"
B. The program will print an empty string
C. The program will fail to compile because the doSomething method is private
D. The program will fail to compile because you cannot access a non-static method from a static method

Answer: D.

You can only invoke a non-static method by first creating an instance of the class containing the method. In order for the class to compile, you can either change **doSomething** to static like this:

```
private static void doSomething() {
    System.out.println("Hello, World!");
}
```

Or, you can create an instance of **Demo100** and call the method:

```
Demo100 demo = new Demo100();
demo.doSomething();
```

You can access a private method from the same class, so there is no need to change the method's access modifier.

Question 25 (2.1. Declare and initialize variables (including casting of primitive data types))

Consider the following code snippet:

```
1. package util;
2. public class NumberUtil {
3.     public int getTodaysNumber() {
4.         private int i = 9;
5.         return i;
6.     }
7. }
```

Which statement is true with regard to the class above?

A. The program will compile
B. The getTodaysNumber method returns 9
C. The getTodaysNumber method can be accessed from static methods
D. The program will not compile

Answer: D.

Access modifiers can only be applied to class-level variables or fields. You will therefore get a compile error at line 4.

Question 26 (3.1. Use Java operators; including parentheses to override operator precedence)

Examine the following code:

```
package com.example.test;
public class Test101 {
    public static void main(String[] args) {
        int i = 10;
        System.out.println(i < 11);
    }
}
```

What is the output of this class?

A. 10<11
B. 1011
C. true
D. false

Answer: C.

The boolean expression (i < 11) is evaluated and the result is passed to **System.out.println**. Since i = 10, i < 11 evaluates to true.

Question 27 (6.1. Create methods with arguments and return values; including overloaded methods)

Consider this code snippet:

```
 1. public class MathUtil {
 2.     public static int add(int a, int b) {
 3.         a++;
 4.         b++;
 5.         return a + b;
 6.     }
 7.     public static void main(String[] args) {
 8.         int m = 10;
 9.         int n = 20;
10.         int o = add(m, n);
11.         //
12.     }
13. }
```

Which of the following statement(s) is/are true?

A. At line 11 the value of m is 11
B. At line 11 the value of n is 21
C. At line 11 the value of m is 10
D. At line 11 the value of n is 20

Answer: C, D.

Primitives are passed to methods as values. Changes to the method arguments do not affect the passed-in primitives.

Question 28 (6.3. Create and overload constructors; including impact on default constructors)

What can be said about this class?

```
public class Printer {
    private String name;
    public Printer() {
        this("Default");
    }
    public Printer(String name) {
        this.name = name;
    }
    public static void main(String[] args) {
        Printer printer = new Printer();
    }
}
```

A. The code creates two instances of **Printer**
B. The code creates one instance of **Printer**
C. The code calls the no-argument constructor and then the one-argument constructor
D. The name field will be assigned the value "Default"

Answer: B, C, D.

The program creates an instance of **Printer** by calling its no-argument constructor. The **this** keyword is used to call the other constructor, passing the string "Default". As a result, the **name** field will be given a value.

Question 29 (5.1. Create and use while loops)

What is the output of the following class?

```
public class Loop1 {
    public static void main(String[] args) {
        int x = 0;
        while (x < 5)
            while (x < 3)
                System.out.print(x++);
    }
}
```

A. 012 then stops
B. 123 then stops
C. 012 then loops indefinitely
D. 123 then loops indefinitely

Answer: C.

The value of **x** is 0 when the first **while** loop is evaluated. Since 0 is less than 5, the interpreter enters the second loop. In the second loop, it prints the value of **x** and increments it. As a result, 012 is printed and the code exits the second loop with the value of x equal to 3. Since the interpreter cannot reenter the second loop and **x** does not increment further, the program will run indefinitely.

Question 30 (3.4. Use a switch statement)

Given the following code

```
 1. public class Printer {
 2.     public static void main(String[] args) {
 3.         int x1 = 1;
 4.         int x2 = 2;
 5.         int y = 4;
 6.         switch (y) {
 7.         case x1:
 8.             System.out.println("one");
 9.             break;
10.         case x2:
11.             System.out.println("two");
12.             break;
13.         default:
14.             System.out.println("unknown");
15.         }
16.     }
17. }
```

Which of the statement(s) is/are true?

A. The program prints "one"
B. The program prints "two"
C. The program prints "unknown"
D. Compile error

Answer: D.

Each case in a **switch** statement must be given a constant to evaluate. As the first and second cases are given a variable, there will be compile errors at lines 7 and 10.

Question 31 (7.2. Develop code that demonstrates the use of polymorphism; including overriding and object type versus reference type)

Given the following code:

```
interface Printable {}
class Document{}
class EBook extends Document implements Printable {}
```

Which of the following statements will not cause a compile error?

A. Printable printable1 = new Printable();
B. Printable printable2 = new Document();
C. Printable printable3 = new EBook();
D. Document document1 = new Document();
E. Document document2 = new EBook();
F. EBook ebook1 = new EBook();
G. EBook ebook2 = new Document();

Answer: C, D, E, F.

A is invalid because you cannot instantiate an interface.

B is illegal because there is no is-a relationship between **Printable** and **Document**. Therefore, assigning an instance of **Document** to a reference variable of type **Printable** is not allowed.

C is correct because **EBook** is an implementation of **Printable**. You can therefore assign an **EBook** instance of a variable of type **Printable**.

D is correct because this is just creating an instance of a class and assign the instance to a reference variable of the same type.

E is also correct because **EBook** is a subclass of **Document**. **EBook** and **Document** have an is-a relationship: An **EBook** is a **Document**.

F is definitely correct because you are creating an instance of a class and assign it to a reference variable of the same type.

G is not allowed because a **Document** is not necessarily an **EBook**.

Question 32 (1.3. Create executable Java applications with a main method; run a Java program from the command line; including console output)

Consider the following code:

```
package test;
public class TasteOfMain {
    public static void main(String[] args) {
        System.out.println(args.length);
    }
}
```

The class is invoked with this command line command

```
java test.TasteOfMain \ \\\ \\
```

What is the value of **args.length**?

A. 1
B. 2
C. 3
D. 4

Answer: A.

There is only one argument passed to the program for the following reason. The backslash character (\) can be used to escape another character. The first backslash character escapes the space and the second escapes the third escape. The fourth backslash escapes another space and the fifth escapes the sixth backslash. The argument received is four characters long and consists of two spaces and two backslashes:

```
 \ \
```

Question 33 (2.4. Explain an object's lifecycle (creation, "dereference by assignment" and garbage collection))

Given

```
1.  class Resident {
2.      public void live() {
3.      }
4.  }
5.
6.  public class Printer {
7.      public static void main(String[] args) {
8.          Resident r1 = new Resident();
9.          Resident r2 = new Resident();
10.         r1 = null;
11.         System.out.println(r1);
12.         r2 = r1;
13.         System.out.println(r2);
14.     }
15. }
```

Which of the following statements are true?

A. Two objects will be garbage collected at line 14.
B. One object will be garbage collected at line 12.
C. The object referenced by **r1** is eligible for garbage collection at line 11.
D. The object referenced by **r2** is eligible for garbage collection at line 13.

Answer: C, D.

An object is eligible for garbage collection if it is no longer referenced by any variable. Assigning null to an reference variable removes the reference to an object. Therefore, C and D are correct.

A and B are incorrect because there is no guarantee if or when an object that is eligible for garbage collection will be garbage-collected. The garbage collector runs on a low-priority thread and an intelligent garbage collector will not start destroying objects unless the heap is close to full.

Question 34 (9.1. Manipulate data using the StringBuilder class and its methods)

Given

```
package test;
public class StatementComposer {

    public String getStatement(int id, String name) {
        StringBuilder s = new StringBuilder();
        s.append("SELECT * FROM employees WHERE ");
        s.append("id = " + id);
        s.append(" OR ");
```

```
        if (name == null) {
            s.delete(s.length() - 4, s.length());
        } else {
            s.append("name = '" + name + "'");
        }
        return s.toString();
    }
    public static void main(String[] args) {
        StatementComposer sc = new StatementComposer();
        System.out.println(sc.getStatement(3, null));
    }
}
```

What is the output of the class?

A. SELECT * FROM employees WHERE id = 3
B. SELECT * FROM employees WHERE id =
C. SELECT * FROM employees WHERE id = 3 OR name = 'null'
D. SELECT * FROM employees WHERE id = 3 OR name = null

Answer: A.

The **StringBuilder** object in the **getStatement** method is first given the value "SELECT * FROM employees WHERE ". Then, "id = 3" is added to it and the length of the **StringBuilder** becomes 40. Because **name** is null, the **if** statement evaluates to true and the following line of code is executed:

```
s.delete(36, 40);
```

The **delete** method removes the characters in a substring of the **StringBuilder**. The substring begins at the specified start and extends to the character at index (end - 1) or to the end of the sequence if the length is shorter than (end - 1). This line of code effectively removes the last four characters in the **StringBuilder**.

Question 35 (3.2. Test equality between Strings and other objects using == and equals())

What is the output of this program?

```
package test;
public class StringTest {
    public static void main(String[] args) {
        String s1 = "Java";
        String s2 = "Rocks";
        String s3 = "JavaRocks";
        System.out.print(s3 == s1 + s2);
        System.out.print(".");
        System.out.print(s3.equals(s1 + s2));
    }
}
```

A. false.false
B. false.true
C. true.true

D. true.false

Answer: B.

Comparing string variables with == tests if the variables point to the same object. Comparing string variables with equals tests if the string objects have the same value. Most of the time, when you compare strings, you are interested in knowing whether or not the string values are equal.

Question 36 (2.7. Creating and manipulating Strings)

Consider the following method:

```
public String getSubstring(String s) {
    int index1 = s.indexOf(".");
    int index2 = -1;
    if (index1 != -1) {
        index2 = s.indexOf(".", index1 + 1);
    }
    if (index2 == -1) {
        return s.substring(index1);
    } else {
        return s.substring(index1, index2);
    }
}
```

What is the method's return value if the string "Hello.World" is passed to it?

A. Hello
B. World
C. .World
D. HelloWorld

Answer: C.

The **indexOf** method returns the zero-based position (meaning the first character is at position 0) of the first occurrence of a substring in a string. In this case, **"Hello.World".indexOf(".")** returns 5. Because there is only one dot in "Hello.World", the value of **index2** will be -1 and **"Hello.World".substring(5)** returns ".World".

Question 37 (3.3. Create if and if/else and ternary constructs)

What is the value of **y** after this code is executed?

```
int i = 10;
int y = 50;
if (i + y < 70) {
    if (i + y < 60) {
        y = 500;
    } else {
        y = 5000;
    }
}
```

A. 50
B. 500
C. 5000
D. 10

Answers: C.

The code starts by setting **x** to 10 and **y** to 50. The boolean expression to the first if statement evaluates to true because 10 + 50 < 70. The expression to the second if evaluates to false, so the else block is executed, in effect setting y to 5000.

Question 38 (9.4. Declare and use an ArrayList of a given type)

Which statement(s) creates an **ArrayList** of **String**s with an initial capacity of 20? (Choose all that apply)

A. ArrayList<String> names = new ArrayList<>();
B. ArrayList<String> names = new ArrayList<>(20);
C. ArrayList<String> names = new ArrayList<String>();
D. ArrayList<String> names = new ArrayList<String>(20);

Answers: B, D.

By default, an **ArrayList** is created with an initial capacity of 10 elements. To reserve a space for 20 elements, pass 20 to the constructor. A and C are incorrect because the resulting **ArrayList** will have an initial capacity of 10. B and D are correct.

Question 39 (4.2. Declare, instantiate, initialize and use multi-dimensional array)

Here is a multidimensional array:

```
int[][] tableCells = {{1, 2, 3, 4}, {5, 6, 7, 8}, {9, 10, 11}};
```

What is the value of **tableCells[1][3]**?

A. 3
B. 9
C. 8
D. 11

Answer: C.

tableCells[1] refers to the second row, which contains {5, 6, 7, 8}. **tableCells[1][3]** refers to the fourth member of the row, which is 8.

Question 40 (4.2. Declare, instantiate, initialize and use multidimensional array)

Which of the following are valid declarations of multidimensional arrays? (Choose all that apply)

A. int[][] tableCells = new int[0][0];

B. String names[][] = {};
C. String[] employees[] = {{"Henry Wong", "Hendrick Takada"}};
D. long diameters[] = null;
E. long wheels[][] = null;
F. Object[][] cars = new cars[][];

Answer: A, B, C, E.

A is a valid declaration of a multidimensional array even though the dimensions are 0.

B is also valid and is assigned an empty array.

C is legal. Square brackets after the type and square brackets after the variable name make it multidimensional.

D is a legal declaration of a one-dimensional array. It is therefore not a correct answer.

E is also valid even though it is assigned null.

F is invalid as cars in new cars[][] is not a type.

Question 41 (4.2. Declare, instantiate, initialize and use multidimensional array)

Consider the following class:

```
1. package test;
2. public class MultiDimArray {
3.
4.     public static void main(String[] args) {
5.         int[][] stickers = new int[4][];
6.         for (int i = 0; i < stickers.length; i++) {
7.             stickers[i] = new int[4];
8.         }
9.         System.out.println(stickers[0][0]);
10.    }
11.}
```

What happens if you try to compile and run this class?

A. Compile error at line 5
B. Compile error at line 7
C. It compiles and prints 0
D. It compiles and throws a runtime exception

Answer: C.

A is incorrect as you can declare an array that has zero dimension.

B is incorrect because stickers was initialized and given proper values.

C is correct as by elements of an array of primitives are assigned the default value of the type. In this case, since it is an int array, each of its elements is assigned 0.

D is incorrect as it does not throw an exception.

Question 42 (5.3. Create and use do/while loops)

Consider the following code.

```
package test;
public class Repeater {
    public static void main(String[] args) {
        if (args.length == 0) return;
        int input = 0;
        try {
            input = Integer.parseInt(args[0]);
            do {
                System.out.print(input + " ");
                input += 5;
            } while(input < 5);
        } catch (NumberFormatException e) {
            System.out.println("Not an integer");
        }
    }
}
```

What does the class print if it is invoked using this command line command?

```
java test.Repeater 50 20
```

A. Nothing
B. 50 55 60 65 70
C. 5
D. 50

Answer: D.

The first argument (50) is converted to an **int** and assigned to **input**. The **do** block will be executed at least once, so it will print "50 " and increment **input** by 5. Next, the value of **input** is compared to 5. Since 50 is not less than 5, the **do** block is not executed again.

Question 43 (5.4. Compare loop constructs)

Consider the following while loop:

```
1. int x = 0;
2. while (true) {
3.     x++;
4.     if (x > 5) break;
5.     System.out.println(x);
6. }
```

Which of the following **for** statement can be used to replace line 2 without changing what the code does?

A. for (int x = 0; x < 5; x++) {
B. for (; x < 5;) {
C. for (; ;) {

D. for (int y = 0; y < 5; y++) {

Answer: B, C, D.

A is incorrect because x is redefined in the for statement and it will cause a compile error.

B is correct because the for block will loop until x is equal to 5, which will make the loop iterates five times.

C is correct because for (;;) is the same as while(true)

D is correct and will cause the loop iterates five times.

Question 44 (5.5. Use break and continue)

Consider this **for** loop:

```
for (int i = 0; i < 10; i++) {
    if (i % 2 == 0) continue;
    if (i % 5 == 0) break;
    System.out.print(i + " ");
}
```

What is printed on the console if the code snippet is executed?

A. 1 2 3 4 5 6 7 8 9
B. 1 3 5 7 9
C. 1 3 5
D. 1 3

Answer: D.

A **continue** statement in a **for** loop causes the code below the **continue** statement to be skipped. A **break** statement in a **for** loop causes the loop to terminate.

The first **if** statement tests if **i** is evenly divisible by 2. If it is, the **continue** statement is called and this causes the rest of the **for** block to be skipped. Consequently, if **i** equals 0, 2, 4, 6 or 8, **continue** will be called.

The second **if** statement tests if **i** is evenly divisible by 5, which it is when i = 5. When this happens, the **break** statement is called and the loop terminates. The **print** method is only called when i equals 1 and i equals 3.

Question 45 (6.5. Apply encapsulation principles to a class)

Which of the following statements are true about encapsulation?

A. Instance variables are made private
B. For each instance variable, there is a get method that returns the instance variable. This method is public
C. For each instance variable that is writable, there is a set method that is public.
D. Class fields are made protected.

Answer: A, B, C.

A, B and C are correct. D is incorrect because protected fields are accessible from child classes and classes in the same package.

Question 46 (6.6. Determine the effect upon object references and primitive values when they are passed into methods that change the values)

Consider the following code:

```
package test;
public class MathGenius {
    public void printDouble(int a, int b) {
        a *= 2;
        b *= 2;
        System.out.print(a + "__");
        System.out.print(b);
    }
    public static void main(String[] args) {
        int x = 10;
        int y = 20;
        new MathGenius().printDouble(x, y);
        System.out.print("__" + x + "__" + y);
    }
}
```

What is the output of the program?

A. 20__40__20__40
B. 20__40__10__20
C. 10__20__10__20
D. 10__20__20__40

Answer: B.

Primitive variables are passed to a method by value, which means a copy of the primitive is created. As such, the values of **x** and **y** do not change.

Question 47 (6.6. Determine the effect upon object references and primitive values when they are passed into methods that change the values)

Consider the following code:

```
package test;
class Point {
    int x, y;
    Point(int x, int y) {
        this.x = x;
        this.y = y;
    }
    public void setX(int x) {
        this.x = x;
```

```
    }
    public void setY(int y) {
        this.y = y;
    }
    public int getX() {
        return x;
    }
    public int getY() {
        return y;
    }
    public String toString() {
        return x + "__" + y;
    }
}

public class PointDemo {
    public void enlargeAndPrintPoint(Point point) {
        point.setX(point.getX() * 2);
        point.setY(point.getY() * 2);
        System.out.print(point);
    }
    public static void main(String[] args) {
        Point point = new Point(100, 200);
        new PointDemo().enlargeAndPrintPoint(point);;
        System.out.print("__" + point);
    }
}
```

What is the output of the program?

A. 200__400__200__400
B. 200__400__100__200
C. 100__200__100__200
D. 100__200__200__400

Answer: A.

Point is a reference type, which means if it is passed in to a method, it is passed by reference. In other words, the **Point** object created in the **main** method and the one referenced in the **enlargeAndPrintPoint** method are the same object. Changing it in **enlargeAndPrintPoint** affects the object referenced in the **main** method.

Question 48 (7.2. Develop code that demonstrates the use of polymorphism; including overriding and object type versus reference type)

Given

```
package temporary;
class Animal {
    public void walk() {
        System.out.print("Animal.walk()");
    }
```

```
}
class Giraffe extends Animal {
    public int getLegCount() {
        return 4;
    }
}
public class Main {
    public static void main(String[] args) {
        Animal animal = new Giraffe();
        // some code
        int legCount = animal.getLegCount();
    }
}
```

Which of the following statements are true?

A. This is polymorphism in action.
B. The code will compile
C. The code will not compile because the **getLegCount** method is not part of **Animal**.
D. The code will compile but will thrown a **NullPointerException**

Answer: C.

The code will not compile because the **Animal** class does not contain **getLegCount**. To get around this, cast **animal** to **Giraffe**, like so:

```
int legCount = ((Giraffe) animal).getLegCount();
```

Question 49 (7.3. Determine when casting is necessary)

Consider the following code:

```
package test;
class Request {
    public void parse(String request) {
        System.out.print("Request.parse()");
    }
}
class HttpRequest extends Request {
    public String getHttpMethod() {
        return "post";
    }
}
public class Server {
    public static void main(String[] args) {
        Request request1 = new Request();
        HttpRequest httpRequest1 = (HttpRequest) request1;
        HttpRequest httpRequest2 = new HttpRequest();
        httpRequest2.parse("");
    }
}
```

Which of the following methods are untrue?

A. Compile error at line 15
B. Compile error at line 17
C. No compile error, but there will be a runtime error if the class is executed
D. No compile error and no runtime error if the class is execute

Answer: A, B, D.

Note that the question wants you to point out which statements are false. A is false because there is no compile error at line 15. It is clear that request1 is of type **Request** and cannot be cast to **HttpRequest**. However, the compiler does not know that, so it does not generate a compile error.

B is false because there is no compile error at line 17. It is clear that **httpRequest2** is of type **HttpRequest** and **parse** is a public method defined in a parent class.

C is true because line 15 will throw a runtime error. You cannot cast a parent class to a subclass. Remember, an **Animal** is not necessarily a **Lion**, so you cannot cast an **Animal** to **Lion**. For the same reason, you cannot cast a **Request** to **HttpRequest**. However, you are not looking for true statements, so this option is not included in the answer.

D is false because there is a runtime error when the code is executed.

Question 50 (8.1. Differentiate among checked exceptions, unchecked exceptions, and Errors)

Which of the following statements are true?

A. A checked exception is internal to the program
B. Errors should not be caught
C. A runtime exception is an unchecked exception
D. A runtime exception is a checked exception
E. Applications can recover from checked exceptions

Answer: A, B, C, E.

A checked exception is an exceptional condition that a well-written program should anticipate and try to recover from. All exceptions are checked exceptions except **Error**, **RuntimeException**, and those derived from either of the two classes.

An error is an exceptional condition that is external to the program that it is unable to anticipate or recover from. Errors are represented by **java.lang.Error** and its subclasses.

A runtime exception is an exceptional condition that is internal to the program, and that the program usually cannot anticipate or recover from. A runtime exception is normally caused by a programming bugs. Runtime exceptions are unchecked exceptions.

Question 51 (8.2. Create a try-catch block and determine how exceptions alter normal program flow)

Consider the following code:

```
package test;
public class VideoGame {
```

```
    public static void main(String[] args) {
        int playerCount = 1;
        try {
            playerCount = Integer.parseInt(args[0]);
            if (playerCount > 1) {
                System.out.println("Multiple players found.");
            } else {
                System.out.println("One player");
            }
        } catch (ArrayIndexOutOfBoundsException e) {
            System.out.println("Please determine the number of players");
        } catch (NumberFormatException e) {
            System.out.println("Unrecognized number of players");
        }
    }
}
```

What is the output of the program if invoked using "**java test.VideoGame 1.0**"?

A. A runtime exception occurs
B. The program prints "Multiple players found"
C. The program prints "One player"
D. The program prints "Unrecognized number of players"

Answer: D.

The argument "1.0" cannot be parsed to an int. As such, a **NumberFormatException** will be thrown.

Question 52 (8.5. Recognize common exception classes (such as NullPointerException. ArithmeticException, ArrayIndexOutOfBoundsException, ClassCastException))

Which of the following are not runtime exceptions?

A. ClassCastException
B. NullPointerException
C. ArrayIndexOutOfBoundsException
D. NumberFormatException
E. OutOfMemoryError

Answer: E.

A, B, C and D are incorrect as **NullPointerException**, **ArrayIndexOutOfBoundsException** and **NumberFormatException** are derived from **RuntimeException**.

E is correct because **OutOfMemoryError** is an error and not a runtime exception.

Question 53 (8.5. Recognize common exception classes (such as NullPointerException. ArithmeticException, ArrayIndexOutOfBoundsException, ClassCastException))

Which of the following are caused by external errors?

A. ClassCastException
B. OutOfMemoryError
C. RuntimeException
D. StackOverflowError
E. Throwable

Answer: B, D.

A is incorrect because **ClassCastException** is a runtime exception and not an error.

B is correct because **OutOfMemoryError** is an error.

C is incorrect because **RuntimeException** is an exception.

D is correct because **StackOverflowError** is an error.

E is incorrect because **Throwable** is the parent class of all exceptions and errors and is not an error.

Question 54 (7.2. Develop code that demonstrates the use of polymorphism; including overriding and object type versus reference type)

Let class **Circle** extend class **Shape**. Given the following code

```
Circle circle = new Circle();
Shape shape = new Shape();
```

Which of the following expressions evaluate to true?

A. circle instanceof Shape
B. circle instanceof Object
C. shape instanceof Circle
D. (Shape) circle instanceof Circle

Answers: A, B, D.

A is true because a subclass has an is-a relationship with its parents.

B is true as all classes are directly or indirectly derived from **java.lang.Object**.

C is false because Shape is the parent class of Circle and a shape is not necessarily a circle.

D is true. Upcasting a **Circle** to its parent does not obscure the fact that it is still of type **Circle**.

Question 55 (7.1. Describe inheritance and its benefits)

Consider the following two classes:

```
package inheritance;
class Parent {
    public void print() { ... }
```

```
    String describe() { ... }
    protected String[] copyNames(String[] sources) { ... }
    private boolean isResident() { ... }
}

class Sub extends Parent {
    public void doIt() {
        ...
    }
}
```

Which methods can be used in the **Sub** class?

A. print, describe, doIt
B. print, describe, copyNames, isResident
C. print, describe, copyNames
D. print, describe, copyNames, toString

Answer: A, C, D.

A subclass has access to the public, protected and default methods of its parents.

A is correct because **print** and **describe** have public and default access, respectively, and **doIt** is defined in **Sub**.

B is incorrect because **isResident** is private so it cannot be accessed from a child class.

C is correct a subclass can access the public and protected methods of its parents. In addition, **Parent** and **Sub** are in the same package, so **Sub** can access default methods in **Parent**.

D is correct because **Parent** implicitly extends **java.lang.Object**, As such, **Parent** inherits methods from **java.lang.Object** including its **toString** method. All methods that **Parent** inherit from its parent are also inherited to **Sub**.

Question 56 (2.3. Know how to read or write to object fields)

Consider the following code:

```
package test;
public class Holder {
    float length = 100F;
    static {
        width = 23.00F;
    }
    static {
        width = 25.00F;
    }
    static float width = 12.30F;
    public static void main(String[] args) {
        Holder h1 = new Holder();
        h1.length++;
        h1.width++;
        Holder h2 = new Holder();
```

```
        System.out.print(h2.width + ", ");
        System.out.print(h2.length);
    }
}
```

What is the output of the program?

A. 25.0, 100.0
B. 12.3, 100.0
C. 26.0, 100.0
D. 26.0, 110.0
E. 13.3, 100.0
F. 13.3, 110.0

Answer: E.

First off, static blocks and static variable initialization are called once when the class is loaded in the order they appear in the code. As such, the value of **width** is 12.30F as it is the last in the order. Second of all, static members are shared by all instances. Therefore, **h1.width++** increments the same static variable shared by all instances.

Question 57 (3.1. Use Java operators; including parentheses to override operator precedence)

What is the value of **b**?

```
byte b = 2 ^ 6;
```

A. 64
B. 8
C. 4
D. 2

Answer: C.

The bitwise exclusive OR operator (^) works by comparing bits in the two operands. It returns true if the bits are different. Otherwise, it returns false.

Here is the bitwise exclusive OR operation of 2 and 6 in bit level:

```
2: 0000 0010
6: 0000 0110
------------
   0000 0100 (4)
```

Question 58 (9.4. Declare and use an ArrayList of a given type)

Given the following code:

```
package test;
import java.util.ArrayList;
public class Roller {
    public static void main(String[] args) {
        ArrayList<String> collector = new ArrayList<String>();
        collector.add("Study");
```

```
        collector.add(Integer.toOctalString(Integer.MAX_VALUE));

        ArrayList<String> names = new ArrayList<>();
        names.addAll(collector);
        names.add("Study");
        names.add(null);
        System.out.println(names.size());
    }
}
```

What is printed on the console?

A. 0
B. 2
C. 3
D. 4

Answer: D.

An **ArrayList** allows duplicates and null values. Therefore, the size of **names** after adding **collector**, a **String** and a null is 4.

Question 59 (7.5. Use abstract classes and interfaces)

Consider the following code:

```
 1. package test;
 2. abstract class Base {
 3.     public Base() {}
 4.     public Base(String s) {}
 5. }
 6. final class Impl extends Base {
 7. }
 8. public class Tester {
 9.     public static void main(String[] args) {
10.         Base base1 = new Base();
11.         Base base2 = new Impl();
12.         new Impl().toString();
13.         ((Base) new Impl()).toString();
14.     }
15. }
```

Does the code compile?

A. It compiles
B. No, compile error at line 10
C. No, compile error at line 12
D. No, compile error at line 13

Answer: B.

A is incorrect because the code does not compile for the reason outlined below.

B is correct because you cannot instantiate an abstract class. Line 10 is therefore causes a compile error.

C is incorrect because you can create an object and call its method without first assigning the object to a reference variable.

D is incorrect because **Impl** can be instantiated and upcast to its parent class.

Question 60 (6.1. Create methods with arguments and return values; including overloaded method)

Consider the following class:

```
class Engineer {
    public double calculate(double a, double b) { return 0; }
    private double calculate(double[] numbers) { return 0; }
    private void demandPayRise() {}
    public static void demandPayRise(BigDecimal byHowMuch) {}
    public long thinkInNumbers(int... numbers) { return 0; }
    public long thinkInNumbers(int a, int b) {return 1; }
}
```

Which of the following statements are true?

A. calculate are method overloads
B. demandPayRise are method overloads
C. thinkInNumbers are method overloads
D. calculate are not method overloads because they don't have the same access modifiers.
E. demandPayRise are not method overloads because one is static and the other is not.
F. thinkInNumbers are not method overloads because it is ambiguous which method will be called when two **int**s are passed in.

Answer: A, B, C.

A, B and C are true statements.

D is false because overloaded methods may have different access modifiers.

E is false because overloaded methods may be static or otherwise.

F is false because in the case of two arguments, the method that take two arguments will be called.

Question 61 (4.1. Declare, instantiate, initialize and use a one-dimensional array)

Given

```
public class ArrayUtil2 {
    public static void main(String[] args) {
        char[] characters = { '1', '2', '3', '4'};
        int[] numbers = characters;
        for (char c : characters) {
            System.out.print(c);
        }
```

```
8.      }
9. }
```

A. The code prints 1234
B. Compile error at line 4
C. Compile error at line 5
D. Compile error at lines 4 and 5

Answer: B.

Just because a **char** can be assigned to an **int** does not mean a **char** array can be assigned to an **int** array. Because a **char** array and an **int** array are different types, there will be a compile error at line 4.

Question 62 (5.2. Create and use for loops including the enhanced for loop)

Given

```
1. public class ArrayUtil2 {
2.     public static void main(String[] args) {
3.         Character[] characters = { '1', '2', '3', '4'};
4.         Object[] numbers = characters;
5.         for (char c : characters) {
6.             System.out.print(c);
7.         }
8.     }
9. }
```

Which of the following statement(s) is/are true?

A. The code prints 1234
B. Compile error at line 4
C. Compile error at line 5
D. Compile error at lines 4 and 5

Answer: A.

java.lang.Object is the root of all Java classes. Assigning an array of any reference type to an **Object** array variable is allowed. However, you cannot assign an array of a primitive type to an **Object** array.

Question 63 (2.2. Differentiate between object reference variables and primitive variables)

Which of the following are primitive wrappers?

A. Boolean
B. Char
C. Character
D. Int
E. Integer
F. Double

G. String
H. float

Answer: A, C, E, F.

The wrapper classes are **Byte**, **Short**, **Integer**, **Long**, **Float**, **Double**, **Character** and **Boolean**. A, C, E and F are therefore correct.

B is incorrect because there is no type **Char**. The wrapper class for **char** is **Character**.

D is incorrect because there is no type **Int**. The wrapper class for **int** is **Integer**.

G is incorrect because even though **String** is a reference type, it isn't a primitive wrapper class.

H is incorrect because float is a primitive, not a wrapper class.

Question 64 (8.3. Describe the advantages of Exceptions handling)

Which of the following statements are true?

A. The **try** statement can be used to handle errors in your program
B. The **try-with-resources** statement closes all resources that implements **AutoCloseable**
C. You should catch all errors in your program
D. All exception classes are subclasses of **java.lang.Throwable**

Answer: A, B, D.

C is incorrect because you should not try to catch serious errors such as **java.lang.StackOverflowError** and **java.lang.OutOfMemoryError**.

Question 65 (8.4. Create and invoke a method that throws an exception)

Consider the following code:

```
public class VideoGame {
    public static void execute() {}
    public static void exit() {}
    public static void main(String[] args) {
        switch (args[0]) {
        default:
            exit();
            break;
        case "1":
        case "2":
        case "3":
            execute();
            break;
        }
    }
}
```

Which of the following statements are true?

A. The program may throw an exception
B. The **execute** method will be called if the value of the first argument to the program is “1”, “2” or “3”.
C. There is a compile error because the default case must be the last case in a switch statement
D. Nothing will be invoked if the value of the first argument to the program is “1” or “2”

Answer: A, B.

A is true because if the program is executed without an argument, accessing the first argument to the program using the expression **args[0]** will throw an **ArrayIndexOutOfBoundsException**.

B is also true because there is no **break** statement after cases labeled “1” and “2”. As such, in either case, control will fall through the case labeled “3” and the **execute** method will be called.

C is false because the default case may appear anywhere in the **switch** block.

D is false because if the value of the first argument to the program is “1” or “2”, the case labeled “3” will be invoked.

Question 66 (6.1. Create methods with arguments and return values; including overloaded method)

Given the following code:

```
1. package science;
2. public class MathGenius {
3.     public int add(int... numbers) {
4.         int result = 0;
5.         for (int n : numbers) {
6.             result += n;
7.         }
8.         return result;
9.     }
10.    public static void main(String[] args) {
11.        MathGenius mathGenius = new MathGenius();
12.        // some code
13.        System.out.println(result);
14.    }
15. }
```

Which of the following statements may replace the code in line 12 so the program will print **10**. (Choose all that apply).

A. int result = mathGenius.add({1, 2, 3, 4});
B. int result = mathGenius.add(new int[] {1, 2, 3, 4});
C. int result = mathGenius.add(1, 2, 3, 4);
D. int result = mathGenius.add(4, 3, 2, 1);

Answer: B, C.

First note that the varargs used as the argument to the **add** method is equivalent to an **int** array. A is false because even though { 1, 2, 3, 4 } can be used to create an int array, it cannot by itself be used as a method argument. If you want to use this format, you could use these two statements to replace line 12:

```
int[] input = {1, 2, 3, 4};
int result = mathGenius.add(input);
```

B is correct. To create an array and use it as a method argument without first assigning the array to a variable, you can use this syntax:

```
new type[] { ... }
```

C is correct because you are passing a series of **int**s, which is expected for a varargs.

D is correct because you are passing a series of **int**s, which is expected for a varargs.

Question 67 (2.3. Know how to read or write to object fields)

Consider the following code:

```
public class Employee {
    protected String firstName;
    public int age;
    private String lastName;
    boolean member;
}
-----------------------------------
import test.sense.Employee;
public class Manager extends Employee {
    public void configure() {
        this.age = 12;
        this.firstName = "Aurora";
        this.lastName = "Valentino";
        this.member = false;
    }
}
```

Assuming **Employee** and **Manager** are not in the same package, which of the following statements in the **Manager** class will generate a compile error?

A. this.age = 12;
B. this.firstName = "Aurora";
C. this.lastName = "Valentino";
D. this.member = false;

Answer: C, D.

A is valid because **age** is a public field and can be accessed from anywhere.

B is also correct because **firstName** is a protected field and can therefore be accessed from classes in the same package as **Employee** as well as from classes that extend **Employee**.

C is invalid because **lastName** is private and cannot be accessed from outside its own class.

D is invalid because **member** has the default access and thus can be accessed by classes in the same package as **Employee**. Since **Employee** and **Manager** are not in the same package, **member** is not visible from **Manager**.

Question 68 (2.3. Know how to read or write to object fields)

Examine the following code.

```
class Person {
    protected String firstName;
    public int age;
    private String lastName;
    boolean member;
}

class HR {
    public static void main(String[] args) {
        Person person = new Person();
        person.age = 30;
        person.firstName = "Brad";
        person.lastName = "Sumitomo";
        person.member = false;
    }
}
```

Assuming **Person** and **HR** are classes in the same package, which statements will not generate a compile error?

A. person.age = 30;
B. person.firstName = "Brad";
C. person.lastName = "Sumitomo";
D. person.member = false;

Answer: A, B, D.

Note that the question is which statements will *not* generate a compile error.

A is valid because **age** is a public field and can be accessed from anywhere.

B is also correct because **firstName** is a protected field and can therefore be accessed from classes in the same package as **Person** as well as from classes that extend **Person**.

C is invalid because **lastName** is private and cannot be accessed from outside the **Person** class.

D is correct because member has the default access and thus can be accessed by classes in the same package as **Person**.

Question 69 (6.1. Create methods with arguments and return values; including overloaded method)

Consider the signature of the following method:

```
public int handle(int a, int b)
```

Which of these method signatures are the overloads of the method above?

A. public static int handle(int a, int b)
B. public void handle(int[] args)
C. private String handle(int x, int y)
D. public Object handle(long a, long b)

Answer: B, D.

A is incorrect because simply making a method static does not create an overload. B is correct because it has a different set of arguments. C is incorrect because it has the same set of arguments. D is also correct because it has a different set of arguments.

Question 70 (7.5. Use abstract classes and interfaces)

Consider these two interfaces:

```
interface Printable {
    float getCost();
}

interface Uploadable {
    double getCost();
}
```

Is it possible for a class to implement both interfaces?

A. Yes, a class can always implement any set of interfaces
B. Yes, and you must provide two implementations of getCost()
C. Yes, and you must only provide one implementation of getCost()
D. No, it is not possible. The class will not compile

Answer: D.

A class implementing both interfaces would have to provide the implementations of both **getCost** methods. However, the compiler would consider these implementations duplicate methods. If it were allowed and you made a call to **getCost** without assigning its return value to a variable, it would not be clear which **getCost** method should be invoked.

Question 71 (1.5. Compare and contrast the features and components of Java such as: platform independence, object orientation, encapsulation, etc.)

Which of the following options are part of what makes Java platform-independent? (Choose all that apply)

A. Java programs are compiled into bytecode
B. Small programs are compiled into native code
C. The JVM is available in many platforms
D. The JVM can run Java bytecode

Answer: A, C, D.

Unlike the conventional programming paradigm, Java programs are compiled into bytecode. This bytecode cannot be executed directly but needs a Java Virtual Machine to run. By providing a JVM in a supported platform, the same bytecode can run in multiple platforms. Currently the JVM is available in Windows, Linux, Unix, Mac OS X, and others.

B is incorrect because even small programs are compiled into bytecode.

Question 72 (2.5. Develop code that uses wrapper classes such as Boolean, Double, and Integer)

Which of the following statements are valid? (Choose all that apply)

A. double w = Double.MAX_VALUE;
B. Integer s = new Integer(123);
C. Long t = new Integer(9);
D. long u = new Integer(99);

Answer: A, B, D.

A is valid because the **Double** object will be unboxed and its value assigned to **w**.

B is valid because assigning an **Integer** to a variable of the same type is valid.

C is invalid because **Long** and **Integer** are different classes and no unboxing will be attempted.

D is valid because the **Integer** will be unboxed and its int value assigned to **u**, which is a **long**.

Question 73 (2.5. Develop code that uses wrapper classes such as Boolean, Double, and Integer)

What is the value of s after the following line of code is executed?

```
int s = new Double(23.8).intValue();
```

A. 23.8
B. 23
C. 24
D. 0

Answer: B.

The **intValue** method of the **Double** class converts the internal double value to an **int**. No rounding will be performed, therefore the value of **s** will be 23.

Question 74 (9.3. Create and manipulate calendar data using classes from java.time.LocalDateTime, java.time.LocalDate, java.time.LocalTime, java.time.format.DateTimeFormatter, java.time.Period)

Consider the following code snippet:

```
String pattern = ...;
DateTimeFormatter formatter = DateTimeFormatter.ofPattern(pattern);
LocalDate date = LocalDate.parse("24 04 2019", formatter);
```

Which date pattern can be used to parse "24 04 2019" to April 24, 2019? (Choose all that apply)

A. dd mm yyyy
B. dd MM yyyy
C. d M yyy
D. dd MMM yyyy

Answer: B, C.

The letter "d" indicates the date and "m" the minute. As such, A is incorrect.

The letter M indicates the month. M and MM indicate the month in number, such as 01 or 1. MMM indicates the month in text, such as "Dec." Therefore, the pattern in D cannot be used to parse a month represented by a number.

B and C are both correct as they use d, M and y. "d" and "dd" are different. "d" allows one and two digit dates and "dd" only allows two digit dates. There is also a difference between M and MM. M accepts one or two digit months. MM only allows two-digit months.

For the year part, the following rules apply which can be found in the documentation for **java.text.SimpleDateFormat**.

For parsing, if the number of pattern letters is more than 2, the year is interpreted literally, regardless of the number of digits. So using the pattern "MM/dd/yyyy", "08/21/12" parses to August 21, 12 A.D.

Question 75 (9.3. Create and manipulate calendar data using classes from java.time.LocalDateTime, java.time.LocalDate, java.time.LocalTime, java.time.format.DateTimeFormatter, java.time.Period)

Which of the following lines of code can be used to create a date representing yesterday?

A. LocalDate yesterday = LocalDate.now().minusDays(1);
B. LocalDate yesterday2 = LocalDate.now().plusDays(-1);
C. LocalDate yesterday3 = LocalDate.now().plus(1, TemporalUnit.DAYS);
D. LocalDate yesterday4 = LocalDate.now().minus(1, ChronoUnit.DAYS);

Answer: A, B, D.

A is correct because **LocalDate.now()** returns a date representing today and **minusDays** decrements the date.

B is also correct because the **plusDays(-1)** decrements the date by one day.

C is incorrect because **TemporalUnitlDAYS** does not exist.

D is correct because the **minus** method can be used to decrement any component of the date by passing a number and a **TemporalUnit**. **ChronoUnit** implements **TemporalUnit** and therefore an instance of **ChronoUnit** can be passed to the **minus** method.

Question 76 (9.5. Write a simple Lambda expression that consumes a Lambda Predicate expression)

Which statements are true with regard to **java.util.function.Predicate**?

A. **Predicate** is a predefined functional interface
B. **Predicate** can take primitive arguments
C. **Predicate** can take an array argument
D. **Predicate** can take one or two arguments

Answer: A, C.

A is correct because **Predicate** is one of the predefined functional interfaces in **java.util.function**.

B is incorrect because **Predicate** cannot take a primitive argument.

C is correct because **Predicate** can take any reference type, including an array.

D is incorrect because **Predicate** can only take one argument. You can use **BiPredicate** if you need a predicate that takes two arguments.

Question 77 (9.5. Write a simple Lambda expression that consumes a Lambda Predicate expression)

Which of the following are valid statements?

A. Predicate<Integer> abc = x -> x == 0;
B. Predicate<Void> s = (x) -> 2 == 1;
C. Predicate<> w = (x) -> 2 == 1;
D. Predicate<Long> t = x -> {return true};

Answer: A, B.

A is correct as **Predicate** can take an **Integer**.

B is correct as **Void** can be used as an argument to **Predicate**.

C is incorrect because **Predicate** must take an argument.

D is incorrect because braces in a lambda expression must contain statements. “return true” is not a statement as it is missing a semicolon.

Appendix C
Mock Exam 2

The following are questions for the second mock exam. Each question may have more than one correct answer and you have to choose all the correct answers.

Question 1 (1.3. Create executable Java applications with a main method; run a Java program from the command line; including console output)

Consider the following code.

```
package demo;
public class MainDemo {
    public static void main(String[] args) {
        System.out.println(args[0]);
    }
}
```

It is invoked with this command line command:

```
java demo.MainDemo 20+30
```

What is printed on the standard out?

A. 50
B. 20
C. 30
D. 20+30

Question 2 (1.3. Create executable Java applications with a main method; run a Java program from the command line; including console output)

Consider the following code snippet:

```
package test;

public class Device {
    void main() {
    }
}
```

What will happen if you try to compile this class? (Choose all that apply)

A. You will get a compile error at line 4 because **main** must be static.
B. You will get a compile error at line 4 because **main** must be public and static.
C. You will get a compile error at lines 3 and 4.
D. The class compiles without issues.

Question 3 (1.3. Create executable Java applications with a main method; run a Java program from the command line; including console output)

Given

```
package smalldevice;
public class Counter {
    public static void main(String[] args) {
        System.out.print(args[1]);
        System.out.print(args[2]);
    }
}
```

The program is invoked using this command.

```
java smalldevice.Counter zero "one" two
```

What is printed on the console?

A. zeroone
B. zero"one"
C. onetwo
D. "one"two

Question 4 (1.4. Import other Java packages to make them accessible in your code)

Which sets of **import** statements would allow you to use **java.util.List**, **java.util.ArrayList** and **java.lang.System** in your class?

A. import java.util.*;
B. import java.util.List; import java.util.ArrayList;
C. import java.util.List; import java.util.ArrayList; import java.lang.System;
D. import java.lang.*;
E. import java.lang.System;

Question 5 (1.4. Import other Java packages to make them accessible in your code)

Which sets of **import** statements would allow you to use **java.util.List**, **java.util.ArrayList** and **java.lang.annotation.Documented** in your class?

A. import java.util.*;
B. import java.util.List; import java.util.ArrayList;
C. import java.util.*; import java.lang.annotation.Documented;

D. import java.util.*; import java.lang.annotation.*;
E. import java.lang.*;

Question 6 (4.1. Declare, instantiate, initialize and use a one-dimensional array)

Assuming **stringArray** is a one-dimensional array, which of the following expressions returns the number of element in **stringArray**?

A. stringArray.size
B. stringArray.size()
C. stringArray.length
D. stringArray.length()
E. stringArray.capacity
F. stringArray.capacity()

Question 7 (2.1. Declare and initialize variables (including casting of primitive data types))

What is the output of this program?

```
1. public class Utility {
2.     public static void main(String[] args) {
3.         int i = 9;
4.         char c = '3';
5.         i = c;
6.         c = i;
7.         System.out.print(i);
8.         System.out.print(c);
9.     }
10. }
```

A. The code prints 93
B. Compile error at line 5
C. Compile error at line 6
D. Compile error at lines 5 and 6

Question 8 (7.5. Use abstract classes and interfaces)

What is the result of compiling this code?

```
interface Viewable {
    public List<String> getAllScreenNames();
    public static int getWidth() {
        return 1024;
    }
    public default int getScreenCount() {
        return 1;
    }
    String getDefaultScreenName();
}
```

A. Compile error because an interface may not contain static methods
B. Compile error because an interface may not contain method implementations
C. Compile error because the **getDefaultScreenName** method has no access modifier
D. It compiles without issues

Question 9 (9.5. Write a simple Lambda expression that consumes a Lambda Predicate expression)

What is the possible outcome of this code?

```
package test;
import java.util.function.Predicate;
public class Tester {
    public static void main(String[] args) {
        Predicate<String> isNumber = x -> {
            for (int i = 0; i < x.length(); i++)
                if ("0123456789".indexOf("" + x.charAt(i)) == -1)
                    return false;
            return true;
        };
        System.out.println(isNumber.test(args[0]) ? "TRUE" : "FALSE");
    }
}
```

A. The code may print TRUE
B. The code may print FALSE
C. The code may throw an exception
D. The code will not compile

Question 10 (9.1. Manipulate data using the StringBuilder class and its methods)

What does this code fragment print on the console?

```
StringBuilder buffer = new StringBuilder("Reversible");
for (int i = 0; i < buffer.length(); i++)
    if (buffer.charAt(i) == 'e')
        buffer.replace(i - 1, i, "E");
System.out.println(buffer);
```

A. REvErsiblE
B. REVERSIBLE
C. EeEersibEe
D. EEEErsibEE

Question 11 (2.5. Develop code that uses wrapper classes such as Boolean, Double, and Integer)

What is the outcome of the following class?

```
package example.test;
public class SmartUtility {
```

```
    public static double average(Integer... numbers) {
        long temp = 0;
        for (Integer i : numbers)
            temp += i;
        return temp / numbers.length;
    }
    public static void main(String[] args) {
        int[] ints = {1, 2, 6, 7};
        System.out.println(average(ints));
    }
}
```

A. The class prints 4.0
B. The code generates a compile error
C. The code throws a runtime exception
D. The class prints 4

Question 12 (6.1. Create methods with arguments and return values; including overloaded methods)

Consider the following code.

```
class Car extends java.lang.Object {
    private void brake() {}
    protected void brake(float decelaration) {}
    public int run(int speed) {
        int currentSpeed = 100;
        return currentSpeed < speed? currentSpeed : speed;
    }
    public static int run(int speed, int accelaration) {
        return speed + accelaration;
    }
    public String toString() {
        return "Car";
    }
}
```

Which statement(s) is or are true regarding the code?

A. The run methods are overloaded methods
B. The run methods are not overloaded methods since you cannot overload a static method with an instance method
C. The brake methods are overloaded methods.
D. The toString method in Car is an overload of the toString method in java.lang.Object.
E. The Car class will generate a compile error because of duplicate method names

Question 13 (1.2. Define the structure of a Java class)

Which of the following can appear within a class? (Choose all that apply)

A. Comments
B. Methods

C. Fields
D. Embedded files
E. Import statements

Question 14 (1.5. Compare and contrast the features and components of Java such as: platform independence, object orientation, encapsulation, etc.)

Which of the following are features of Java?

A. Java is just like the conventional programming paradigm, after a program is compiled you get an executable file
B. Java programs can run in multiple platforms
C. To achieve platform independence, Java programs are compiled into different forms that work in multiple platforms
D. Java programs are compiled into bytecode

Question 15 (2.1. Declare and initialize variables (including casting of primitive data types))

Given

```
int i = 257;
byte b = (byte) i;
```

What is the value of **b** after the code is executed?

A. 255
B. 256
C. 257
D. 1
E. -1

Question 16 (3.2. Test equality between Strings and other objects using == and equals())

Consider this code.

```
Double d = new Double(12.34);
Double e = new Double(12.34);
Double f = 12.34;
Double g = 12.34;
```

Which of the following expressions return true? (Choose all that apply)

A. d==e
B. f==g
C. d.equals(e)
D. f.equals(g)

Question 17 (2.2. Differentiate between object reference variables and primitive variables)

Consider this code:

```
Long a = new Long(1000);
Long b = new Long(1000);
long c = 1000;
long d = 1000;
```

Which of the following expressions evaluate to true? (Choose all that apply)

A. a==b
B. a==c
C. c==d
D. a!=d

Question 18 (8.4. Create and invoke a method that throws an exception)

What is the output of the following program?

```
package test.math;
public class MathTester {
    public static double average(Integer... numbers) throws Exception {
        double total = 0;;
        for (Integer i : numbers) {
            if (i == null) {
                throw new Exception("Number cannot be null");
            }
            total += i;
        }
        return total/numbers.length;
    }

    public static void main(String[] args) {
        Integer[] numbers = {Integer.MIN_VALUE, Integer.MAX_VALUE, 0, 0};
        try {
            System.out.println(average(numbers));
        } catch (Exception e) {
            System.err.println(e.getMessage());
        }
    }
}
```

A. 0.00
B. -0.00
C. -0.25
D. Number cannot be null

Question 19 (7.2. Develop code that demonstrates the use of polymorphism; including overriding and object type versus reference type)

Consider this class declaration:

```
class Entertainment implements java.io.Serializable {

}
```

Which of the following expressions evaluates to true?

A. (new Entertainment() instanceof Object)
B. (new Entertainment() instanceof Serializable)
C. (new Entertainment() instanceof Entertainment)
D. (new Object() instanceof Entertainment)
E. (new Object() instanceof Serializable);

Question 20 (9.2. Creating and manipulating Strings)

Which of the following expressions case-insensitively compare two strings?

A. a.equals(b)
B. a.toUpperCase().equals(b.toUpperCase())
C. a.toLowerCase().equals(b.toLowerCase())
D. a.equalsIgnoreCase(b)

Question 21 (3.3. Create if and if/else and ternary constructs)

What is printed on the console if the following class is executed without an argument?

```
package test;
public class Argument {
    public static void main(String[] args) {
        String comment = args.length > 0 ? args[0].equals("file") ?
                "accept" : "ignore" : "invalid";
        System.out.println(comment);
    }
}
```

A. file
B. accept
C. ignore
D. invalid

Question 22 (5.1. Create and use while loops)

Given

```
package exercise;
public class EternalLoop {
    public static void main(String[] args) {
```

```
        int[] a = { 10, 20, 30, 40, 50, 10 };
        int i = a.length - 3;
        while (i > 0) {
            System.out.print(a[a.length - i]);
            i--;
        }
    }
}
```

What is printed on the console?

A. 123456
B. 102030405010
C. 405010
D. 10203040
E. 2030405010

Question 23 (2.4. Explain an object's lifecycle (creation, "dereference by assignment" and garbage collection))

Given

```
 1.  public class Skill {
 2.      public static void main(String[] args) {
 3.          Skill s1 = new Skill();
 4.          Skill s2 = new Skill();
 5.          if (args.length > 0) s1 = null;
 6.          System.out.println(s1);
 7.          if (args.length > 1) s2 = new Skill();
 8.          System.out.println(s2);
 9.      }
10.  }
```

Which of the following statements are true?

A. Two objects will be garbage collected at line 8.
B. One object will be garbage collected at line 6.
C. The object referenced by **s1** may be eligible for garbage collection at line 5.
D. The object referenced by **s2** is eligible for garbage collection at line 7.

Question 24 (6.3. Create and overload constructors; including impact on default constructors)

Given the following code

```
package sample;
class Event {
    private String name;
    private String description;
    public Event(String name) {
        this.name = name;
    }
```

```
    public Event(String name, String description) {
        this.name = name;
        this.description = description;
    }
    public String getName() {
        return name;
    }
    public String getDescription() {
       return description;
    }
    public String toString() {
        return name + ", " + description;
    }
}

public class EventOrganizer {
    public static void main(String[] args) {
        Event e1 = new Event("New Year's Eve", "Sponsored event");
        Event e2 = new Event("101th Birthday");
        Event e3 = new Event(); // empty event
        System.out.print(e2);
        System.out.print(e3);
    }
}
```

Which of the following statements are correct?

A. The code will print "New Year's Eve, Sponsored event 101th Birthday"
B. The code will not compile
C. The code will print an empty string
D. The code will throw a runtime exception

Question 25 (1.1. Define the scope of variables)

Consider the following code snippet that contains named regions A, B, C, D, E and F.

```
int m = 0;
long x = 1001;
// ------- A --------
if (m == 0) {
    // ------- B --------
    for (int n = 0; n < 9; n++) {
        // ------- C --------
        System.out.println(x - n);
        System.out.println(n);
        if (n == 2) m++;
        // ------- D --------
    }
    // ------- E --------
    x++;
}
// ------- F --------
```

Which of the following statements are true?

A. *n* cannot be used in region F.
B. *m* and *n* can be used in region B
C. *m* and *n* can be used in region D
D. *m* and *n* can be used in region F

Question 26 (2.3. Know how to read or write to object fields)

Consider the following code.

```
package com.example;
class Event {
    public String name;
    private String description;
    public Event(String name) {
        this.name = name;
    }

    public Event(String name, String description) {
        this.name = name;
        this.description = description;
    }

    public String getDescription() {
        return description;
    }

    public void setDescription(String description) {
        this.description = this.description;
    }
    public String toString() {
        return name + ", " + description;
    }
}

public class Organizer {
    public static void main(String[] args) {
        Event e = new Event("Summer Festival", "New York & Toronto");
        e.name = "Winter is coming early";
        e.setDescription("Summer Festival canceled");
        System.out.println(e);
    }
}
```

What is the outcome of the code?

A. The code generates a compile error
B. The code prints “Summer Festival, New York & Toronto”
C. The code prints “Winter is coming early, Summer Festival canceled”
D. The code prints “Winter is coming early, New York & Toronto”

Question 27 (3.1. Use Java operators; including parentheses to override operator precedence)

What is the output of the following code snippet?

```
public class Tester {
    public static void main(String[] args) {
        int i = 3, j = 3;
        System.out.print(++i + i);
        System.out.print(" ");
        System.out.print(j++ + j);
        System.out.print(" ");
        System.out.print(i);
        System.out.print(" ");
        System.out.print(j);
    }
}
```

A. 8 8 4 4
B. 7 7 4 4
C. 7 8 4 4
D. 8 7 4 4

Question 28 (3.4. Use a switch statement)

What is the output of the following code?

```
package base;

public class SwitchTester {
    public static void main(String[] args) {
        int n = 100;
        switch (++n) {
        case 100:
            System.out.print("100");
        default:
            System.out.print("default");
        }
    }
}
```

A. 100default
B. 100
C. default
D. default100

Question 29 (4.2. Declare, instantiate, initialize and use multi-dimensional array)

Consider the following class:

```
public class Test100 {
```

```
    public static void main(String[] args) {
        int[][][] matrix = {{{1, 2, 3},{4, 5, 6}}, {
            {10, 20, 30},{40, 50, 60}}};
        System.out.print(matrix[0][0][0] * matrix[1][1][1]);
    }
}
```

What is printed on the console when the class is executed?

A. 8
B. 10
C. 40
D. 50
E. 80
D. 120

Question 30 (5.2. Create and use for loops including the enhanced for loop)

Given

```
package test;
import java.util.ArrayList;
import java.util.List;
public class Test200 {
    public static void main(String[] args) {
        String[] names = { "Henri", "Borousa" };
        String[] cities = { "Melbourne", "Wilton" };
        List<String> mix = new ArrayList<>();
        for (String name : names) {
            mix.add(name);
            for (String city : cities) {
                mix.add(city);
            }
        }
        String[] namesCities = new String[]{};
        namesCities = mix.toArray(namesCities);
        System.out.println(namesCities.length);
    }
}
```

What is printed on the console when the class is run?

A. 2
B. 4
C. 6
D. 7
E. 8

Question 31 (9.3. Create and manipulate calendar data using classes from java.time.LocalDateTime, java.time.LocalDate, java.time.LocalTime, java.time.format.DateTimeFormatter, java.time.Period)

Consider the following code.

```
package tester;
import java.time.LocalDate;
import java.time.LocalDateTime;
import java.time.LocalTime;
import java.time.format.DateTimeFormatter;

public class FlightTime {
    public static void main(String[] args) {
        LocalDate depDate = LocalDate.of(2015, 12, 12);
        LocalTime depTime = LocalTime.of(10, 20);
        LocalDateTime departure = LocalDateTime.of(depDate, depTime);
        LocalDateTime arrival = departure.plusHours(8).plusMinutes(30);
        System.out.println(arrival.format(
            DateTimeFormatter.ofPattern("yyyy mm dd hh:MM")));
    }
}
```

What is printed on the console?

A. 2015 12 12 06:50
B. 2015 50 12 06:12
C. 2015/12/12 06:50
D. 2015/06/12 12:50
E. 2015 12 12 18:50

Question 32 (9.4. Declare and use an ArrayList of a given type)

Consider the following class:

```
package com.brainysoftware.server;
import java.util.ArrayList;
public class Gauge {
    public static void main(String[] args) {
        ArrayList<Long> collection = new ArrayList<>();
        collection.add(459);
        collection.add(new Long("123"));
        for (long l : collection) {
            System.out.print(l);
        }
    }
}
```

What is the result of this class?

A. Compilation error

B. Runtime error
C. It prints 459123 when run
D. It prints 459 when run

Question 33 (7.1. Describe inheritance and its benefits)

Which of the following statements are true? (Choose all that apply)

A. Inheritance is a feature of object-oriented programming
B. You implement inheritance using the extend keyword
C. All methods in a parent class can be used in a child class
D. Certain fields in a parent class can be accessed in a child class.

Question 34 (7.3. Determine when casting is necessary)

Consider this code.

```
long l = 4321238398434234 34L;
int i = (int) l;
long l2 = (long) i;
byte b = (byte) i;
short s = (short) b;
short t = (short) s;
```

Which explicit castings are not optional? (Choose all that apply)

A. int i = (int) l;
B. long l2 = (long) i;
C. byte b = (byte) i;
D. short s = (short) b;
E. short t = (short) s;

Question 35 (8.5. Recognize common exception classes (such as NullPointerException. ArithmeticException, ArrayIndexOutOfBoundsException, ClassCastException))

Which of the following are runtime exceptions? (Choose all that apply)

A. CannotLoadException
B. NullPointerException
C. IllegalArgumentException
D. NumberFormatException
E. OutOfMemoryError

Question 36 (8.3. Describe the advantages of Exceptions handling)

Which of the following statements are true?

A. A potential error can be isolated using the **try** statement
B. The **try-with-resources** statement closes all resources that implements **AutoCloseable**

C. You should catch all errors in your program
D. All exception classes are subclasses of **java.lang.Exception**

Question 37 (8.2. Create a try-catch block and determine how exceptions alter normal program flow)

Consider the following code fragment.

```
package rewardprogram;
public class Reward {
    public static void main(String[] args) {
        int j = 0;
        try {
            j = Integer.parseInt(args[0]);
        } catch (NumberFormatException e) {
            System.out.println("Incorrect number format");
        } catch (NullPointerException e) {
            System.out.println("Null argument");
        } catch (ArrayIndexOutOfBoundsException e) {
            System.out.println("No argument found");
        }
        System.out.println(j);
    }
}
```

What is printed on the console if the class is invoked without an argument.

A. No argument found
B. Null argument
C. 0
D. Incorrect number format

Question 38 (7.4. Use super and this to access objects and constructors)

Given

```
package test;
class Super {
    @Override
    public String toString() {
        return "Super " + this.toString();
    }
}

class Sub extends Super {
    @Override
    public String toString() {
        return "Sub " + super.toString();
    }
}

public class Tester {
```

```
    public static void main(String[] args) {
        Sub sub = new Sub();
        System.out.println(sub);
    }
}
```

What happens when the class **Tester** is executed?

A. An error will be thrown
B. It will print "Sub Super Object"
C. It will print "Sub Super"
D. It will print "Sub Super" followed by a random string

Question 39 (5.3. Create and use do/while loops)

Given

```
package com.example.test;
import java.util.ArrayList;
import java.util.List;

public class LoopExample {
    public static void main(String[] args) {
        List<String> list = new ArrayList<>();
        String[] favCities = { "Berlin", "Boston", "Chicago" };
        for (String city : favCities) list.add(city);
        do {
            System.out.print(list.get(0) + "--");
            list.remove(0);
        } while (list.size() > 0);
    }
}
```

What is the result of running this class?

A. Berlin--Boston--Chicago--
B. An empty string
C. Berlin--Boston--
D. Berlin--

Question 40 (3.4. Use a switch statement)

What is the output of the following code if ?

```
public class Util {
    public static void main(String[] args) {
        int a = args.length;
        switch (a) {
        case 0:
            System.out.print("No argument");
        case 1:
            System.out.print("One argument");
            break;
```

```
            case 2:
                System.out.print("Two arguments or more");
                break;
                default:
                    System.out.print("Default");
            }
        }
}
```

A. No argument
B. One argument
C. No argumentOne argument
D. Default

Question 41 (5.5. Use break and continue)

What is the output of the following class?

```
public class FunnyGame {
    public static void main(String[] args) {
        int b = 15;
        Loop1:
        for (int a = 0; a < 5; a += 2) {
            Loop2:
                b--;
                for (int c = 6; c > 0; c--) {
                    if (c==4) continue;
                    System.out.print(c+" ");
                    if (c==3) continue Loop1;
                    if (c==2) break;
                }
        }
    }
}
```

A. 6 5 3 2 6 5 3 2 6 5 3 2
B. 6 5 3 6 5 3 6 5 3
C. 6 5 3 6 5 3 6 5 3 5
D. 6 5 3 6 5 3 6 5 2

Question 42 (5.4. Compare loop constructs)

Consider the following code snippet that is supposed to print 234:

```
1. ...
2. {
3.     System.out.print(a++);
4. }
```

Which of the following statements can be inserted into line 1 so that the code does what is expected of it?

A. for (int a=2; i<5;)

B. int a=2; while(a<5)
C. for (int a=2; a<5; a++)
D. for (int a=2; i<5; i++)

Question 43 (6.2. Apply the static keyword to methods and fields)

What will happen if you try to compile and run this code?

```
package test;
class Bottle {
    public static int weight = 10;
}
public class Bartender {
    public static void main(String[] args) {
        Bottle bottle = new Bottle();
        bottle.weight = 123;
        Bottle.weight = 654;
        System.out.println(bottle.weight);
    }
}
```

A. You will get a compilation error for trying to access a static field as an instance field
B. The code will compile fine and it will print 123
C. The code will compile fine and it will print 654
D. The code will throw a runtime error

Question 44 (6.4. Apply access modifiers)

Which of the following statements are true? (Choose all that apply)

A. Public methods in a protected class can only be accessed from subclasses of the class
B. The private methods of a class cannot be accessed from other top-level classes
C. Static private methods in a class can be access from other classes
D. Methods with the default access can be called from the class's subclasses and other classes in the same package

Question 45 (6.5. Apply encapsulation principles to a class)

Which of the following are steps to implementing encapsulation? (Choose all that apply)

A. All fields are made private
B. Access to fields are done through public methods
C. Read-only fields must have get methods but not set methods
D. Write-only fields must have get methods but not set methods

Question 46 (8.1. Differentiate among checked exceptions, unchecked exceptions, and Errors)

Which of the following statements are true with regard to exception handling in Java?

A. A well-written program should try to catch both checked exceptions and unchecked exceptions
B. Unchecked exceptions are runtime exceptions
C. Errors are caused by external factors to the program
D. Errors should be caught

Question 47 (6.6. Determine the effect upon object references and primitive values when they are passed into methods that change the values)

Consider this code:

```
package com.example.geniemanager;
import java.util.ArrayList;
import java.util.List;
class Genie {
    public String grantWishes(int requestCode, List<String> wishes) {
        for (int i = wishes.size() - 1; i >= 0; i--) {
            String wish = wishes.get(wishes.size() - 1);
            // do something to grant wish
            wishes.remove(wish);
        }
        requestCode++;
        return "OK";
    }
}
public class GenieManager {
    public static void main(String[] args) {
        Genie genie = new Genie();
        List<String> wishes = new ArrayList<>();
        wishes.add("I want to pass all exams without studying");
        wishes.add("I want a flashy electric car");
        byte requestCode = 100;
        genie.grantWishes(requestCode, wishes);
        System.out.println(requestCode);
        for (String wish : wishes) {
            System.out.println(wish);
        }
    }
}
```

What are the variable values right after the for loop in **main** is executed?

A. The value of requestCode is 100
B. The List contains two elements
C. The List is empty
D. The value of requestCode is 101

Question 48 (7.5. Use abstract classes and interfaces)

Which of the following are correct implementations of the interface **WithWings**?

```
public abstract interface WithWings {
    void fly(int speed);
}

class DragonFly implements WithWings { }

abstract class Bird implements WithWings {
}

abstract class Bat implements WithWings {
    public void fly(int speed) {}
}

abstract class Moth implements WithWings {
    public abstract void fly(int speed);
}

final class Bee implements WithWings {
    protected void fly(int speed) {}
}
```

A. Dragonfly
B. Bird
C. Bat
D. Moth
E. Bee

Question 49 (7.2. Develop code that demonstrates the use of polymorphism; including overriding and object type versus reference type)

Consider the following code:

```
 1. class Combatant {
 2.    public void fight() {}
 3. }
 4. class Gladiator extends Combatant {
 5.     public void changeEmployer() {}
 6. }
 7.
 8. public class Test1000 {
 9.     public static void main(String[] args) {
10.         Combatant c1 = new Combatant();
11.         Combatant c2 = new Gladiator();
12.         Gladiator c3 = new Gladiator();
13.         ...
14.     }
15. }
```

What can be inserted into line 13 without generating a compilation error?

A. c1.changeEmployer();
B. c2.changeEmployer();

C. (Gladiator)c2.changeEmployer()
D. ((Gladiator)c2).changeEmployer();

Question 50 (9.4. Declare and use an ArrayList of a given type)

What is the output of the following code?

```
public class Numerator {
    public static void main(String[] args) {
        List<Integer> numbers = new ArrayList<>();
        for (int i = 0; i < 5; i++) {
            numbers.add(i + numbers.size());
        }
        for (int i = 0; i < 5; i++) {
            if (numbers.contains(i))
                numbers.remove(new Integer(i));
        }
        System.out.println(numbers);
    }
}
```

A. [1, 2, 3, 4, 5]
B. [1, 3, 5, 7, 9]
C. [9, 7]
D. [6, 8]

Question 51 (9.5. Write a simple Lambda expression that consumes a Lambda Predicate expression)

Given

```
Predicate<Void> xyz = (x) -> 3 == 1;
```

Which statement(s) can be used to invoke the Predicate?

A. xyz.test(null);
B. xyz.test("");
C. xyz.test();
D. xyz.test(xyz);

Question 52 (9.1. Manipulate data using the StringBuilder class and its methods)

Given

```
public class StringUtil {
    public static String process(String s) {
        StringBuilder sb = new StringBuilder();
        for (int i = s.length() - 1; i >= 0; i--) {
            sb.append(i % 2 == 0? Character.toUpperCase(s.charAt(i)) :
                    s.charAt(s.length() - i));
        }
```

```
        return sb.toString();
    }
    public static void main(String[] args) {
        String s = "New Age";
        System.out.println(process(s));
    }
}
```

What is the output of the class?

A. NEW AGE
B. Ega weN
C. EEgnwen
D. EwAAWeN

Question 53 (3.4. Use a switch statement)

Consider the following code:

```
public class DataAccess {
    public static void main(String[] args) {
        String s = "\\\\temp\\\\data";
        switch (s.substring(1, 2)) {
        case "\\":
            s = "slash" + s;
        case "\\\\":
            s += "\\\\temp";
            break;
        case "data":
            s += "data";
            break;
        default:
            s += "default";
        }
        System.out.println(s);
    }
}
```

What is printed on the console when the class is executed?

A. \\
B. \\\\
C. slash\\temp\\data\\temp
D. temp\data

Question 54 (8.2. Create a try-catch block and determine how exceptions alter normal program flow)

What is the result of the following class if invoked without an argument?

```
public class TryCatchFinally {
    public static void main(String[] args) {
        String s = null;
```

```
        try {
            s = args[0];
        } catch (Exception e) {
            try {
                s = "exception ";
                throw new Exception();
            } catch (Exception x) {
                s = s + "exception ";
            } finally {
                s = s + "finally ";
            }
        } finally {
            s += "finally ";
        }
        System.out.println(s);
    }
}
```

A. Compilation error
B. Uncaught exception
C. exception exception
D. exception exception finally finally
E. exception finally exception finally

Question 55 (4.1. Declare, instantiate, initialize and use a one-dimensional array)

What is the result of this code?

```
package animalkingdom;
public class Dog {
    private String name;
    public Dog(String name) {
        this.name = name;
    }
    @Override
    public String toString() {
        return name;
    }
    public static void main(String[] args) {
        Dog dog1 = new Dog("Wanda");
        Dog dog2 = new Dog("William Biteman");
        Dog[] dogs = { dog1, dog2 };
        dog1 = new Dog("Shark");
        dog2 = new Dog("Sherri");
        for (Dog dog : dogs) {
            System.out.print(dog + " ");
        }
    }
}
```

A. Compilation error
B. Runtime exception

C. Wanda William Biteman
D. Shark Sherri

Question 56 (3.1. Use Java operators; including parentheses to override operator precedence)

What is the result of this code?

```
public class Prince {
    public static void main(String[] args) {
        System.out.print(" " + 66 + 2 + " ");
        System.out.print(66 + 2 + " ");
        System.out.print(" " + (66 + 2) + " ");
        System.out.print(66 + 2);
    }
}
```

A. 68 68 68 68
B. 662 662 68 68
C. 662 68 68 68
D. 662 662 662 662

Question 57 (5.1. Create and use while loops)

What is the result of the following code?

```
public class WhileTest {
    public static void main(String[] args) {
        String s= "newworld";
        int i = s.length();
        while (!s.isEmpty()) {
            i++;
            s = s.substring(1);
        }
        System.out.println(i);
    }
}
```

A. NullPointerException
B. newworld
C. 18
D. 16

Question 58 (5.3. Create and use do/while loops)

What is the result of the class?

```
class Roll {
    public static void main(String[] args) {
        String s= "java";
        do {
            System.out.print(s);
```

```
            s = s.substring(0, s.length() - 1);
        } while (s.length() > 1);
    }
}
```

A. javajavajava
B. javajavajav
C. javajavj
D. javajavja

Question 59 (5.2. Create an use for loops including the enhanced for loop)

Given

```
import java.util.ArrayList;
import java.util.List;

public class Kitty {
    public static void main(String[] args) {
        List<String> names = new ArrayList<>();
        names.add("Jay");
        names.add("James");
        names.addAll(names);
        names.addAll(names);
        names.remove(4);
        for (String name : names) {
            System.out.println(name);
        }
    }
}
```

How many names are printed on the console?

A. 7
B. 4
C. 3
D. 8

Question 60 (9.3. Create and manipulate calendar data using classes from java.time.LocalDateTime, java.time.LocalDate, java.time.LocalTime, java.time.format.DateTimeFormatter, java.time.Period)

What is the output of this code?

```
LocalDate start = LocalDate.of(2015, 10, 13);
LocalDate finish = LocalDate.of(2015, 9, 15);
Period period = Period.between(start, finish);
System.out.println(period.getDays());
```

A. -29

B. 29
C. -28
D. 28

Question 61 (7.4. Use super and this to access objects and constructors)

Given

```
class Tier1 {
    public void print() {
        System.out.print("Tier 1...");
    }
}
class Tier2 extends Tier1 {
    public void print() {
        super.print();
        System.out.print("Tier 2...");
    }
}

class Tier3 extends Tier2 {
    public void print(String name) {
        super.print();
        System.out.print("Tier 3...");
    }
}
public class Tiery {
    public static void main(String[] args) {
        Tier2 tier = new Tier3();
        tier.print();
        tier = (Tier3) tier;
        tier.print();
    }
}
```

What is printed on the console when the class is run?

A. Tier1...Tier2...Tier3...
B. Tier1...Tier2...Tier1...Tier2...
C. Tier1...Tier2...Tier1...Tier2...Tier3...
D. Tier1...Tier2...Tier3...Tier1...Tier2...Tier3...

Question 62 (2.4. Explain an object's lifecycle (creation, "dereference by assignment" and garbage collection))

Given

```
public class Solution {
    private void print() {
        System.out.println(new Solution());
        System.out.println(new Solution());
    }
```

```
 6.     public static void main(String[] args) {
 7.         Solution solution = new Solution();
 8.         solution.print();
 9.
10.     }
11. }
```

At line 9, how many objects are eligible for garbage collection?

A. 0
B. 1
C. 2
D. 3

Question 63 (7.1. Describe inheritance and its benefits)

Which of the following statements are true? (Choose all that apply)

A. A class can implement another class
B. An interface can extend another interface
C. A class can extend any class
D. A class can implement multiple interfaces

Question 64 (5.5. Use break and continue)

What is the result of this code?

```
public class LoopTest {
    public static void main(String[] args) {
        int i = 0;
        while (true) {
            if (i == 1) continue;
            if (i == 2) break;
            System.out.print(i + " ");
            i++;
        }
        System.out.println("done");
    }
}
```

A. 1
B. 1 2
C. 1 done
D. Indefinite loop

Question 65 (2.1. Declare and initialize variables (including casting of primitive data types)

Given

```
public class USB {
    public static void main(String[] args) {
```

```
3.          int e = 0;
4.          float f = 123.3f;
5.          float h = f + (int) 12.3;
6.          float j = f = h;
7.          float k = j + 100.00;
8.      }
9. }
```

Which line(s) of code contain invalid declaration?

A. Line 4
B. Line 5
C. Line 6
D. Line 7

Question 66 (9.2. Creating and manipulating Strings)

What is the output of the following class?

```
package test;
public class Splitter {
    public static void main(String[] args) {
        String a = "aabraacadabra";
        String[] tokens = a.split("a");
        System.out.print(tokens.length);
        for (String token : tokens) {
            System.out.print(token + "|");
        }
    }
}
```

A. 6b|r|c|d|b|r|
B. 7||br||c|d|br|
C. 13a|a|b|r|a|a|c|a|d|a|b|r|a|
D. 8a|b|r|a|c|d|b|r|

Question 67 (2.5. Develop code that uses wrapper classes such as Boolean, Double, and Integer)

What are the wrapper classes for char, short, int, long and boolean, respectively?

A. Char, Short, Int, Long and Bool
B. Character, Short, Int, Long and Boolean
C. Character, Short, Integer, Long and Bool
D. Character, Short, Integer, Long and Boolean

Question 68 (6.4. Apply access modifiers)

Which access modifiers can be used for constructors?

A. public
B. protected

C. private
D. static

Question 69 (6.6. Determine the effect upon object references and primitive values when they are passed into methods that change the values)

Which of the following statements are true?

A. Objects and arrays are passed by reference
B. Primitives are passed by value
C. Arrays of primitives are passed by value
D. Arrays of objects are passed by reference

Question 70 (4.2. Declare, instantiate, initialize and use multi-dimensional array)

Consider the following code snippet:

```
public class Image {
    public static void main(String[] args) {
        int[][] pixels = {{0, 1, 0, 1}, {2, 2, 2}, {5, 6, 5}};
        int rows = pixels.length;
        int cols = pixels[0].length;
        for (int i = 0; i < rows; i++) {
            for (int j = 0; i < cols; j++) {
                System.out.print(pixels[i][j]);
            }
        }
    }
}
```

What is the result of the code?

A. Compilation error
B. The code throws an exception
C. 0101222565
D. 0251260250

Question 71 (6.1. Create methods with arguments and return values)

Which of the following shows the signature of a method that takes an **int** array and returns no value? (Choose all that apply)

A. public void method1(int... dots)
B. public null method2(int[] array)
C. private void method3(int... varargs)
D. method4(int[] array) as void

Question 72 (8.1. Differentiate among checked exceptions, unchecked exceptions, and Errors)

Which of the following is not an exception category?

A. Checked exceptions
B. Bugs
C. Unchecked exceptions
D. Errors

Question 73 (7.3. Determine when casting is necessary)

Consider the following code:

```
class Parent {}
class Child extends Parent {}
class GrandChild extends Child {}
```

Which of the following will generate a compile error? (Choose all that apply)

A. Parent p = new Child();
B. Child c = (Child) new Parent();
C. GrandChild g = (GrandChild) new Parent();
D. g = (Child) c;

Question 74 (6.2. Apply the static methods and fields)

Which of the following statements are true?

A. A static method is shared by all instances
B. A static field is a good way to store a value that is unique throughout all instances.
C. A static method can be called from an instance method in the same class.
D. An instance method can be called from a static method defined in the same class.

Question 75 (2.3. Know how to read or write to object fields)

Examine the following code.

```
public class Coder {
    private static short x;
    public long y;

    public static void main(String[] args) {
        Coder s = new Coder();
        x = (short) 7;
        y = 10;
        s.y = 12478;
        s.x = 100;
    }
}
```

Which of the following cause(s) a compile error?

A. x = (short) y;
B. y = 10;
C. s.y = 12478;
D. s.x = 100;

Question 76 (6.5. Apply encapsulation principles to a class)

A Java class has a field (named **x** and of type **long**) that needs to be protected against direct access from other classes. Which of the following line(s) of code complies with the OOP encapsulation principles?

A. private long x;
B. public void setX(long value)
C. public void getX()
D. protected long x;

Question 77 (9.4. Declare and use an ArrayList of a given type)

Which statement(s) creates an **ArrayList** of **File**s with an initial capacity of 36? (Choose all that apply)

A. ArrayList<File> names = new ArrayList<>();
B. List<File> names = new ArrayList<>(36);
C. List<File> names = new List<File>();
D. ArrayList<File> names = new ArrayList<File>(36);

Appendix D
Mock Exam 2 Answers

The following are answers to the questions in the second mock exam. Each question may have more than one correct answer and you have to choose all the correct answers.

Question 1 (1.3. Create executable Java applications with a main method; run a Java program from the command line; including console output)

Consider the following code.

```
package demo;
public class MainDemo {
    public static void main(String[] args) {
        System.out.println(args[0]);
    }
}
```

It is invoked with this command line command:

```
java demo.MainDemo 20+30
```

What is printed on the standard out?

A. 50
B. 20
C. 30
D. 20+30

Answer: D.

Program arguments are not evaluated. Thus, 20+30 is passed on to the **main** method as is.

Question 2 (1.3. Create executable Java applications with a main method; run a Java program from the command line; including console output)

Consider the following code snippet:

```
1.   package test;
2.
3.   public class Device {
```

```
4.          void main() {
5.          }
6.    }
```

What will happen if you try to compile this class? (Choose all that apply)

A. You will get a compile error at line 4 because **main** must be static.
B. You will get a compile error at line 4 because **main** must be public and static.
C. You will get a compile error at lines 3 and 4.
D. The class compiles without issues.

Answer: D.

You can create a public static void **main** method to make a class executable. However, nothing prevents you from naming a non-static non-public method **main**.

Question 3 (1.3. Create executable Java applications with a main method; run a Java program from the command line; including console output)

Given

```
package smalldevice;
public class Counter {
    public static void main(String[] args) {
        System.out.print(args[1]);
        System.out.print(args[2]);
    }
}
```

The program is invoked using this command.

```
java smalldevice.Counter zero "one" two
```

What is printed on the console?

A. zeroone
B. zero"one"
C. onetwo
D. "one"two

Answer: C.

The first element of **args** is args[0]. The program therefore prints the second and third arguments. Quotes around an argument are removed before the argument is passed to the program.

Question 4 (1.4. Import other Java packages to make them accessible in your code)

Which sets of **import** statements would allow you to use **java.util.List**, **java.util.ArrayList** and **java.lang.System** in your class?

A. import java.util.*;
B. import java.util.List; import java.util.ArrayList;
C. import java.util.List; import java.util.ArrayList; import java.lang.System;
D. import java.lang.*;
E. import java.lang.System;

Answer: A, B, C.

You can use members of the **java.lang** package without importing them, so you do not need to import **java.lang.System** even though doing so will not generate a compile error. On the other hand, members of other packages must be imported before use. You can import the whole package by using the asterisk as in option A. Alternatively, you can import individual types as in option B.

Question 5 (1.4. Import other Java packages to make them accessible in your code)

Which sets of **import** statements would allow you to use **java.util.List**, **java.util.ArrayList** and **java.lang.annotation.Documented** in your class?

A. import java.util.*;
B. import java.util.List; import java.util.ArrayList;
C. import java.util.*; import java.lang.annotation.Documented;
D. import java.util.*; import java.lang.annotation.*;
E. import java.lang.*;

Answer: C, D.

You can use members of the **java.lang** package without importing them, but members of its subpackages, such as **java.lang.annotation**, must be imported before use. Therefore, you need to import **java.lang.annotation.Documented** and the two members of **java.util**. You can import the whole package by using the asterisk as in D. Alternatively, you can import individual types as in C.

Question 6 (4.1. Declare, instantiate, initialize and use a one-dimensional array)

Assuming **stringArray** is a one-dimensional array, which of the following expressions returns the number of element in **stringArray**?

A. stringArray.size
B. stringArray.size()
C. stringArray.length
D. stringArray.length()
E. stringArray.capacity
F. stringArray.capacity()

Answer: C.

A and B are incorrect because arrays do not have a member called **size**.

C is correct because every array object has a field named **length**, which contains the number of elements in the array.

D is incorrect because an array object has no **length** method.

E and F are incorrect because array objects have no member called **capacity**.

Question 7 (2.1. Declare and initialize variables (including casting of primitive data types))

What is the output of this program?

```
 1. public class Utility {
 2.     public static void main(String[] args) {
 3.         int i = 9;
 4.         char c = '3';
 5.         i = c;
 6.         c = i;
 7.         System.out.print(i);
 8.         System.out.print(c);
 9.     }
10. }
```

A. The code prints 93
B. Compile error at line 5
C. Compile error at line 6
D. Compile error at lines 5 and 6

Answer: B.

A **char** can be assigned to an **int** without casting. However, an **int** cannot be assigned to a **char**.

Question 8 (7.5. Use abstract classes and interfaces)

What is the result of compiling this code?

```
interface Viewable {
    public List<String> getAllScreenNames();
    public static int getWidth() {
        return 1024;
    }
    public default int getScreenCount() {
        return 1;
    }
    String getDefaultScreenName();
}
```

A. Compile error because an interface may not contain static methods
B. Compile error because an interface may not contain method implementations
C. Compile error because the **getDefaultScreenName** method has no access modifier
D. It compiles without issues

Answer: D.

A is incorrect because Java 8 interfaces may contain static methods.

B is incorrect because starting from Java 8, interfaces may contain implementations in default methods.

C is incorrect because by default all methods are public even when no access modifier is present.

D is correct because the interface compiles without issues.

Question 9 (9.5. Write a simple Lambda expression that consumes a Lambda Predicate expression)

What is the possible outcome of this code?

```
package test;
import java.util.function.Predicate;
public class Tester {
    public static void main(String[] args) {
        Predicate<String> isNumber = x -> {
            for (int i = 0; i < x.length(); i++)
                if ("0123456789".indexOf("" + x.charAt(i)) == -1)
                    return false;
            return true;
        };
        System.out.println(isNumber.test(args[0]) ? "TRUE" : "FALSE");
    }
}
```

A. The code may print TRUE
B. The code may print FALSE
C. The code may throw an exception
D. The code will not compile

Answer: A, B, C.

A is correct. It will print TRUE if the class is invoked with at least one argument that consists of numbers only.

B is correct. It will print FALSE if the class is invoked with at least one argument and the argument is not a whole number.

C is correct. It will throw an exception if the class is run without an argument.

D is incorrect as the code compiles without issues.

Question 10 (9.1. Manipulate data using the StringBuilder class and its methods)

What does this code fragment print on the console?

```
StringBuilder buffer = new StringBuilder("Reversible");
for (int i = 0; i < buffer.length(); i++)
    if (buffer.charAt(i) == 'e')
        buffer.replace(i - 1, i, "E");
System.out.println(buffer);
```

A. REvErsiblE

B. REVERSIBLE
C. EeEersibEe
D. EEEErsibEE

Answer: C.

The code inspects each character in the **StringBuilder** and upon encountering an 'e' calls this line:

```
buffer.replace(i - 1, I, "E");
```

This replaces the character to the left of every 'e' with E.

Question 11 (2.5. Develop code that uses wrapper classes such as Boolean, Double, and Integer)

What is the outcome of the following class?

```
package example.test;
public class SmartUtility {
    public static double average(Integer... numbers) {
        long temp = 0;
        for (Integer i : numbers)
            temp += i;
        return temp / numbers.length;
    }
    public static void main(String[] args) {
        int[] ints = {1, 2, 6, 7};
        System.out.println(average(ints));
    }
}
```

A. The class prints 4.0
B. The code generates a compile error
C. The code throws a runtime exception
D. The class prints 4

Answer: B.

The **average** method takes an array of **Integers**. The **main** method passes it an array of **ints**. Since an array of **ints** is not compatible with an array of **Integers**, the class will generate a compile error.

Question 12 (6.1. Create methods with arguments and return values; including overloaded methods)

Consider the following code.

```
class Car extends java.lang.Object {
    private void brake() {}
    protected void brake(float decelaration) {}
    public int run(int speed) {
        int currentSpeed = 100;
```

```
        return currentSpeed < speed? currentSpeed : speed;
    }
    public static int run(int speed, int accelaration) {
        return speed + accelaration;
    }
    public String toString() {
        return "Car";
    }
}
```

Which statement(s) is or are true regarding the code?

A. The run methods are overloaded methods
B. The run methods are not overloaded methods since you cannot overload a static method with an instance method
C. The brake methods are overloaded methods.
D. The toString method in Car is an overload of the toString method in java.lang.Object.
E. The Car class will generate a compile error because of duplicate method names

Answer: A, C.

The **run** and **brake** methods are overloaded methods, so A and C are correct.

B is incorrect because you can overload an instance and a static methods.

D is incorrect. The **toString** method overrides the method in java.lang.Object and is not an overload of it.

E is incorrect since the class compiles fine.

Question 13 (1.2. Define the structure of a Java class)

Which of the following can appear within a class? (Choose all that apply)

A. Comments
B. Methods
C. Fields
D. Embedded files
E. Import statements

Answer: A, B, C.

A, B and C are correct as comments, methods and fields can appear in a Java class.

D is incorrect because a Java class cannot embed files.

E is incorrect because import statements cannot appear within a class.

Question 14 (1.5. Compare and contrast the features and components of Java such as: platform independence, object orientation, encapsulation, etc.)

Which of the following are features of Java?

A. Java is just like the conventional programming paradigm, after a program is compiled you get an executable file
B. Java programs can run in multiple platforms
C. To achieve platform independence, Java programs are compiled into different forms that work in multiple platforms
D. Java programs are compiled into bytecode

Answer: B, D.

A is incorrect because Java is unlike the conventional programming paradigm. In fact, a Java program is compiled to bytecode and not an executable file. This bytecode can only run on a Java virtual machine.

B is correct, platform independence is one of the allures of Java that make Java very popular.

C is incorrect. To achieve platform independence, Java programs are compiled into bytecodes, which can run on a Java virtual machine. By making JVMs available in multiple platforms, the same bytecode can be run in different operating systems, including Windows, Linux, Unix and Mac OS X.

D is correct. Java programs are compiled into bytecodes.

Question 15 (2.1. Declare and initialize variables (including casting of primitive data types))

Given

```
int i = 257;
byte b = (byte) i;
```

What is the value of **b** after the code is executed?

A. 255
B. 256
C. 257
D. 1
E. -1

Answer: D.

257 is too big for a byte and the value is truncated to 1 when narrowing conversion occurred.

Question 16 (3.2. Test equality between Strings and other objects using == and equals())

Consider this code.

```
Double d = new Double(12.34);
Double e = new Double(12.34);
Double f = 12.34;
Double g = 12.34;
```

Which of the following expressions return true? (Choose all that apply)

A. d==e
B. f==g
C. d.equals(e)
D. f.equals(g)

Answer: C, D.

Applied on reference types, the == operator tests if two variables are pointing to the same object. In this case, **d** and **e** are referring to different objects. Therefore, d==e evaluates to false and A is incorrect.

B is also incorrect because **f** and **g** are assigned different objects that are created by boxing the primitive value 12.34. f==g therefore evaluates to false.

C is correct as the **equals** methods in **String** and primitive wrapper classes compares the value of an object with the value of the current object.

For the same reason, D is also correct.

Question 17 (2.2. Differentiate between object reference variables and primitive variables)

Consider this code:

```
Long a = new Long(1000);
Long b = new Long(1000);
long c = 1000;
long d = 1000;
```

Which of the following expressions evaluate to true? (Choose all that apply)

A. a==b
B. a==c
C. c==d
D. a!=d

Answer: B, C.

A is incorrect because the == operator on reference variables test whether the variables are pointing to the same object. In this case, they are clearly not because **a** and **b** are assigned different objects (even though both have the same value).

B is correct because comparing a **Long** and a **long** forces the former to be unboxed and the primitive value retrieved from the unboxing process to be compared to the **long**.

C is correct because two **long**s having the same value are equal.

D is incorrect because a==d evaluates to true. Therefore, a!=d evaluates to false.

Question 18 (8.4. Create and invoke a method that throws an exception)

What is the output of the following program?

```
package test.math;
```

```
public class MathTester {
    public static double average(Integer... numbers) throws Exception {
        double total = 0;;
        for (Integer i : numbers) {
            if (i == null) {
                throw new Exception("Number cannot be null");
            }
            total += i;
        }
        return total/numbers.length;
    }

    public static void main(String[] args) {
        Integer[] numbers = {Integer.MIN_VALUE, Integer.MAX_VALUE, 0, 0};
        try {
            System.out.println(average(numbers));
        } catch (Exception e) {
            System.err.println(e.getMessage());
        }
    }
}
```

A. 0.00
B. -0.00
C. -0.25
D. Number cannot be null

Answer: C.

D is incorrect because 0 in the array declaration in the **main** method is boxed to an **Integer**. As such, the **average** method will not throw an exception.

C is correct. The value of **Integer.MIN_VALUE** is -2,147,483,648 and the value of Integer.MAX_VALUE is 2,147,483,647, so Integer.MIN_VALUE + Integer.MAX_VALUE = -1. Since there are four members in numbers, the average is -0.25 (1 / 4).

A and B are incorrect because the output is -0.25.

Question 19 (7.2. Develop code that demonstrates the use of polymorphism; including overriding and object type versus reference type)

Consider this class declaration:

```
class Entertainment implements java.io.Serializable {
}
```

Which of the following expressions evaluates to true?

A. (new Entertainment() instanceof Object)
B. (new Entertainment() instanceof Serializable)
C. (new Entertainment() instanceof Entertainment)

D. (new Object() instanceof Entertainment)
E. (new Object() instanceof Serializable);

Answer: A, B, C.

A is correct because all classes are implicitly derived from **java.lang.Object**. As such, an instance of any class is implicitly an instance of **Object**.

B is correct because **Entertainment** implements **java.io.Serializable**. As such, an instance of **Entertainment** is a type of **Serializable**.

C is correct for the obvious reason that the object you get by instantiating a class is an instance of that class.

D is incorrect as **Object** is not a type of **Entertainment**.

E is incorrect because **Object** and **Serializable** have no parent-child relationship.

Question 20 (9.2. Creating and manipulating Strings)

Which of the following expressions case-insensitively compare two strings?

A. a.equals(b)
B. a.toUpperCase().equals(b.toUpperCase())
C. a.toLowerCase().equals(b.toLowerCase())
D. a.equalsIgnoreCase(b)

Answer: B, C, D.

A is incorrect because the **String** class's **equals** method compares two strings case-sensitively.

B, C and D are correct. You can either use **equalsIgnoreCase** to compare two strings case-insensitively or convert the strings to either upper case or lower case before comparing.

Question 21 (3.3. Create if and if/else and ternary constructs)

What is printed on the console if the following class is executed without an argument?

```
package test;
public class Argument {
    public static void main(String[] args) {
        String comment = args.length > 0 ? args[0].equals("file") ?
                "accept" : "ignore" : "invalid";
        System.out.println(comment);
    }
}
```

A. file
B. accept
C. ignore
D. invalid

Answer: D.

The ternary construct will be easier to understand if written with parentheses:

```
args.length > 0 ? (args[0].equals("file")? "accept" : "ignore")
        : "invalid";
```

Since the class is invoked without arguments, **args.length** is 0 and the expression in the parentheses will be ignored and "invalid" printed.

Question 22 (5.1. Create and use while loops)

Given

```
package exercise;
public class EternalLoop {
    public static void main(String[] args) {
        int[] a = { 10, 20, 30, 40, 50, 10 };
        int i = a.length - 3;
        while (i > 0) {
            System.out.print(a[a.length - i]);
            i--;
        }
    }
}
```

What is printed on the console?

A. 123456
B. 102030405010
C. 405010
D. 10203040
E. 2030405010

Answer: C.

Since **a.length** = 6, the initial value of **i** is 3 and the loop iterates three times. The code prints 405010.

Question 23 (2.4. Explain an object's lifecycle (creation, "dereference by assignment" and garbage collection))

Given

```
public class Skill {
    public static void main(String[] args) {
        Skill s1 = new Skill();
        Skill s2 = new Skill();
        if (args.length > 0) s1 = null;
        System.out.println(s1);
        if (args.length > 1) s2 = new Skill();
        System.out.println(s2);
    }
}
```

Which of the following statements are true?

A. Two objects will be garbage collected at line 8.
B. One object will be garbage collected at line 6.
C. The object referenced by **s1** may be eligible for garbage collection at line 5.
D. The object referenced by **s2** is eligible for garbage collection at line 7.

Answer: C, D.

A and B are incorrect because there is no guarantee if or when an object that is eligible for garbage collection will be garbage-collected. The garbage collector runs on a low-priority thread and an intelligent garbage collector will not start destroying objects unless the heap is close to full.

An object is eligible for garbage collection if it is no longer referenced by any variable. Assigning null to a reference variable removes the reference to an object. C is correct because if the class is executed with at least one argument, **s1** will be null at line 5 and the object it referenced will be eligible for garbage collection.

D is also correct. If the class was executed with at least two arguments, **s2** will be assigned a new object and the old object will be eligible for garbage collection.

Question 24 (6.3. Create and overload constructors; including impact on default constructors)

Given the following code

```
package sample;
class Event {
    private String name;
    private String description;
    public Event(String name) {
        this.name = name;
    }
    public Event(String name, String description) {
        this.name = name;
        this.description = description;
    }
    public String getName() {
        return name;
    }
    public String getDescription() {
       return description;
    }
    public String toString() {
        return name + ", " + description;
    }
}

public class EventOrganizer {
    public static void main(String[] args) {
        Event e1 = new Event("New Year's Eve", "Sponsored event");
        Event e2 = new Event("101th Birthday");
        Event e3 = new Event(); // empty event
        System.out.print(e2);
```

```
        System.out.print(e3);
    }
}
```

Which of the following statements are correct?

A. The code will print "New Year's Eve, Sponsored event 101th Birthday"
B. The code will not compile
C. The code will print an empty string
D. The code will throw a runtime exception

Answer: B.

The Event class has two non-default constructors. As such, the compiler will not create a default constructor for it. As a result, attempting to create an **Event** by using this statement will generate a compilation error:

```
Event e3 = new Event();
```

Question 25 (1.1. Define the scope of variables)

Consider the following code snippet that contains named regions A, B, C, D, E and F.

```
int m = 0;
long x = 1001;
// ------- A --------
if (m == 0) {
    // ------- B --------
    for (int n = 0; n < 9; n++) {
        // ------- C --------
        System.out.println(x - n);
        System.out.println(n);
        if (n == 2) m++;
        // ------- D --------
    }
    // ------- E --------
    x++;
}
// ------- F --------
```

Which of the following statements are true?

A. *n* cannot be used in region F.
B. *m* and *n* can be used in region B
C. *m* and *n* can be used in region D
D. *m* and *n* can be used in region F

Answer: A, C.

A is correct because the scope of **n** is only in the **for** block. Therefore, **n** cannot be used in region F.

B is incorrect because **n** is not yet declared in region B.

C is correct because **m** and **n** are visible in region D.

D is incorrect because **n** is not visible in region F.

Question 26 (2.3. Know how to read or write to object fields)

Consider the following code.

```
package com.example;
class Event {
    public String name;
    private String description;
    public Event(String name) {
        this.name = name;
    }

    public Event(String name, String description) {
        this.name = name;
        this.description = description;
    }

    public String getDescription() {
        return description;
    }

    public void setDescription(String description) {
        this.description = this.description;
    }
    public String toString() {
        return name + ", " + description;
    }
}

public class Organizer {
    public static void main(String[] args) {
        Event e = new Event("Summer Festival", "New York & Toronto");
        e.name = "Winter is coming early";
        e.setDescription("Summer Festival canceled");
        System.out.println(e);
    }
}
```

What is the outcome of the code?

A. The code generates a compile error
B. The code prints “Summer Festival, New York & Toronto”
C. The code prints “Winter is coming early, Summer Festival canceled”
D. The code prints “Winter is coming early, New York & Toronto”

Answer: D.

The **name** field in the **Event** class can be set directly because it is public. The **setDescription** method looks like it has been designed to write to the **description** field. However, there is a bug. The **this** keyword in **this.description** refers to the **description** field. As such, this line of code in **setDescription** does not change the value of the

description field.

```
this.description = this.description
```

Question 27 (3.1. Use Java operators; including parentheses to override operator precedence)

What is the output of the following code snippet?

```
public class Tester {
    public static void main(String[] args) {
        int i = 3, j = 3;
        System.out.print(++i + i);
        System.out.print(" ");
        System.out.print(j++ + j);
        System.out.print(" ");
        System.out.print(i);
        System.out.print(" ");
        System.out.print(j);
    }
}
```

A. 8 8 4 4
B. 7 7 4 4
C. 7 8 4 4
D. 8 7 4 4

Answer: D.

This is an easy question if you know the difference between i++ and ++i:

The expression i++ returns the value of i and then increments i. By contrast, the expression ++i increments i and then returns its value. Therefore, (++i + i) is equal to (4 + 4) whereas (j++ + j) is equal to (3 + 4).

Question 28 (3.4. Use a switch statement)

What is the output of the following code?

```
package base;

public class SwitchTester {
    public static void main(String[] args) {
        int n = 100;
        switch (++n) {
        case 100:
            System.out.print("100");
        default:
            System.out.print("default");
        }
    }
}
```

A. 100default

B. 100
C. default
D. default100

Answer: C.

Note that **++n** increments **n** and then return its value. In other words, in the code above, switch (++n) is equivalent to switch (101). Since there is no case for 101, the default case is executed.

Question 29 (4.2. Declare, instantiate, initialize and use multi-dimensional array)

Consider the following class:

```
public class Test100 {
    public static void main(String[] args) {
        int[][][] matrix = {{{1, 2, 3},{4, 5, 6}}, {
            {10, 20, 30},{40, 50, 60}}};
        System.out.print(matrix[0][0][0] * matrix[1][1][1]);
    }
}
```

What is printed on the console when the class is executed?

A. 8
B. 10
C. 40
D. 50
E. 80
D. 120

Answer: D.

matrix[0][0][0] is 1 and **matrix[1][1][1]** is 50. Therefore, 50 will be printed on the console when the program is run.

Question 30 (5.2. Create and use for loops including the enhanced for loop)

Given

```
package test;
import java.util.ArrayList;
import java.util.List;
public class Test200 {
    public static void main(String[] args) {
        String[] names = { "Henri", "Borousa" };
        String[] cities = { "Melbourne", "Wilton" };
        List<String> mix = new ArrayList<>();
        for (String name : names) {
            mix.add(name);
            for (String city : cities) {
```

```
                mix.add(city);
            }
        }
        String[] namesCities = new String[]{};
        namesCities = mix.toArray(namesCities);
        System.out.println(namesCities.length);
    }
}
```

What is printed on the console when the class is run?

A. 2
B. 4
C. 6
D. 7
E. 8

Answer: C.

The question asks the length of **namesCities**. These loops add elements to the **List**:

```
for (String name : names) {
    mix.add(name);
    for (String city : cities) {
        mix.add(city);
    }
}
```

The outer loop iterates twice, adding two elements to **mix**. For each iteration, the inner **for** loop is called, adding two more elements each time. Therefore, the number of elements in **mix** is six after the outer loop terminates, and so is the length of **namesCities**.

Question 31 (9.3. Create and manipulate calendar data using classes from java.time.LocalDateTime, java.time.LocalDate, java.time.LocalTime, java.time.format.DateTimeFormatter, java.time.Period)

Consider the following code.

```
package tester;
import java.time.LocalDate;
import java.time.LocalDateTime;
import java.time.LocalTime;
import java.time.format.DateTimeFormatter;

public class FlightTime {
    public static void main(String[] args) {
        LocalDate depDate = LocalDate.of(2015, 12, 12);
        LocalTime depTime = LocalTime.of(10, 20);
        LocalDateTime departure = LocalDateTime.of(depDate, depTime);
        LocalDateTime arrival = departure.plusHours(8).plusMinutes(30);
        System.out.println(arrival.format(
            DateTimeFormatter.ofPattern("yyyy mm dd hh:MM")));
```

```
    }
}
```

What is printed on the console?

A. 2015 12 12 06:50
B. 2015 50 12 06:12
C. 2015/12/12 06:50
D. 2015/06/12 12:50
E. 2015 12 12 18:50

Answer: B.

Note that the pattern is very unusual. mm represents minutes and MM the month. This pattern basically tells the date time to be displayed in this format: year minute date hour:month.

Question 32 (9.4. Declare and use an ArrayList of a given type)

Consider the following class:

```
package com.brainysoftware.server;
import java.util.ArrayList;
public class Gauge {
    public static void main(String[] args) {
        ArrayList<Long> collection = new ArrayList<>();
        collection.add(459);
        collection.add(new Long("123"));
        for (long l : collection) {
            System.out.print(l);
        }
    }
}
```

What is the result of this class?

A. Compilation error
B. Runtime error
C. It prints 459123 when run
D. It prints 459 when run

Answer: A.

The **ArrayList** can only store **Long**s and cannot be given an **int** (of value 459).

Question 33 (7.1. Describe inheritance and its benefits)

Which of the following statements are true? (Choose all that apply)

A. Inheritance is a feature of object-oriented programming
B. You implement inheritance using the extend keyword
C. All methods in a parent class can be used in a child class
D. Certain fields in a parent class can be accessed in a child class.

Answer A, D.

A is correct because inheritance is a feature of OOP.

B is incorrect. You use the keyword **extends** to create a subclass, not **extend**.

C is incorrect. Private methods in a parent class are not accessible from within a child class.

D is correct. Only protected and public fields in a parent class are guaranteed to be accessible from a child class. In addition, default fields in a parent class can also be accessed from a child class if the child class resides in the same package as the parent class.

Question 34 (7.3. Determine when casting is necessary)

Consider this code.

```
long l = 4321238398434234 34L;
int i = (int) l;
long l2 = (long) i;
byte b = (byte) i;
short s = (short) b;
short t = (short) s;
```

Which explicit castings are not optional? (Choose all that apply)

A. int i = (int) l;
B. long l2 = (long) i;
C. byte b = (byte) i;
D. short s = (short) b;
E. short t = (short) s;

Answer: A, C.

Narrowing conversions require explicitly casting.

Question 35 (8.5. Recognize common exception classes (such as NullPointerException. ArithmeticException, ArrayIndexOutOfBoundsException, ClassCastException))

Which of the following are runtime exceptions? (Choose all that apply)

A. CannotLoadException
B. NullPointerException
C. IllegalArgumentException
D. NumberFormatException
E. OutOfMemoryError

Answer: B, C, D.

A is incorrect as it does not exist.

B, C and D are correct as **NullPointerException**, **IllegalArgumentException** and **NumberFormatException** are derived from **RuntimeException**.

E is incorrect because **OutOfMemoryError** is an error and not a runtime exception.

Question 36 (8.3. Describe the advantages of Exceptions handling)

Which of the following statements are true?

A. A potential error can be isolated using the **try** statement
B. The **try-with-resources** statement closes all resources that implements **AutoCloseable**
C. You should catch all errors in your program
D. All exception classes are subclasses of **java.lang.Exception**

Answer: A, B.

C is incorrect because you should not try to catch serious errors such as **java.lang.StackOverflowError** and **java.lang.OutOfMemoryError**.

D is incorrect because all exception classes are derived from **java.lang.Throwable**.

Question 37 (8.2. Create a try-catch block and determine how exceptions alter normal program flow)

Consider the following code fragment.

```
package rewardprogram;

public class Reward {
    public static void main(String[] args) {
        int j = 0;
        try {
            j = Integer.parseInt(args[0]);
        } catch (NumberFormatException e) {
            System.out.println("Incorrect number format");
        } catch (NullPointerException e) {
            System.out.println("Null argument");
        } catch (ArrayIndexOutOfBoundsException e) {
            System.out.println("No argument found");
        }
        System.out.println(j);
    }
}
```

What is printed on the console if the class is invoked without an argument.

A. No argument found
B. Null argument
C. 0
D. Incorrect number format

Answer: A.

The **main** method of a class invoked without an argument will received an empty String array. Since the array is empty, trying to read an argument in it will throw an **ArrayIndexOutOfBoundsException**.

Question 38 (7.4. Use super and this to access objects and constructors)

Given

```
package test;
class Super {
    @Override
    public String toString() {
        return "Super " + this.toString();
    }
}

class Sub extends Super {
    @Override
    public String toString() {
        return "Sub " + super.toString();
    }
}

public class Tester {
    public static void main(String[] args) {
        Sub sub = new Sub();
        System.out.println(sub);
    }
}
```

What happens when the class **Tester** is executed?

A. An error will be thrown
B. It will print "Sub Super Object"
C. It will print "Sub Super"
D. It will print "Sub Super" followed by a random string

Answer: A.

The class will throw a **java.lang.StackOverflowError** because the **toString** method in **Super** calls itself recursively until a stack overflow occurs.

Question 39 (5.3. Create and use do/while loops)

Given

```
package com.example.test;
import java.util.ArrayList;
import java.util.List;

public class LoopExample {
    public static void main(String[] args) {
        List<String> list = new ArrayList<>();
        String[] favCities = { "Berlin", "Boston", "Chicago" };
        for (String city : favCities) list.add(city);
        do {
            System.out.print(list.get(0) + "--");
```

```
            list.remove(0);
        } while (list.size() > 0);
    }
}
```

What is the result of running this class?

A. Berlin--Boston--Chicago--
B. An empty string
C. Berlin--Boston--
D. Berlin--

Answer: A.

The class starts by adding the elements in the string array to the **List**. It then uses a do-while loop to iterate over the **List**, removing the first element at each iteration until there is no more element in the **List**.

Question 40 (3.4. Use a switch statement)

What is the output of the following code if ?

```
public class Util {
    public static void main(String[] args) {
        int a = args.length;
        switch (a) {
        case 0:
            System.out.print("No argument");
        case 1:
            System.out.print("One argument");
            break;
        case 2:
            System.out.print("Two arguments or more");
            break;
            default:
                System.out.print("Default");
        }
    }
}
```

A. No argument
B. One argument
C. No argumentOne argument
D. Default

Answer: C.

If the class is invoked without an argument, **args.length** will be 0 and the first case of the **switch** statement will be executed. Because there is no break at the end of the code for the case, the case next to it will also be called.

Question 41 (5.5. Use break and continue)

What is the output of the following class?

```
public class FunnyGame {
    public static void main(String[] args) {
        int b = 15;
        Loop1:
        for (int a = 0; a < 5; a += 2) {
            Loop2:
                b--;
                for (int c = 6; c > 0; c--) {
                    if (c==4) continue;
                    System.out.print(c+" ");
                    if (c==3) continue Loop1;
                    if (c==2) break;
                }
        }
    }
}
```

A. 6 5 3 2 6 5 3 2 6 5 3 2
B. 6 5 3 6 5 3 6 5 3
C. 6 5 3 6 5 3 6 5 3 5
D. 6 5 3 6 5 3 6 5 2

Answer: B.

The second for loop will iterate until **c** is equal to 3 and then continue to the outer loop. As a result, the second loop will only iterate three times, printing 6 5 3. The outer loop iterates three times (for a = 0, a = 2 and a = 4), so 6 5 3 will be printed three times.

Question 42 (5.4. Compare loop constructs)

Consider the following code snippet that is supposed to print 234:

```
1. ...
2. {
3.     System.out.print(a++);
4. }
```

Which of the following statements can be inserted into line 1 so that the code does what is expected of it?

A. for (int a=2; i<5;)
B. int a=2; while(a<5)
C. for (int a=2; a<5; a++)
D. for (int a=2; i<5; i++)

Answer: A, B.

A and B are correct.

C is incorrect because a is incremented twice.

D is incorrect because it uses variable i without declaring it. It will generate a compile error.

Question 43 (6.2. Apply the static keyword to methods and fields)

What will happen if you try to compile and run this code?

```
package test;
class Bottle {
    public static int weight = 10;
}
public class Bartender {
    public static void main(String[] args) {
        Bottle bottle = new Bottle();
        bottle.weight = 123;
        Bottle.weight = 654;
        System.out.println(bottle.weight);
    }
}
```

A. You will get a compilation error for trying to access a static field as an instance field
B. The code will compile fine and it will print 123
C. The code will compile fine and it will print 654
D. The code will throw a runtime error

Answer: C.

You can access a static field as an instance field, however the field will still be shared by all instances.

Question 44 (6.4. Apply access modifiers)

Which of the following statements are true? (Choose all that apply)

A. Public methods in a protected class can only be accessed from subclasses of the class
B. The private methods of a class cannot be accessed from other top-level classes
C. Static private methods in a class can be access from other classes
D. Methods with the default access can be called from the class's subclasses and other classes in the same package

Answer: B.

A is incorrect because a method's accessibility is determined by the method's access modifier, and not by the access modifier of its enclosing class. As long as you can instantiate the enclosing class, you can access its public methods.

B is correct because private methods can only be accessed from within the class itself.

C is incorrect because private methods can only be accessed from within the class itself, even though the methods are static.

D is incorrect because methods with the default access can only be accessed from other classes in the same package.

Question 45 (6.5. Apply encapsulation principles to a class)

Which of the following are steps to implementing encapsulation? (Choose all that apply)

A. All fields are made private
B. Access to fields are done through public methods
C. Read-only fields must have get methods but not set methods
D. Write-only fields must have get methods but not set methods

Answer: A, B, C.

A, B and C are correct.

D is incorrect because write-only fields must have set methods but not get methods.

Question 46 (8.1. Differentiate among checked exceptions, unchecked exceptions, and Errors)

Which of the following statements are true with regard to exception handling in Java?

A. A well-written program should try to catch both checked exceptions and unchecked exceptions
B. Unchecked exceptions are runtime exceptions
C. Errors are caused by external factors to the program
D. Errors should be caught

Answer: B, C.

A is incorrect because programmers are supposed to catch checked exceptions only.

B and C are correct.

D is incorrect because errors are not supposed to be caught.

Question 47 (6.6. Determine the effect upon object references and primitive values when they are passed into methods that change the values)

Consider this code:

```
package com.example.geniemanager;
import java.util.ArrayList;
import java.util.List;
class Genie {
    public String grantWishes(int requestCode, List<String> wishes) {
        for (int i = wishes.size() - 1; i >= 0; i--) {
            String wish = wishes.get(wishes.size() - 1);
            // do something to grant wish
            wishes.remove(wish);
        }
        requestCode++;
        return "OK";
```

```
    }
}
public class GenieManager {
    public static void main(String[] args) {
        Genie genie = new Genie();
        List<String> wishes = new ArrayList<>();
        wishes.add("I want to pass all exams without studying");
        wishes.add("I want a flashy electric car");
        byte requestCode = 100;
        genie.grantWishes(requestCode, wishes);
        System.out.println(requestCode);
        for (String wish : wishes) {
            System.out.println(wish);
        }
    }
}
```

What are the variable values right after the for loop in **main** is executed?

A. The value of requestCode is 100
B. The List contains two elements
C. The List is empty
D. The value of requestCode is 101

Answer: A, C.

A is correct because **requestCode** in the **main** method is not affected by the change made in **grantWishes**.

B is incorrect because the **List** is emptied and since **List** is a reference type, the changes made in a method affect the object passed. The **List** is empty after **grantWishes** is executed.

C is correct.

D is incorrect because primitives passed to a method are first copied. Changes are only made to the copies.

Question 48 (7.5. Use abstract classes and interfaces)

Which of the following are correct implementations of the interface **WithWings**?

```
public abstract interface WithWings {
    void fly(int speed);
}

class DragonFly implements WithWings { }

abstract class Bird implements WithWings {
}

abstract class Bat implements WithWings {
    public void fly(int speed) {}
}
```

```
abstract class Moth implements WithWings {
    public abstract void fly(int speed);
}

final class Bee implements WithWings {
    protected void fly(int speed) {}
}
```

A. Dragonfly
B. Bird
C. Bat
D. Moth
E. Bee

Answer: B, C, D.

A is incorrect because **DragonFly** implements **WithWings** but does not provide an implementation for its **fly** method.

B is correct. Even though the class **Bird** implements **WithWings** and does not provide an implementation for its **fly** method, the class itself is declared abstract. An abstract class does not have to provide implementations for the methods of the interfaces it implements.

C and D are also correct for the same reason B is correct.

E is incorrect because the **fly** implementation in **Bee** reduces the visibility of the method from public to protected. This is illegal in Java.

Question 49 (7.2. Develop code that demonstrates the use of polymorphism; including overriding and object type versus reference type)

Consider the following code:

```
 1. class Combatant {
 2.    public void fight() {}
 3. }
 4. class Gladiator extends Combatant {
 5.     public void changeEmployer() {}
 6. }
 7.
 8. public class Test1000 {
 9.     public static void main(String[] args) {
10.         Combatant c1 = new Combatant();
11.         Combatant c2 = new Gladiator();
12.         Gladiator c3 = new Gladiator();
13.         ...
14.     }
15. }
```

What can be inserted into line 13 without generating a compilation error?

A. c1.changeEmployer();

B. c2.changeEmployer();
C. (Gladiator)c2.changeEmployer()
D. ((Gladiator)c2).changeEmployer();

Answer: D.

A is incorrect because **c1** is pointing to an instance of **Combatant** and the **Combatant** class does not have a **changeEmployer** method.

B is incorrect because even though **c2** is pointing to an instance of **Gladiator**, **c2** is of type **Combatant**, which does not provide a **changeEmployer** method.

C is an attempt to downcast **c2** to **Gladiator**. However, its syntax is wrong. C is therefore incorrect.

D is correct, **c2** is downcast to **Gladiator**.

Question 50 (9.4. Declare and use an ArrayList of a given type)

What is the output of the following code?

```
public class Numerator {
    public static void main(String[] args) {
        List<Integer> numbers = new ArrayList<>();
        for (int i = 0; i < 5; i++) {
            numbers.add(i + numbers.size());
        }
        for (int i = 0; i < 5; i++) {
            if (numbers.contains(i))
                numbers.remove(new Integer(i));
        }
        System.out.println(numbers);
    }
}
```

A. [1, 2, 3, 4, 5]
B. [1, 3, 5, 7, 9]
C. [9, 7]
D. [6, 8]

Answer: D.

In the first **for** loop, the values of **i** in the iterations are 0, 1, 2, 3 and 4, for which the values of **numbers.size()** are also 0, 1, 2, 3, 4, respectively. After the first loop, the content of **numbers** is [0, 2, 4, 6, 8]. The second loop will remove elements in numbers with the value of 0, 2 and 4, leaving 6 and 8.

Question 51 (9.5. Write a simple Lambda expression that consumes a Lambda Predicate expression)

Given

```
Predicate<Void> xyz = (x) -> 3 == 1;
```

Which statement(s) can be used to invoke the Predicate?

A. xyz.test(null);
B. xyz.test("");
C. xyz.test();
D. xyz.test(xyz);

Answer: A.

A **Predicate** that takes **Void** can only be invoked by passing null.

Question 52 (9.1. Manipulate data using the StringBuilder class and its methods)

Given

```
public class StringUtil {
    public static String process(String s) {
        StringBuilder sb = new StringBuilder();
        for (int i = s.length() - 1; i >= 0; i--) {
            sb.append(i % 2 == 0? Character.toUpperCase(s.charAt(i)) :
                    s.charAt(s.length() - i));
        }
        return sb.toString();
    }
    public static void main(String[] args) {
        String s = "New Age";
        System.out.println(process(s));
    }
}
```

What is the output of the class?

A. NEW AGE
B. Ega weN
C. EEgnwen
D. EwAAWeN

Answer: D.

The length of **s** is 7 and the value of **i** in the for loop starts with 6 and ends with 0. The sequence of characters returned by the **process** method is determined by this expression:

```
i % 2 == 0
```

For i = 6, the expression returns true, so the uppercase of the sixth character in **s** (E) is added to the **StringBuilder**.

For i = 5, i%2==0 returns false, so s.charAt(7-5), which is 'w', is added to the StringBuilder.

Since D is the only option that starts with Ew, D is correct.

Question 53 (3.4. Use a switch statement)

Consider the following code:

```
public class DataAccess {
    public static void main(String[] args) {
        String s = "\\\\temp\\\\data";
        switch (s.substring(1, 2)) {
        case "\\":
            s = "slash" + s;
        case "\\\\":
            s += "\\\\temp";
            break;
        case "data":
            s += "data";
            break;
        default:
            s += "default";
        }
        System.out.println(s);
    }
}
```

What is printed on the console when the class is executed?

A. \\
B. \\\\
C. slash\\temp\\data\\temp
D. temp\data

Answer: C.

"\\\\temp\\\\data".substring(1, 2) returns a backslash, which has to be escaped with another backslash if it is to be written as a Java string. Therefore, the first case, "\\" will be executed, which appends the string "slash" to **s**. At this point, the value of **s** is "slash\\\\temp\\\\data". Since there is no break at the end of the first case, execution continues to the second case, appending "\\\\temp" to **s**. As a result, the value of **s** is now "slash\\\\temp\\\\data\\\\temp". Note that "\\\\" is printed simply as \\.

Question 54 (8.2. Create a try-catch block and determine how exceptions alter normal program flow)

What is the result of the following class if invoked without an argument?

```
public class TryCatchFinally {
    public static void main(String[] args) {
        String s = null;
        try {
            s = args[0];
        } catch (Exception e) {
            try {
                s = "exception ";
                throw new Exception();
            } catch (Exception x) {
                s = s + "exception ";
            } finally {
```

```
13.                 s = s + "finally ";
14.             }
15.         } finally {
16.             s += "finally ";
17.         }
18.         System.out.println(s);
19.     }
20. }
```

A. Compilation error
B. Uncaught exception
C. exception exception
D. exception exception finally finally
E. exception finally exception finally

Answer: D.

Since the class is invoked without an argument, calling args[0] at line 5 will throw an **ArrayIndexOutOfBounds** exception, causing the catch block that starts at line 6 to be executed. As a result, at line 8, **s** is assigned "exception " and line 9 throws a new exception. Due to the new exception, the caught block that starts at line 10 is called, followed by the finally block at line 12. Finally, the finally block of the outer try is called.

Question 55 (4.1. Declare, instantiate, initialize and use a one-dimensional array)

What is the result of this code?

```
package animalkingdom;
public class Dog {
    private String name;
    public Dog(String name) {
        this.name = name;
    }
    @Override
    public String toString() {
        return name;
    }
    public static void main(String[] args) {
        Dog dog1 = new Dog("Wanda");
        Dog dog2 = new Dog("William Biteman");
        Dog[] dogs = { dog1, dog2 };
        dog1 = new Dog("Shark");
        dog2 = new Dog("Sherri");
        for (Dog dog : dogs) {
            System.out.print(dog + " ");
        }
    }
}
```

A. Compilation error
B. Runtime exception
C. Wanda William Biteman

D. Shark Sherri

Answer: C.

The dogs named Wanda and Wiliam Biteman are added to the array, then the reference variables for both dogs are assigned new dogs. However, this does not change the fact that the array contains the original dogs that were added to it. As a result, Wanda William Biteman is printed on the console.

Question 56 (3.1. Use Java operators; including parentheses to override operator precedence)

What is the result of this code?

```
public class Prince {
    public static void main(String[] args) {
        System.out.print(" " + 66 + 2 + " ");
        System.out.print(66 + 2 + " ");
        System.out.print(" " + (66 + 2) + " ");
        System.out.print(66 + 2);
    }
}
```

A. 68 68 68 68
B. 662 662 68 68
C. 662 68 68 68
D. 662 662 662 662

Answer: C.

Adding a string with an integer results in a string. Therefore, " " + 6 returns " 6". Therefore, the first **print** method prints " 662 ". The second print method evaluates 66 + 2 before concatenating the result with " ". As a result, it prints "68 ". The third and fourth calls to print evaluates the addition before printing the result.

Question 57 (5.1. Create and use while loops)

What is the result of the following code?

```
public class WhileTest {
    public static void main(String[] args) {
        String s= "newworld";
        int i = s.length();
        while (!s.isEmpty()) {
            i++;
            s = s.substring(1);
        }
        System.out.println(i);
    }
}
```

A. NullPointerException
B. newworld
C. 18

D. 16

Answer: D.

The code starts with i = 8, which is the length of the string **s. s.substring(1)** reduces the length by 1. Each time it happens, i is incremented. Because the initial length of s is 8, the final value for **i** is 16.

Question 58 (5.3. Create and use do/while loops)

What is the result of the class?

```
class Roll {
    public static void main(String[] args) {
        String s= "java";
        do {
            System.out.print(s);
            s = s.substring(0, s.length() - 1);
        } while (s.length() > 1);
    }
}
```

A. javajavajava
B. javajavajav
C. javajavj
D. javajavja

Answer: D.

The **substring** method in the code cuts the last character in the string. As a result, javajavja is printed on the console.

Question 59 (5.2. Create an use for loops including the enhanced for loop)

Given

```
import java.util.ArrayList;
import java.util.List;

public class Kitty {
    public static void main(String[] args) {
        List<String> names = new ArrayList<>();
        names.add("Jay");
        names.add("James");
        names.addAll(names);
        names.addAll(names);
        names.remove(4);
        for (String name : names) {
            System.out.println(name);
        }
    }
}
```

How many names are printed on the console?

A. 7
B. 4
C. 3
D. 8

Answer: A.

The list is created empty and two names are added to it:

```
List<String> names = new ArrayList<>();
names.add("Jay");
names.add("James");
```

Next, the **addAll** method adds all members in the collection. In effect, this doubles the number of elements in **names** to four. It then calls **addAll** for the second time, doubling the number of elements to eight. Finally, the code removes the element at index 4. As a result, just before the for loop is executed, **names** contains 7 elements.

Question 60 (9.3. Create and manipulate calendar data using classes from java.time.LocalDateTime, java.time.LocalDate, java.time.LocalTime, java.time.format.DateTimeFormatter, java.time.Period)

What is the output of this code?

```
LocalDate start = LocalDate.of(2015, 10, 13);
LocalDate finish = LocalDate.of(2015, 9, 15);
Period period = Period.between(start, finish);
System.out.println(period.getDays());
```

A. -29
B. 29
C. -28
D. 28

Answer: C.

The **between** method returns the difference between its two arguments, and there are 28 days between September 15 and October 13. Since **finish** is earlier than **start**, the result is negative.

Question 61 (7.4. Use super and this to access objects and constructors)

Given

```
class Tier1 {
    public void print() {
        System.out.print("Tier 1...");
    }
}
class Tier2 extends Tier1 {
```

```
    public void print() {
        super.print();
        System.out.print("Tier 2...");
    }
}

class Tier3 extends Tier2 {
    public void print(String name) {
        super.print();
        System.out.print("Tier 3...");
    }
}
public class Tiery {
    public static void main(String[] args) {
        Tier2 tier = new Tier3();
        tier.print();
        tier = (Tier3) tier;
        tier.print();
    }
}
```

What is printed on the console when the class is run?

A. Tier1...Tier2...Tier3...
B. Tier1...Tier2...Tier1...Tier2...
C. Tier1...Tier2...Tier1...Tier2...Tier3...
D. Tier1...Tier2...Tier3...Tier1...Tier2...Tier3...

Answer: B.

An instance of **Tier3** is assigned to a reference variable of type **Tier2**. Calling **print** on the object will invoke the **print** method in **Tier2**, not **Tier3**. Then, an attempt is made to downcast the variable to **Tier3**, but it has no effect since **tier** is already an instance of **Tier3** and, more importantly, it is not assigned to a variable of type **Tier3**. As a result, during the execution of the class, the **print** method defined in **Tier2** is called twice.

Question 62 (2.4. Explain an object's lifecycle (creation, "dereference by assignment" and garbage collection))

Given

```
public class Solution {
    private void print() {
        System.out.println(new Solution());
        System.out.println(new Solution());
    }
    public static void main(String[] args) {
        Solution solution = new Solution();
        solution.print();

    }
}
```

At line 9, how many objects are eligible for garbage collection?

A. 0
B. 1
C. 2
D. 3

Answer: D.

At line 8 there are three **Solution** objects created, including two instances created by the **print** method. At line 9, none of the objects is referenced by any variable. As a result, all of them are eligible for garbage collection.

Question 63 (7.1. Describe inheritance and its benefits)

Which of the following statements are true? (Choose all that apply)

A. A class can implement another class
B. An interface can extend another interface
C. A class can extend any class
D. A class can implement multiple interfaces

Answer B, D.

A is incorrect because a class can implement interfaces, not another class.

B is correct because an interface can extend another interface.

C is incorrect because a class cannot extend a final class.

D is correct. A class can implement multiple interfaces.

Question 64 (5.5. Use break and continue)

What is the result of this code?

```
public class LoopTest {
    public static void main(String[] args) {
        int i = 0;
        while (true) {
            if (i == 1) continue;
            if (i == 2) break;
            System.out.print(i + " ");
            i++;
        }
        System.out.println("done");
    }
}
```

A. 1
B. 1 2
C. 1 done
D. Indefinite loop

Answer: D.

The **continue** statement in the **while** loop moves control to the beginning of the loop and causes an indefinite loop.

Question 65 (2.1. Declare and initialize variables (including casting of primitive data types)

Given

```
1. public class USB {
2.     public static void main(String[] args) {
3.         int e = 0;
4.         float f = 123.3f;
5.         float h = f + (int) 12.3;
6.         float j = f = h;
7.         float k = j + 100.00;
8.     }
9. }
```

Which line(s) of code contain invalid declaration?

A. Line 4
B. Line 5
C. Line 6
D. Line 7

Answer: D.

Options A, B and C are valid. Option D is invalid as 100.00 is a **double** and j + 100.00 is also a **double**. Assigning a **double** to a **float** is invalid.

Question 66 (9.2. Creating and manipulating Strings)

What is the output of the following class?

```
package test;
public class Splitter {
    public static void main(String[] args) {
        String a = "aabraacadabra";
        String[] tokens = a.split("a");
        System.out.print(tokens.length);
        for (String token : tokens) {
            System.out.print(token + "|");
        }
    }
}
```

A. 6b|r|c|d|b|r|
B. 7||br||c|d|br|
C. 13a|a|b|r|a|a|c|a|d|a|b|r|a|
D. 8a|b|r|a|c|d|b|r|

Answer: B.

The string is split into tokens using “a” as the delimiter. Two consecutive characters that are equal to the delimiter will result in an empty string. As such, there will be seven tokens since there are seven "a"s.

Question 67 (2.5. Develop code that uses wrapper classes such as Boolean, Double, and Integer)

What are the wrapper classes for char, short, int, long and boolean, respectively?

A. Char, Short, Int, Long and Bool
B. Character, Short, Int, Long and Boolean
C. Character, Short, Integer, Long and Bool
D. Character, Short, Integer, Long and Boolean

Answer: D.

The wrapper classes for char, short, int, long and boolean are **Character**, **Short**, **Integer**, **Long** and **Boolean**, respectively.

Question 68 (6.4. Apply access modifiers)

Which access modifiers can be used for constructors?

A. public
B. protected
C. private
D. static

Answer: A, B, C.

Constructors can have the following access modifiers: public, protected, the default access modifier and private. Therefore, A, B and C are correct.

D is incorrect because **static** is not an access modifier.

Question 69 (6.6. Determine the effect upon object references and primitive values when they are passed into methods that change the values)

Which of the following statements are true?

A. Objects and arrays are passed by reference
B. Primitives are passed by value
C. Arrays of primitives are passed by value
D. Arrays of objects are passed by reference

Answer: A, B, D.

Objects are passed by reference and primitives are passed by value. Arrays (even arrays of primitives) are objects so arrays are also passed by reference.

Question 70 (4.2. Declare, instantiate, initialize and use multi-dimensional array)

Consider the following code snippet:

```
public class Image {
    public static void main(String[] args) {
        int[][] pixels = {{0, 1, 0, 1}, {2, 2, 2}, {5, 6, 5}};
        int rows = pixels.length;
        int cols = pixels[0].length;
        for (int i = 0; i < rows; i++) {
            for (int j = 0; i < cols; j++) {
                System.out.print(pixels[i][j]);
            }
        }
    }
}
```

What is the result of the code?

A. Compilation error
B. The code throws an exception
C. 0101222565
D. 0251260250

Answer: B.

The code author assumed that all rows would have the same number of elements as the first row, which is not the case. The second and third rows only have three elements instead of four. As a result, an **ArrayIndexOutOfBoundsException** is thrown.

Question 71 (6.1. Create methods with arguments and return values)

Which of the following shows the signature of a method that takes an **int** array and returns no value? (Choose all that apply)

A. public void method1(int... dots)
B. public null method2(int[] array)
C. private void method3(int... varargs)
D. method4(int[] array) as void

Answer: A, C.

A and C are correct. A varargs argument is basically an array.

B is incorrect because null is not a valid return value.

D is incorrect because of the syntax.

Question 72 (8.1. Differentiate among checked exceptions, unchecked exceptions, and Errors)

Which of the following is not an exception category?

A. Checked exceptions
B. Bugs
C. Unchecked exceptions
D. Errors

Answer: B.

Java exceptions fall into three categories: checked exceptions, unchecked exceptions and errors. Bugs are not exceptions.

Question 73 (7.3. Determine when casting is necessary)

Consider the following code:

```
class Parent {}
class Child extends Parent {}
class GrandChild extends Child {}
```

Which of the following will generate a compile error? (Choose all that apply)

A. Parent p = new Child();
B. Child c = (Child) new Parent();
C. GrandChild g = (GrandChild) new Parent();
D. g = (Child) c;

Answer: D.

A will not cause a compile error because it is legal to assign an instance of a subclass to a reference variable that is of the type of the parent class.

B will not cause a compile error either, but will throw a **ClassCastException** because **Parent** cannot be downcast to **Child**.

C will not cause a compile error either, but will throw a **ClassCastException** because **Parent** cannot be downcast to **GrandChild**.

D will generate a compile error because Java does not permit the casting of a class to a subclass.

Question 74 (6.2. Apply the static methods and fields)

Which of the following statements are true?

A. A static method is shared by all instances
B. A static field is a good way to store a value that is unique throughout all instances.
C. A static method can be called from an instance method in the same class.
D. An instance method can be called from a static method defined in the same class.

Answer: A, C.

Static methods and static fields are shared by all instances. A is therefore correct.

B is incorrect because a static field is shared by all instances.

C is also correct. A static method can be invoked from an instance method.

D is incorrect because an instance method needs an object. A static method cannot call an instance method.

Question 75 (2.3. Know how to read or write to object fields)

Examine the following code.

```
public class Coder {
    private static short x;
    public long y;

    public static void main(String[] args) {
        Coder s = new Coder();
        x = (short) 7;
        y = 10;
        s.y = 12478;
        s.x = 100;
    }
}
```

Which of the following cause(s) a compile error?

A. x = (short) y;
B. y = 10;
C. s.y = 12478;
D. s.x = 100;

Answer: B.

A is not a correct option because **x** is a static method so it can be set from a static method. And, even though it is private, it can be accessed from the same class, so it will not cause a compilation error.

B is correct. **y** is an instance field so it cannot be accessed from a static method without an instance of the class encapsulating **y**.

C and D will not cause a compile error because both **x** and **y** can be accessed through an instance even though **x** is static.

Question 76 (6.5. Apply encapsulation principles to a class)

A Java class has a field (named **x** and of type **long**) that needs to be protected against direct access from other classes. Which of the following line(s) of code complies with the OOP encapsulation principles?

A. private long x;
B. public void setX(long value)
C. public void getX()

D. protected long x;

Answer: A, B.

To encapsulate a piece of data, a field needs to be made private and access to it is done through a get and a set methods. A and B are therefore correct.

C is incorrect because a get method should return a value;

D is incorrect because this would make **x** accessible from subclasses and from classes in the same package.

Question 77 (9.4. Declare and use an ArrayList of a given type)

Which statement(s) creates an **ArrayList** of **File**s with an initial capacity of 36? (Choose all that apply)

A. ArrayList<File> names = new ArrayList<>();
B. List<File> names = new ArrayList<>(36);
C. List<File> names = new List<File>();
D. ArrayList<File> names = new ArrayList<File>(36);

Answers: B, D.

By default, an **ArrayList** is created with an initial capacity of 10 elements. To reserve a space for 36 elements, pass 36 to the constructor. A is incorrect because the resulting **ArrayList** will have an initial capacity of 10.

B and D are correct.

C is incorrect because **List** is an interface and cannot be instantiated.

Index

Made in the USA
Monee, IL
05 November 2026

67845293R00216